To Tim
a young man —

ANGLING IN THE SMILE
OF THE GREAT SPIRIT

Good angling!
Harold C. Lyon Jr.

Deep Waters Press
77 Court Street, Suite 100
Laconia, New Hampshire 03246
Phone: (603) 524-2585
FAX: (603) 825-0399
http://www.deepwaterspress.com

© Copyright 2004, Harold C. Lyon, Jr.
All rights reserved.
No part of this book may be reproduced, stored in a retrieval system, or transmitted by any means, electronic, mechanical, photocopying, recording, or otherwise, without written permission from the author.

ISBN 0-9748171-0-4 hardback
ISBN 0-9748171-1-2 paperback

Standard Address Number (SAN): 2 5 5 - 8 7 7 7
Library of Congress Control Number: 2004090768

Lyon, Harold C. Jr., 1935-
Angling in the Smile of the Great Spirit: Six Centuries of Wisdom from the Master Anglers of Lake Winnipesaukee

Book Cover Design by C. Andrew French
Cover Tech Consultant: Phil Stephenson
Book and cover Layout: Jonathan Gullery at Budget Book Design

Descriptions of fish are generously taken from:
John F. Scarola's book, *Freshwater Fishes of New Hampshire*,
published by the New Hampshire Fish & Game Department and
Jack Noon's book, *Fishing in New Hampshire — a History*,
published by Moose Country Press

Photographs included here are by my friends William Beetham and Vincent Giuliano
Photos of the spring Winni Salmon Derby are by Wayne Carter
10 9 8 7 6 5 4 3 2 1
Printed in the United States of America

Other books by Harold Lyon

Tenderness Is Strength

It's Me & I'm Here!

Learning to Feel — Feeling to Learn

For my children:
Eric, Gregg, Dan, Dian, Laural, Roy, and John
and my grandchildren:
Miranda, Hans, Heidi, Jessie, Amanda, Crystal, Brittany, Taylor, Jordan, Tiiersten, Jaymie, and James

*May each learn to love to angle and to walk
in the Smile of the Great Spirit ...*

Acknowledgments

Many thanks to those who have contributed to this labor of love, especially my great group of Master Anglers: Barbara Cotton, Rick Davis, Mario DeCarolis, Chuck French, Jim Warner, Carl Gephardt, Alan Nute, Bill Martel, Jason Parent, Ted St. Onge, Stephen Perry, the late Paul Philippe, Al Stewart, Travis Williams, and Bill Whall ("Mighty MO 2") who has helped me more than I care to admit and many other boaters and anglers on the Lake.

Thanks to Jack Noon for his support, reading of the manuscript, suggestions, and the material quoted from his excellent books, *The Bassing of New Hampshire* and *Fishing in New Hampshire, a History*.

Thanks to John F. Scarola for his book *Fresh Water Fishes of New Hampshire*, published by the New Hampshire Fish & Game Department, and for his excellent descriptions of fish, frequently quoted in this book.

I am very grateful to angler artist, C. Andrew French, for his cover art for this book and to Phil Stephenson, for his much needed technical consultation on the cover.

A special thanks to my brother, Robert Lyon, an accomplished author and fly fishing guide, for his inspiration, reading, and suggestions for improving the manuscript of this book.

Thanks, also, to Jennifer Plum, of Words & Numbers for her diligent copy editing, and to Jonathan Gullery for the creative design of this book.

Special thanks to Don Miller and John Viar, two dedicated Fish & Game biologists, who carefully read through the manuscript and whose work helps preserve Lake Winnipesaukee, as the angling paradise, it is, and will continue to be.

Last but not least, thanks to my wife, Edith, for putting up with an angler who is not only frequently out fishing, but who, when home, is also often busy writing about it! "She is the catch of my life!"

ANGLING IN THE SMILE OF THE GREAT SPIRIT

Six Centuries of Wisdom from the Master Anglers of Lake Winnipesaukee

Dr. Harold C. Lyon, Jr.

Deep Waters Press

New Hampshire

www.deepwaterspress.com

CONTENTS

Foreword
by Vincent Giuliano
xiii

Chapter 1
The Formative Years
1

Chapter 2
Smallmouth Black Bass
23

Chapter 3
Landlocked Atlantic Salmon
41

Chapter 4
Lake Trout
63

Chapter 5
Rainbow Trout
75

Chapter 6
White Fish, Pickerel and Largemouth Black Bass
81

Chapter 7
Yellow Perch and White Perch
91

Chapter 8
Cusk, Horned Pout (Bull Heads), Black Crappie, and Other fish
97

Chapter 9
Ice Fishing
109

Chapter 10
The Lake Winni Fishing Derbies
• The Spring Salmon Derby with pictures of the winners
• The Great Rotary Ice Fishing Derby
• The Bass tournaments
117

Chapter 11
The Senior Master Anglers
(Paul Philippe — in memoriam, Barbara Cotton, Bill Martel, Jim Warner, Al Stewart, Ted St. Onge, and Mario DeCarolis)
135

Chapter 12
The Old (but not oldest) Master Anglers
(Hal Lyon, Chuck French, Carl Gephardt, Rick Davis, and Steve Perry)
189

Chapter 13
The Younger Master Anglers
(Alan Nute, Jason Parent, and Travis Williams)
243

Chapter 14
The Chart of Secrets and the Top Lake Winni Salmon Lures
273

Chapter 15
State of New Hampshire Record Fresh Water Fish
281

Epilogue
286

FOREWORD

by Dr. Vincent Giuliano

In the course of Hal's work on this book, I had an opportunity to be with him and a number of the Master Anglers presented in this book in different contexts. I was out with them in fishing boats at 5AM as dawn was breaking and with them as the glaring heat of the day turned into the cool of the night. They were always fishing and always telling stories, in their island or mainland homes with furnishings and décor right out of the 1920s. I heard them talk over CB radio and videoed them in their funky bait shops, their plain or fancy fishing boats and in their basement fly-tying shops. I inspected old photos with them and looked at stuffed fish hanging on their den walls. Many of these people are in their 70s, and one is in her 90s. There is a rich background of folk history here, just waiting to be read by you.

What struck me in these individuals was their folk-charisma accompanied by modesty, and their expression of the subtle interplay of the physical and humanistic sides of fishing. Fishing is ever-elusive. It can be recreation or meditation. It can be constant action or waitful inaction. It can be expression of community or an opportunity to experience one's solitude. Fishing can be art, and fishing can be science. It can be an irrational activity pursued rationally, or the other way around. It can be a rich person's hobby or a poor person's solace. It can be an opportunity to tell stories, to accompany somebody who is in pain. It is an opportunity to witness dawns and dusks of incredible beauty, to be with nature, to know the lives of fish. It can be to get fish to feed the grandkids at dinner. Or, the fisherman may take extra care not to harm the fish in the process of catch-and-release.

Above all, fishing is a major folk opportunity for subtle story-telling, indications of a folk culture from the past that is still with us. The fishing stories in this book are about much more than fishing. They are about trivial events — a dog that drinks beer on the fishing boat, how to keep a 50 year-old outboard motor running, what to do about going to the toilet when out ice fishing, ways to smoke lake salmon, about where the fish are and aren't when and how and under what weather conditions. And they are about times remembered, about the human condition as expressed on the waters of New Hampshire's greatest lake, remembered parents and old friends, and philosophies developed in the course of life itself.

Along with forgivable lies, the stories contain great truths. There are moments of sadness, of remembrance, of re-creating old tales told by long-dead grandparents. There are worries and concerns about children and grandchildren, and whether they too will be able to experience the good simple life of angling. And there are concerns about our own aging as the cycle of life continues.

Folk history and wisdom as expressed through the medium of fishing is thus the intellectual content of this book. The images tell important parts of the stories, photos from the 1920s and 1930s, wrinkled faces on the DVDs which will follow this book. They show the insides of dwellings whose walls are rough unpainted boards, and painted floors that are covered with rag rugs. There is the beautifully simple cottage on Two-Mile Island belonging to one Master Angler with no electricity and a white picket fence. There are wooden rowboats propelled by oars and the insides of bob houses in February.

Our task as artists is to capture, re-create and convey the essence of this history and wisdom while at the same time conveying a lot of practical information. This draws fully on our skills as writers and videographers, as well as on the collective wisdom of our own long lives and our many years of angling. I spend as much time as I can in my lake camp as I have done for 29 years now, as Hal Lyon's next door neighbor on Bear Island.

This is about capturing the essences of these stories, preserving them, re-creating them in writing and video media and making the results available to you. Because fishing is so variable in its essence, we have elected to do the project on a scale that captures much of the subtle variability involved. We have interviewed not only Master Anglers but also bait-shop owners, fly tiers, and even "Donald Duck," (or "Mighty Mo 2") the blind ex-navy man known to all serious Lake Winni fishermen who devotes his days to monitoring the CB radio on Lake Winnipesaukee and coordinating responses to emergencies. Coverage of winter through-the-ice fishing is another part of the story.

Hal started this project as a labor of love 20 years ago… and it continues in this mode. I'm proud to be his friend and partner in this story telling and sharing.

—Vincent E. Giuliano, Ph.D.

CHAPTER 1

THE FORMATIVE YEARS

"The charm of fishing is that it is the pursuit of what is elusive, but attainable: a perpetual series of occasions for hope."
— John Buchan —

FOR SIX DECADES I have been fishing the healing waters of Lake Winnipesaukee. It is said that Winnipesaukee translates from the native Abenaki into "The Smile of the Great Spirit." There is also another translation, reportedly from another tribe: "Beautiful water in a high place." Both are apt descriptions. I fancy the first translation. God's spirit is smiling down on me through the beauty he has created around this special New Hampshire Lake. Angling in these pristine waters, especially on a peaceful, calm morning with views of Mt. Washington and the Ossipees to the north is a spiritual experience. But fishing is not only about catching fish. What is it about? Read on and see as 14 other Master Anglers and I share our thoughts, not only about catching fish, but also about what drives us to angle in the smile of the Great Spirit.

Lake Winnipesaukee is the second largest lake in New England and the 6th largest natural lake in the United States containing 274 inhabitable islands and a shore line of 283 miles for a total of 44,586 acres. It is approximately 28 miles from Alton Bay to Center Harbor and about 13 miles wide at its widest. It is characteristic of many glacial lakes in the United States. What we share in this book is equally relevant to all New England lakes and especially the great Maine lakes like Moosehead, the Sebago Region, the Belgrade and Rangeley Lakes Regions, the Down East Lakes, the Penobscot River Valley, and the Kennebec River Valley. What we share in this book will help you significantly if you angle in any glacial lake.

A Lake Winnipesaukee angler and outdoor writer, Bob Harris, shares one version of history on how it got its name from the natives who lived here when the first white men from a survey party from Boston discovered it in 1652:

> According to the story, "The Naming of Winnipesaukee," I learned that on the northern shores of the big lake there lived a great chief, Wanaton, who was well known for his courage in war and for the beauty of his daughter, Mineola. Mineola had many suitors, but she refused them all. Adiwando, a young chief from a hostile tribe to the south, heard so much about the fair Mineola, that he paddled his canoe over the great lake and fearlessly entered the village of his enemies. Luckily, Mineola's father was away at the time. Admiring his daring courage, Mineola and Adiawando fell desperately in love. Upon his return, Chief Wonaton was angered to find the chief of the enemy tribe in his camp and the suitor for the hand of his daughter. He immediately raised his tomahawk and started to attack the young man. But Mineola rushed in between them, pleading with her father to spare Adiwando's life and finally succeeded in reconciling them. The couple were married and left the village to return to Adiwando's tribe. The sky was overcast and the waters of the lake were black, as the whole tribe, paddling canoes, accompanied the two lovers halfway across the big lake. Just as the natives were about to turn back toward their camp, leaving the couple on their own, the sun came out and the waters of the lake sparkled around the canoe of Adiwando and Mineola. "This is a good omen," proclaimed Chief Wonaton, "and hereafter these waters shall be called Winnipesaukee, The Smile of the Great Spirit.[1]

An occasional spiritual thread may be found in this book's angling tales and tips. Angling on "Lake Winni," as we fondly call our clear deep glacial lake, provides a sanctuary for renewal for the fish as well as for me. It is a meeting place between the busyness of my everyday world, and a peaceful, spiritual way of being. This process of renewal helps me escape from the burden of people, conflicts, and worries. An inner experience of peace grows while I angle in the "Smile of the Great Spirit." I find my stress transforming into a rich variety of opportunities when God makes his presence known to me on the Lake. As the late theologian, Henri Nouwen put it so well in writing of the spiritual life:

Gramp Hines (father of my mentor) with trout in 1934

Our conflicts and pains, our tasks and promises, our families and friends, our activities and projects, our hopes and aspirations, no longer appear to us as a fatiguing variety of things which we can barely keep together, but rather as affirmations and revelations of the new life of the Spirit in us. All these other things, which so occupied and preoccupied us, now come as gifts or challenges that strengthen and deepen the new life which we have discovered.[2]

I confess that I'm trying to capture some of the elusive essence, spiritual and otherwise, of angling. Angling satisfies many needs. Some practice it as part of that progression from generation to generation, passed on to us by our fathers and forefathers. Some angle as a kind of therapy, which has its roots, perhaps, in primitive times, never questioning or understanding how it heals us. Some go fishing to escape from the stress of our relationships, jobs, and the toils of life. For some, there may be a genetic programming to be anglers, hunters, gathers, and to provide for our families, but, if that's so, then why do we practice "catch and release?" Some become addicted to the powerful strike of the fish and the anticipated life-death struggles transmitted from an eight-pound salmon through our 6 pound-test line to our rod and through our hands and arms to our brains where synapses fire to satisfy some complex longing - perhaps an unconscious desire for a connection with our universe. Some "Type A's" do it as just another form of competition — driven to out-fish other anglers. Is it any wonder, then, why so many of us make angling an obsession? Among some anglers there is no clear line between religion and fishing!

What about the social nature of fishing? Do we find the counterparts of primitive hunting-and-fishing bands of males? And what about women fishing?

Aunt Eloine and Gramp Hines ready for trolling 1937

In 2002, while teaching in Europe on a Fulbright Professorship, I had the rare opportunity of going on a fishing and hunting trip to a small village in the Hohe Tatra Mountains of Slovakia on the Polish border — a place where no other American had visited, according to my hosts. Though we spoke different languages and these fellow anglers and hunters had been raised under Communism, there was an instant bond among us sportsmen. When word got around that an American angler and hunter was in a hunting hut high in the mountains, other anglers and hunters hiked up through the snow, carrying in their rucksacks wine, schnapps, food, and musical instruments to share with an unknown American comrade. Though we had just met and I did not understand all the lyrics, I knew their message. Until the wee hours we sang classic Slovakian folk songs in candle-light with tears of fellowship and joy running down our cheeks, linking arms with one another ... about the monster trout that broke the line and got away, the sad tale of the man who lost his beautiful girl friend because he was always out angling, and the missed shot at the biggest stag of a life-time. What are these deep, natural angler bonds of love and fellowship about?

Why is fishing a life-long passion for so many fishermen? Now, in my late 60s, I still steal every hour I can, getting out on my boat on the peaceful lake: fishing, fishing, fishing. I'm not sure I really know why. It's certainly not just about catching fish.

In this book, each of the Master Anglers and I offer our unique answers to these questions along with our tips for catching each fish - our tales and our stories. The pages which follow offer angling knowledge from a select group of anglers. We, fifteen, who have collectively fished Lake Winnipesaukee for over 6 centuries, share practical tips, secrets, stories, histories, lies, and techniques learned over lifetimes of angling which can save novice or expert anglers decades of trials and errors.

The author smiling after a successful day on the Lake whether or not catching fish.

My son, Eric, an ardent angler and Master Angler Mario DeCarolis advised me to forget about trying to analyze angling. "Enjoying it is enough! Don't pick away at something so special!" they said. "Just let us enjoy it without the analysis!" Somehow, they fear, I might spoil it. My Brother, Robert, is an outdoor writer and fly fishing guide on the West Coast. A writer with deep introspection and more metaphysical orientation than I usually have, he recently authored an article entitled, "Death of a Fisherman." This is the story of an angler who, while trying to examine the mystical allure of angling in an introspective self-portrait of himself, has gradually contemplated the "whys of angling" and suddenly finds his passions for angling disappearing and being displaced by another deep longing — hunting fever:

> I was working the flies hard and fast in the quick water and a breeze with the smell of late autumn was drifting up river when it happened. There it was! Off like a chased burglar at a full out clip and heading toward Mikey down river. Zzzzzzzzzzzzzz from the battered CFO and the rod bucking while I kept a fine touch on the rim, not daring any more pressure.
> I held the rod up just enough to exert some small pressure on the streaking fish. It turned sharply in center channel, maybe 75 yards out and jumped, meanwhile the current had pushed me sideways and I had to jerk around with water splashing over my wader bib and lean hard upriver to keep my balance.
> It was a heavy fish. I'd seen the burnished gill plates and dusky belly even from that distance. Meanwhile —my awareness segued quickly to objective: *Flat line, breathing steady, heart calm . . . no ju ju in the pulsing rod*
> I fought the fish hard, bringing it quickly as possible to hand, all the

while muttering a litany of apology under my breath. My dropper fly was lodged in cartilage in the corner of its jaw. I removed it, feeling a depth of empathy I had not allowed before. The fish flurried in my grip. I worked it back and forth to flush water through it's gills, then opened my hand and watched it melt from sight. *Never again*, I decided, *unless it was destined for the table.*

What a gorgeous creature it was . . . in my mind's eye I could still see the painting of a steelhead in *A Book of Fishes*, by S. Kip Farrington Junior, an image that had sustained my passion for fishing and created a mystique about the west as a youth. It had been one of my bibles in fact, along with the *Little Book of Fishes*, as a kid growing up in the suburbs of D.C. The vivid water color paintings on those pages forged a deep, lifelong love of the mysterious, beautiful creatures that swim up rivers and none more so than the noble looking "steelhead trout," as Farrington refers to it. Backdrop to the painting, incidentally, is a rock wall plunging vertically into a raging river, as if this fish is swimming through the most inviolate of canyons . . . *not far from the truth this day.* The sun peeked over the rim of the canyon at that moment and I set down my rod and lay back Prometheus style, back deeply arched, over a large, gray, cold, river-smooth boulder and offered myself to its rays.

It was just not the same anymore and it boiled down simply, I figured, to magic. Where there was magic there was passion and a period of grace. Without it, fishing was a mechanical act. Like your favorite meal without bon appetit. For me it boiled down to the electricity of the hookup, that smooth, raw nerve feeling — that was the essential thing for this fisherman . . . that quickening instant of first connection .... The moment of strike and the life-death struggle had been unbearably compelling once. Now the honeymoon was over, replaced by the reality of a passionate animal frantically seeking release.

The image occurred to me and brought a smile: one iron cold trip in late October, near the end of our guiding season. Ed Henry, guiding with me at the time, had brought along his gun, a well loved, well worn, double barrel 20 gauge, as I recall. And one night he returned to our camp on a forested island with a partridge in his pocket. He had my full attention, and like a slowly germinating disease I would have seasonal outbreaks of a yearning to hunt over the next ten years. Several times I had gone as far as buying a shotgun, even getting out once or twice to try it out. But in the end each attempt to take up hunting was aborted by the resident passion to fish.

Now the fever was fully upon me. I walked out of the river, through a weathered Russian Thornberry and hiked back to camp. Along the way my eyes strayed to the canyon rim. Beyond the ridge line, the thousand foot hills, was no man's land—at least until a few years back when we had good reason to go up and check it out. Even having stood upon the windy ridge line with the canyon yawning below, while to the east a farmer on a Siberian sized farm implement threw a massive apostrophe of brown dust against a sterling sky, and a lonely road ridge top, gravel road led to scattered ranches and a military looking microwave station on a bump on the spine of the thirty mile ridge line . . . it was still always like another world at the bottom of the canyon.

There was no one around when I arrived. I put a cold coffeepot on the Coleman and fired it up, walking over to the bank to look out on the river. I could see Max working the riffle across the way; we caught each other's eye and waved.

I walked back and sat down, shucked my waders. Instead of stashing my rod in the bushes, I snipped off my flies and reeled in my line. I dug out my case and put my trusty old, dinged up, true running Orvis CFO IV neatly away. As though it was my father's body I carefully prepared the embalming. I wiped down the rod with a tuck of my tee shirt until the resin gleamed in the morning light. I unscrewed the brass cap to my rod tube, took out the sleeve and slipped two slender segments into their case. Twisting the cap until it was snug, I walked with it down to the raft, slipping it securely under the tubular aluminum brace of the rowing frame, then lashed it snug with two short straps.

I stood up on the cooler looking out on the water. Moved by the clear finality of the moment, tears suddenly welled into my eyes. I folded my hands gently in front of my chest and bowed my head in homage to the passing of an old and well loved friend.

In camp, I slipped into my threadbare shorts and put on my hunting vest, enjoying the familiar procedures, the small hunting rituals that replaced the fishing. I sipped at my coffee. I took my shotgun out of its dusty canvas case, slipped it over my head on its strap and onto my back. I noticed I was smiling. As I hiked up the trail through camp and crossed the wooden stair onto the old railroad grade, I felt a familiar small buoyancy. No more was I ambivalent and muddied feeling, not something I had easily suffered; now I was doing again exactly what I lived and breathed . . . .

Less than an hour later, after a demanding but satisfying effort, I stood high on a rocky ridgeback over a deep golden canyon. *God, but I love it high up on the ridge top.* I had even pushed my mountain bike to the top once and cruised like hell on wheels along the rim. I would rather hunt chukar up on the top o' the world with the wind in my face and a view to forever, than spend the day mucking through brambled, wooded draws closer to camp.

I could smell dry cheat grass, sagebrush and a hint of winter on the wind. I felt exhilarated and about as fresh in the spirit of the hunt as a ten-year-old with his first Red Ryder BB gun. A shot caught my attention and there was Scotty on the shoulder of the next canyon over. *I'll be damned.* Half a dozen birds descended in a long swooping glide and I could hear the odd *ping, ping* sound they make sometimes. They coasted out of sight over the flank of my own ridge and I watched Scotty as he scuttled down the slope to retrieve a kill. He might have heard me if I gave a yell, but I didn't.

Instead, looking beyond and down into the yawning canyon, I couldn't help but notice how there was little difference really between the two substances. Air over water, one overlay the other. I was fishing still, only in a different river, a subtler dimension, an ethereal medium where I wouldn't get wet and the fish had wings.

My brother, Robert Lyon, an outdoor writer, adventure guide, and an angler of deep introspection

My brother has captured some of the mystique I seek in my "Whys" without being explicit about it, without digging below the tip of the iceberg and exposing the vulnerable ice to the heat which will destroy it. So, while I cautiously ask some "whys" in this book, perhaps it's enough to just surrender to angling as a past time I love and enjoy for a variety of reasons and seasons, many of which I do not understand and never will. I know that the transformation he writes of is still in process within me, and maybe my Master Anglers. I find myself releasing many more large fish, after contemplating their enigmatic beauty than I did earlier in my life, even though we love to eat them. And like some hunting friends, I can see on the horizon a time when I will sadly shoot my last buck, when my compulsion displaces itself, only to emerge in some new pathology, perhaps.

Though I write from the perspective of *this* special lake in New Hampshire, what I write is applicable to any northern glacial lake on which you might be blessed to fish. How can I write about *more than one* lake, when it's taken me a lifetime to learn *one*? And still I have much more to learn from the fish and fishermen through trials and errors — and the fish are often more reluctant teachers than are the fishermen! This book is more about fishing, than it is about catching fish!

Soon after I embraced the sport of angling, I became convinced that I should never be able to enjoy it if I had to rely on the cooperation of fish. Fortunately,

> I learned long ago that although fish do make a difference — *the* difference — in angling, catching them does not.... — Sparse Grey Hackle —

This book combines both scientifically accurate information with not-so-scientific tales from fishermen friends, offered at face value, since anglers, who are always optimists, tend to exaggerate. As Ed Zern said, "I get all the truth I need in the newspaper every morning, and every chance I get, I go fishing, or swap stories with fishermen, to get the taste of it out of my mouth."

It all started for me in 1938 when I was three years old. My cousin, Bill Hines, and I would lie on our bellies for hours on our dock on Meredith Neck. We wore uncomfortable life jackets and kept our rods close beside us. We held our lines in the sensitive fingers of one hand while peering down into the clear water watching and waiting for yellow perch, hornpout, or even an occasional bass to swim toward our baited hooks, all the time struggling to keep our bait from ravenous sunfish, or "bait snatchers." Occasionally, my patience was rewarded when a big bass swam deliberately toward my night crawler to inhale it. This was followed by a count to five and a hard jerk to set the hook. The fight would begin! We became experts at catching perch and small bass from our dock.

Uncle Gordon's old Laker Boat (1939) with view from Meredith Neck (Lovejoy Lane) to Bear Island

And later when we had passed our swim test by swimming from our dock on Lovejoy Lane to Shep Brown's Boat Basin, we graduated to fish for the monster bass, which lived in the cribbings of Brown's docks. More often than not, they would wrap our lines around the pilings before we could land them. Later when we passed our one-mile final swim test — from LoveJoy Lane to the Bear Island Post Office, we were allowed to take our old wooden rowboat out fishing by ourselves.

So where is the place in the history of angling that we 15 Master Anglers fit, as sportsmen who have pursued angling for the past century?

My old wooden rowboat and Gordon's old Laker boat, 1940

The consummate New Hampshire angler and historian Jack Noon provides some perspective for our place in the angling history:

> Indians were probably fishing for shad at the Weirs at least as early as nine thousand years ago. The anadromous shad continued to spawn in Winnipesaukee until early in the nineteenth century, but dams on the Winnipesaukee River such as that for the Belknap Mill denied them access, and the shad fishery died. Early white settlers pursued subsistence and commercial fishing on Winnipesaukee and in the Winnipesaukee River for shad, lake trout, silver eels, and pickerel. Lake trout were being sent to the Boston market in winter during the 1820s, and commercial fishing for pickerel was still being pursued in the 1880s. Overfishing for native species with nets, spears, and eel weirs resulted in protective legislation specific to the Winnipesaukee River in the eighteenth century and to the lake early in the nineteenth century.
>
> Though Theodore Dwight mentioned sportfishing for yellow perch at Winnipesaukee in his book published in 1829 and Meader's 1869 book on the Merrimack watershed described sportfishermen arriving at Winnipesaukee on trains just as tourism was starting to boom, sportfishing didn't truly hit its stride until the early introduction of smallmouth bass and continuous stocking of landlocked salmon - neither of them native to the state - and the later introduction and continued stocking of rainbow trout. Sportfishing continued to gain ascendancy, and eventually all commercial fishing was banned.

Early twentieth century fishing with hook and line, both with bait and with lures, continued to be catch-and eat fishing. Fish and Game regulations protected the resource with length limits and daily bag limits. The development of the catch-and-release phenomenon for a renewable resource is well worth an in-depth study. Developments from the nineteenth century up to present day have progressed in this fashion:
  - Subsistence and commercial fishing by the most effective means with the goal of catching as many fish as possible.
  - Sport fishing with hook and line and eating all the fish legally caught and of legal length.
  - Sport fishing for catch-and-release. Entertainment only.
  - Sport fishing for competition with a sidelight lottery mentality: bass tournaments and Winnipesaukee derbies in winter and spring.[3]

My uncle and angling mentor, Gordon Hines

This book presents the histories and experiences of a small group of 15 anglers whose lives overlap the last of the three eras mentioned above.

My uncle, Gordon Hines was one of the best fishermen in the Lake. He was well known for his angling prowess, but also had his less savory side with which he wrestled all his life. As one great angling writer expresses it:

The world of angling is richly diverse.... It elicits some of the sweetest and deepest qualities in man — and, occasionally, some of the worst. It can be cooly dispassionate, lyrical, or maddeningly intense. — Nick Lyons —

Uncle Gordon Hines, cooling it, with a big string of lake trout, circa 1929

Fortunately for me, my cousin, Bill, didn't share my love of angling and I was often the one who accompanied my uncle on his evening fishing outings. During these trips I was privileged to experience some of the sweet and deeper qualities of this gifted man. As Washington Irving said, "There is certainly something in angling that tends to produce a gentleness of spirit and a pure serenity of mind."

Left: My father, Col. Harold Lyon, back from WWII, ready for fishing 1945
Right: Colonel Harold Lyon with his son, the author, 1979

My father, an army officer, was away in Europe in World War II during this time from 1941-1945.

It was during these fatherless years that I was blessed to learn from my Uncle Gordon how to fish. He warned me sternly that I should <u>never</u> tell anyone the secret places we fished, or he would never take me out again. I kept that promise until a few decades later when I showed my sons and daughters the same secret spots, which still produce the big fish. Now I am sharing these spots with my 12 grandchildren! Though my "Master Angler" friends and I share time-tested techniques for angling in this beautiful lake, or many others, for that matter, I honor my Uncle Gordon's request (and that of other Master Anglers) not to reveal our secret spots, so in these pages you will find no detailed maps of our sacred hot spots. I catch more good fish within sight of my Bear Island cottage, precisely because I fish it more often than far away places. Mark Twain said, "There is no use in your going five miles away to fish when you can depend on being just as unsuccessful near home." But there is so much structure and so many fish in the Lake, you won't have to look far to find good fishing, especially if you read on to learn what other Master Anglers and I share in these pages.

There is NO Single Best Way to Fish

Henry Beard and Roy McKie define fishing this way:

"The art of casting, trolling, jigging, or spinning while freezing, sweating, swatting, or swearing."

One of my greatest joys is to pass on the old secrets and tips I've learned in my 65 years of angling to my children and grandchildren. It's also satisfying discovering new techniques and learning about why what we were doing in the old days still works today. In my association with the 14 other eclectic Master Anglers in this book, I'm learning that there is no single best way to catch fish. Some troll slow and some fast. Some swear on using certain lures and others catch as many on different lures, depths, and leaders. I've learned new tricks from each of them. Master Anglers are a species apart. We're a dedicated and driven crew — indolent, improvident, and quietly mad. Are we only out there to catch fish? No. We go fishing even after days of catching nothing. Something else is happening when we fish.

*3 generations of Lyons: top left: Son, Gregg Lyon
with 5-pound smallmouth bass, 1971;
Right top: author at age 7, 1942 ; right: Col. H.Lyon, retired, 1975 with bass;
below right: author at age 17 with small mouth bass, 1953,
just before entering West Point:
left lower: Bill Hines and author 1942 with catch from dock*

Why do we angle?

- Is it about escaping from stresses of family and work? Sometimes it's that.
- Is it some atavistic impulse, going back to the primitive hunter-gatherer days, imprinted in our genes to catch food for our families? Maybe something like that is part of it, but since so many practice "catch and release," that's not all that's going on.
- For Type A over-achievers, fishing is competition. These anglers are striving to catch more, bigger fish than others. One angler on Lake Winni won't reveal information on the radio. When called, he'll quickly respond, "Go to Channel 4." Channel 4 doesn't exist on the marine radio, but this is a code to a secret channel where he'll talk cryptically without giving away any secrets. These men are competitors in all aspects of their lives including angling. No wonder there are so many competitive bass tournaments scheduled every summer weekend on Lake Winni!
- Is angling a form of ancient therapy, where people fish to find solitude and refresh themselves from the tensions of life? It's partly that, but it's more.
- Is the feeling of a powerful fish in a life-death struggle on the other end of our line something we're addicted to? I think we can become addicted to angling and that power on the line is part of what we seek, but it's more.
- Is it an excuse to immerse ourselves in nature — to be with our Maker in the beauty of his natural settings? That may be closer than any explanation I can come up with - hence, my title, *Angling in the Smile of the Great Spirit*.

I found that most of the Master Anglers have not contemplated this question much, "Why do you angle?" But they fish every time they have an opportunity and they love it. That's enough for them ... and for me. We tend to analyze things to death! Leave it well enough alone and just go fishing and enjoy!

Lake Winni: the Magnet that Draws Us Back Home

I spent the first thirteen summers of my childhood on this beautiful lake. I then went off with my military family to all the distant places where such families go, followed by West Point, seven years as a Ranger, Airborne Army officer, graduate school, and new careers as an educator and psychologist. I always returned to Lake Winni when I could. I've fished and hunted in places throughout the world where the Lake Winni lessons served me well. But in no other place have I found such fulfillment in angling or more beauty in nature. My children and grandchildren are also drawn back to the shores of this beautiful lake. I discovered in these travels how difficult it is to learn to fish a large, unknown lake without the benefit of a mentor who shares "the secrets" and techniques I learned as a child. There are many ideal looking bass spots on this lake where the structure seems perfect, but where the bass just don't congregate.

Knowing the varied techniques the Master Anglers and I have shared here can save you years of trial and error. I recall from boyhood how the wealthy vacationers with the finest tackle would fish here and count it as successful if they caught during their entire vacation what our family caught in a good afternoon! As young anglers, we loved it when they'd come over to ask for our help.

A Community of Outdoorsmen

This year I was privileged to attend the "Rocky's Rangers" annual game banquet in New Hampshire in honor of sportsmen who have passed on and named in honor of Rocky DeCarolis, who tragically perished in a storm while fishing for salmon on Moosehead Lake, Maine. I had thought that Europe was the only place where such rich outdoor tradition was well preserved and passed down from generation to generation. But this wonderful experience proved otherwise. 50 sportsmen, grandfathers, sons, and grandsons feasted on delicious wild game they had bagged the past season, while fellowshipping with one another. One by one they appeared before the "Judge," Mark DeCarolis, in this true "Kangaroo court" to tell rich stories of their outdoor successes from the previous season. Host, Master Angler Mario DeCarolis, opened the proceedings saying, "Any and everything you say WILL be used against you and there are no excuses or defense." After each testimony, anyone with previous gripes or humorous stories about them was asked by the judge to present any evidence about their behavior or sportsmanship from the past. There were incredibly dedicated outdoorsmen there. Being a former New Hampshire Wild Turkey calling champ, I was asked to give a turkey calling demonstration. I told the 50 people there that giving them a turkey-calling demo was like asking me to sing opera for Pavorati. I have never seen so many guys with incredible hunting and angling dedication and skills.

One 40 year old, Jimmy Gallagher, had shot 10 deer with his bow this past season in New Hampshire, Maine, Connecticut, Massachusetts, and Vermont. He has quit rifle hunting, as it is not enough challenge for him. He always saves deer tarsal glands and pins them on his clothing. He never goes into a stand the same route; to mask his human scent, he always stores his hunting boots in rabbit droppings he saves from his own domestic rabbits before going out (and sometimes sees rabbits sniffing their way to his tree looking for a fellow rabbit!) He sits in his portable silent climbing tree stand at least 20-30 feet high up in a tree and uses a bottle instead of urinating in the woods. And he calls deer in by mouth with bleats, "social" snorts, and grunts. I think this guy practically lives in the woods year round! He says whenever he jumps a buck, he stops, "social snorts", and immediately climbs silently up in his portable tree stand and bleats. He claims the jumped deer will run only a few hundred yards, and then hearing the snort and bleats, work its way back within an hour or so.

Many outdoorsmen like him were there. It was fascinating to see that kind of dedication, which I may have had at his age, but no longer seem to have in such abundance. Hearing his intensity in recalling his hunts is reminiscent of listening to myself or other Ranger buddies recalling patrols just after Army Ranger School! I had almost forgotten how motivated I used to be and I was inspired!

After each lively testimony and tongue-in-cheek rebuttal, the Judge banged his gavel and said, "$50," or any amount he felt the testimony deserved. We defendants opened our wallets and paid the treasurer the specified amount, all of which was then donated to the Crotchet Mountain Fund for disabled children. Trophies were awarded to those with the biggest deer. For the past 42 years this dedicated group of sportsmen has donated over $60,000 to this wonderful cause. And they have bonded as a community.

"Riding the Horse in the Direction it is Going"

During our courting, my wife passed several screening tests to determine if she was an authentic outdoorswoman worthy of marriage. Here's proof of her angling prowess. She did equally well on the hunting tests, bagging game on her first 4 out of 5 shots with the shotgun I bought her during our courting.

Among a small group of us at this banquet, the discussion came up about how our spouses put up with our hunting and angling traditions. There is no problem with those spouses who also love to hunt and fish — except finding baby sitters during opening days when the children are too young to join us. I shared how, while cadets at West Point, we were counseled to carefully pick wives who were independent enough to sell our homes, pack up our furniture and children and move to another state or country while we might be away fighting a war away in some God-forsaken land. Of course the heart invariably defies such logic of the mind. I tested various potential mates by taking them on early morning fishing trips in the rain, or leaving them in a remote tree stand in December and coming back for them after dark to see if they "freaked," as several did.

My wife passed all these preliminary tests. During our courting, I bought her a fishing rod on which she caught the 4-pound smallmouth bass in this picture, and a 20 gauge shot gun — small investments in terms of a lifetime partnership. I was in a hunting club on the Eastern Shore of Maryland and took her on her first hunt. With her first shot she downed a goose, with the second a duck, her third shot downed another goose and she missed the fourth shot. With her fifth shot she shot a deer, four out of five productive shots. She passed my test!

But the old colonel who was head of the club objected to spouses or children hunting with members. I protested saying that it was our legacy to teach our family members outdoorsmanship. He called a vote among the 6 of us in a desperate attempt to ban wives from hunting on our lease. He lost, but immediately dissolved the club! If you are fortunate enough to have a spouse who hunts, it is your good fortune ... and wisdom of forethought. If not, then your spouse has the good fortune of learning to enjoy and savor some space and tranquility during these breaks away from you. One wife shared with me that she is now very grateful for the time to herself or with her lady friends while her husband is away doing his outdoorsman things. That's what I call healthy compromise and the older I get, the more I appreciate the need for compromise. In Zen terms, it is "Riding the horse in the direction it is going." Another apt Zen phrase for accepting what is: "You cannot push the river."

Morning is for Salmon and Trout; Evenings are for Bass

"A bad day of fishing is far better than a good day at work."

For strange reasons, we never fished for bass in the morning. Most likely it was because my Uncle Gordon always slept late. We would not go out for bass until after 5 in the evening, returning at dark. The Lake in the evening has a special mysticism about it, with its pine tree covered islands rising up through the mist and the cries of the loons breaking the stillness.

I seldom take a crowd fishing in my boat as the peacefulness of a Lake Winni sunset or the lonely call of a loon on a misty evening seems to elude me when I am with a crowd. With my large family of 7 children and 12 grandchildren, we found it saner to rotate fishing days for the children. With most of us being ardent fishermen, we planned a calendar during our vacation, with kids participating fully so they would "own" the schedule, which spelled out who could go fishing each day, who did the dishes, set the table, fed the dog, etc. Sometimes they would trade washing dishes for two days, for a day of fishing.

There is such strong nostalgia about the Lake and the familiar islands, which were always such a welcome sight to me as a child in an otherwise lonely childhood. But who could complain when having the blessings of a great fishing mentor on such a lake! After West Point and during my military years, I would always return with my family to our Meredith Neck "Mushroom Camp," as it was called - the same cabin of my childhood. Lake Winni is the only place where I really have roots, moving every two or three years in my life as an Army Brat. Returning to that old cottage on Lovejoy Lane, I found many of the same old pictures, vases, and memorabilia that somehow eased my tensions. The view from the dock across the Lake to Bear Island tranquilized my soul. I explored the rocks I climbed upon and learned to swim from as a child. They had shrunk!

The Lake is still clear enough to see bottom at 20 feet deep on a sunny day. It is pure enough for most people to drink, though slowly that is changing. New laws governing septic systems have cleaned up the Lake in the past decades to the point that the crawfish we used to catch by the dozens in our trap at night, baited with a fish head, are no longer as prevalent. And the Yellow perch seem to have migrated to coves where there is more fertile water. But the shoreline has changed very little. We have lived on East Bear Island since 1979 with the same view of the Ossipee Mountains and Mt. Washington I had as a child, 60 years ago. But most important to me, the smallmouth bass are still in the same secret spots, and, in my opinion, they still out fight, pound for pound, all the other game fish in the Lake and in the other lakes I have been blessed to fish. I can still catch them using the old ways, and my children and grandchildren have learned to catch them too, while I watch and get back in touch with a peacefulness that has eluded me in all other places, except here, where "The Smile of the Great Spirit" is so present in this "beautiful water in a high place."

Too Many High Performance Boats

High Performance craft meant for the ocean now threaten the serenity of Lake Winnipesaukee. What now most threatens this peace and tranquility of our special Lake is the influx of high performance boats which can travel on our once serene waters at a speed of over 100-MPH! These boats do not belong in a lake. They should be restricted to the ocean. And there should be a speed limit established at night of 40 MPH as no one driving one of these performance boats can see well enough after the sun goes down to avoid hitting a small boat. People are now leaving the "Big Lake," selling their properties in fear of the proliferation of these large, fast boats. It is no longer safe to venture out on the lake at night when these craft might be speeding over the waters. A good friend, fellow angler, and retired airline pilot, Jack Hartman was needlessly killed by one of these cigarette boats in the summer of 2002. It ran over his small craft with his family aboard just after dark while the

Hartman family were returning from a restaurant in Meredith. It is no wonder that island and lakefront residents protested the expansion of the once serene Brown's Boat Basin on Meredith Neck when the word got out that they would be expanding and might be selling more of these Baja boats! Several hundred residents turned out in protest in the hopes that this might help motivate the owners of the marina not to specialize in selling these high performance boats which, in my opinion, have changed the character of the lake more than any other development in my 68 years. The good outcome was that the owners decided not to go ahead with the expansion and damage the good will of their residential neighbors. The days of the quiet PUTT-PUT of small boats have sadly been replaced by the deafening roar of 500 HP engines, which can be heard all the way across the lake. I find that sad. Many of us anglers have had several hundred dollars of lines cut by these fast boats whizzing past us much closer than the prescribed 150 feet.

Several years ago during the Spring Winni Salmon Derby, two anglers were trolling near Rattlesnake Island in their 16-foot aluminium boat. According to Master Angler Rick Davis, two high performance "cigarette boats" passed within 20 yards of the men, one on each side of the smaller boat. The unusual dynamic of their two colliding wakes knocked both anglers out of their small craft and into the frigid spring water. The two high performance boats kept speeding on, never looking back at the destructiion they had caused. The two anglers were both fortunate to have been wearing life jackets and were soon rescued by other anglers. Their boat just kept going until it crashed on an island some miles away. Rick Davis, head of the Winni Derby graciously outfitted the two men with entire sets of free fishing tackle, and they were able to fish in their retrieved boat the next day, feeling blessed that they were still alive.

When I was a teenager, I worked pumping gas at Browns, and I have a nostalgic feel for the place. I have caught many fish from its docks while growing up. My cousin, Bill Hines, and I would work for Shep and Adelaide, Gordon, and Bill Quimby at Browns doing odd jobs, helping the Islanders move their summer belongings out to the islands in Shep's home-made taxi boats, testing the small motors the mechanics had fixed…but always being there, thinking about the big fish which made their homes under Shep Brown's docks in the pilings there. So Browns is a nostalgic place for me.

This book is organized to present some information on each fish's life cycle, habitat, and feeding habits along with my own experience with each fish. Angling wisdom and personal secrets will be shared, including tips from my own half-century of angling in these waters. 14 other Master Anglers will present the secrets of their success, their histories, thoughts, ideas, photos, and tips for fishing from over six centuries of angling experience. I will share most of my tales in the early chapters of the book, though I will also present my fishing tips in the Master Angler section.

Uncle Gordon with tie and trout 1933.

Earlier chapters focus on each of the major game fish from my personal perspective: the smallmouth black bass; landlocked Atlantic salmon, lake trout, and the newest game fish, the rainbow trout, introduced in Lake Winni in 1991. Other chapters briefly discuss the other fish: pickerel, horned pout, whitefish or "shad" as the locals call them, yellow perch, white perch, and cusk. Ice fishing techniques are shared, as well as the big derbies with pictures of winners over the years.

For the novice or the experienced angler, In Chapter 14, a "Chart of Secrets" is shared which shows, by month and for each species of cold water game fish, the average depth, trolling speed, and favorite lures of the Master Anglers cumulative 600 years of fishing experience. Also the top flies and top three lures for salmon, as revealed by the Master Anglers, will be shown and discussed. An angler will no longer have to spend 10 years trying to find how to angle for salmon, trout, and bass, if he or she refers to this chart and these secrets!

Photos of angling are offered from each of the Master Anglers, along with the talent of my photographer-physician friend, Bill Beetham, and my long time neighbor and friend on Bear Island, Vince Giuliano, who also shot much of the video of the Master Anglers demonstrating their tips and sharing their stories. This will be offered separately as visual-oral histories in a DVD series on the "Master Anglers of Lake Winni" which will be available at: www.deepwatewrspress.com

Chapter 2

SMALLMOUTH BLACK BASS
MICROPTERUS DOLOMIEUI

"The shadows round the inland sea
Are deeping into night;
Slow up the slopes of Ossipee
They chase the lessening light
Tired of the long day's blinding heat
I rest my languid eye
Lake of the Hills! Where cool and sweet
Thy sunset waters lie!"
—John Greenleaf Whittier—

THE EARLY FRENCH SETTLERS of the St. Lawrence River called the smallmouth bass, "Achigan," an Algonquin Indian word meaning, "ferocious." And I find them to be the most ferocious fresh water fighting fish of all, in spite of some of my Master Angler friends opinions that the landlocked salmon gets their vote.

One morning while trolling a red maribou streamer fly, I caught a respectable 21" three pound salmon that fought valiantly. Ten minutes later I hooked into a big fish on the same fly rod and fly and he would give me no quarter. I had to shut down the boat as he would not allow me any line and I thought I must have a 6 to 8-pound salmon or big laker. But when I finally worked him in closer, I knew by his bull dog savage runs that it was not a laker. He turned out to be a 3 1/2-pound smallmouth, fighting like a 6-pound salmon! This happens quite often in

June that I catch bass while trolling for salmon, when the bass are beginning to settle in to their beds for spawning. What I think is a huge salmon often turns out to be a 3-pound smallmouth. And smallmouths will jump and leap on light lines as well as salmon. So the smallmouth gets my vote as the best fighting fish, pound for pound, along with that vote from former President Grover Cleveland, as you will soon learn.

Though most anglers do not know it, the smallmouth bass is not native to Lake Winni or to New Hampshire waters. There were no bass in Lake Winni before the Civil War. Bass are a native of the Great Lakes. The first New Hampshire bass were privately stocked in Rust Pond and Lake Waukewan. Some might have found their way down the short outlet brooks into Winnipesaukee. They were first officially introduced into Lake Winni in 1873. The stocked bass were either some of the four hundred, taken by hook, from Lake Sunapee, or from Webster Lake, where they had been stocked 5 years earlier.[4] They have thrived here ever since. Angler historian Jack Noon has done a thorough history of how the smallmouth bass came to New Hampshire in his excellent books, *The Bassing of New Hampshire — How Black Bass Came to the Granite State* and his new book, in a series of books on New Hampshire Fishing, *Fishing in New Hampshire - a History.*[5] Jack Noon has written an excellent scholarly work on the fish of New Hampshire, how they got there, and what has happened to them since. Jack's books are liberally quoted in the paragraphs which follow.

The spawning season goes from late April until early June, depending on the water temperature. The water must be at least 59° F to trigger spawning activity. The world record smallmouth was almost 12 pounds and 27" long, caught in Tennessee in 1955. The NH record is 7 pounds, 14.5 oz, 23.25" long, and was caught in 1970 at Goose Pond. My largest is a 6-pounder, caught in Lake Winni in early September of 1986 on a crawfish. Male bass mature and begin spawning at age 4-5 while females mature at age 5-6. A 20" bass is smart enough to have managed escaping being caught for about 9 years! So, like lake trout, they grow slowly.

President Grover Cleveland, an ardent fisherman who fished Lake Winni for bass in the late 1800's, loved the smallmouth bass better than all the other fish:

> The small-mouth family... I consider ... more uncertain, whimsical, and wary in biting, and more strong, resolute and resourceful when hooked, than any other fish ordinarily caught in fresh waters.... It is best and most satisfactory to attempt their capture with bait.... As teachers of patience in fishing, black bass are at the head of the list.
>
>
> *Nice smallmouth doing its aerial acrobatics*
>
> They are so whimsical that the angler never knows whether on a certain day they will take small live fish, worms, frogs, crickets, grasshoppers, crawfish, or some other outlandish bait. ...They will frequently refuse to touch bait of any kind.... They are the most aggravating and profanity-provoking animal which swims in fresh water. Whether they bite or not at any particular time we must freely concede is exclusively their own affair.... Nothing but inherent and tantalizing meanness can account for the manner in which a black bass will ... rush for the bait, and after actually mouthing it, will turn about and insultingly whack it with his tail.[6]

To introduce the Lake Winni smallmouth bass and share my favorite techniques for angling for bass, here's a true account of bass fishing I wrote in the 9th grade, indelibly lodged within my memory:

My line starts running smoothly out through the guides of my fly rod. A good bass must have grabbed my hellgrammite... and I feed him a big loop of line so he can run unimpeded with no resistance. The run is fast now and I can hardly keep up, feeding line! And he's heading out away from the rocks toward deep water, an almost sure sign of a big one.

The first run finally ends and impatiently I hold back my temptation to set the hook, awaiting his second run. Finally, line begins to ease out a second time, accelerating to a fast run. Now's the time! I let him take out the last coil of slack fly line until the line is taut between rod and fish. I sock him hard! He feels solid and bores down deep somewhere out there in the cold dark depths. Then the line slices up.

Up and out of the clear waters of Lake Winnipesaukee catapults a monstrous bass, twisting and splashing back into the water! He's off, then, on a line ripping run, deep and long. I let him run, keeping my fly rod high, but realizing all the time, that he's boss ...for now. He can easily snap my four-pound leader with a toss of his head, if I don't let him run when he wants. I must play him carefully, and wear him down slowly. Five minutes and three spectacular jumps later, I lead him gently, now on his side, over the lip of the net. He is huge! Now he's safely in the boat — all four pounds of him — looking like ten pounds to my cousin, Bill, and me.

Twenty minutes earlier we had just about given up fishing that day after casting our hellgrammites to every likely looking spot. Bill and I, hearty teenagers back in the 1940's, had accompanied Dr. Warren and his son, Sam, out to this spot to dive for his lost anchor. We earned our modest bait, lure, and hook money diving for lost objects in Lake Winni. Hellgrammites, the finest bass bait available in these waters, were 50 cents a dozen back then — an expensive gourmet treat for kids to feed bass. Never the less, as a boy, I almost always spent my allowance and whatever other meager funds I managed to earn pumping gas at Brown's Boat Basin, or unloading vacation supplies, for island residents on Brown's taxi boats, in preparation for my lake Winni fishing.

Dr. Warren had anchored his boat, the night before, just off the "Old South Ledges." After fishing, he found his anchor hopelessly wedged in the rocks and the rope had broken as he tried to free it. As we reached the spot, today, we could clearly see the lost anchor in the clear water twenty feet below us. Dr. Warren suggested we try the fishing before we dived and scared the fish. We were delighted as he opened his hellgrammite box and offered us free access. However the bass were apparently fasting, or not there, as we had no luck. Bill and I then pulled on our swim fins and masks and jumped over. About five dives later, we managed to free the anchor. On the last dive, as I swam up struggling with the anchor to the boat, there they were! Three monster bass were hovering between me and the boat, only five feet away, curiously finning and watching the diving operation. Bill and I struggled to the surface sputtering, "Huge bass! Three of them...right here!" Dr. Warren replied, "Well, we can try 'em again, but they've probably been well spooked by you in the water." One cast later I was fast to the four-pounder, which opened this story.

That event took place 54 years ago. In 2003, when hellgrammites (we call them "helgies"), were going for $6 per dozen, our technique still worked. The bass are still hiding in the depths and shallows (when they come up to feed in about 10-15' of water) off the same rock ledges. Where the structure is close to deep water is where you will find bass in any cold water lake. Hellgrammites, crawfish, live frogs (if you can get them), and even night crawlers are still the best baits. Yet many visiting fishermen are still unsuccessful in their quest for smallmouth bass, fishing with live bait, largely because they do not allow them to run the way we do. Now we also fish with flies and other lures, especially in spring when the bass are on their beds. We fish for them with spinning tackle with light lines, though I prefer to catch them on a long fly rod, either with a bass bug or popper in spring, or with live bait, the way my Uncle Gordon taught me. I remember his bass fly rod of choice being a long "Bristol," tubular telescopic steel rod from a manufacturer which, was in Bristol, Connecticut, back then.

What better witness could I call in support of my choice for the smallmouth as the best fighter than former President Grover Cleveland? He describes the bass' fighting prowess better than any other description I have read:

> Ordinarily when a bass is struck with the hook…he at once enters upon a series of acrobatic performances, which, during their continuance, keep the fisherman in a state of acute suspense. While he rushes away from and toward and around and under the boat, and while he is leaping from the water and turning somersaults with ugly shakes of his head, in efforts to dislodge the hook, there is at the other end of the outfit a fisherman, tortured by the fear of infirmity lurking somewhere in his tackle, and wrought to the point of distress by the thought of a light hook hold in the fish's jaw, and its liability to tear out in the struggle. If in the midst of it all a sudden release of pull and a straightening of his rod give the signal that the bass has won the battle, the vanquished angler has, after a short period of bad behavior and language, the questionable satisfaction of attempting to solve a forever unsolvable problem, by studying how his defeat might have been avoided if he had managed differently.[7]

Jack Noon, in his excellent, book, *Bassing of New Hampshire,* tells a humbling story of Grover Cleveland from 1902, after he had retired from the presidency. He was bass fishing in a small boat one hot July day with his fishing buddy, Dr. Bryant and a farmer. Fishing was slow and finally after some hours, the former president caught a small 7 1/2-inch bass, but the little fish swallowed the hook, and was unable to survive the ordeal.

> Some native on the watch told two deputies that if they wished to obtain evidence of bass being taken under the legal limit that they should follow 'a very fat man in a straw hat' and two others. The two deputies overhauled the corpulent 'old farmer' and asked him to show them the fish they had taken. Grover Cleveland readily complied, though not very proud of his catch. The deputies, when they saw the little specimen, told the fishermen that they had broken the law, and asked who had taken the fish. Both the ex-president and Dr. Bryant claimed that they had caught the specimen, the worthy doctor, anxious to shield his friend.... Mr. Cleveland insisted that the boat and tackle were his, and that he alone was responsible. He told the wardens to do their duty and that he was ready to pay whatever fines the law required. The wardens were shocked when they asked the name of the 'fat man' and were troubled and wanted to back out when told that it was Grover Cleveland of Princeton, New Jersey. The ex-president insisted in appearing in court the next day and paying the fine. This 7 1/2-inch bass was mounted and appears in the archives of the Fish & Game Commission of Massachusetts.[8]

This story does not justify, but helps me a bit with "the egg" I have had on my own face, from having broken the rules from time to time and learning my lessons the hard way.

Jack Noon researched the old records of the New Hampshire Commissioners of Fisheries and here's an interesting entry from 1871, discussing the introduction of bass into New Hampshire waters:

> Some have objected to the enterprise [of stocking bass into New Hampshire] on the ground that the more fish we have, the more we should encourage a set of lazy fellows to fish, who are too lazy to do anything but fish. Now suppose we admit that to be a fact, it is an argument in favor of the enterprise, for we all know that these lazy fellows catch next to nothing now, whereas if fish were plenty, they would catch fish for themselves and others to eat, and would thereby keep themselves from our poor farms. If the number of the lazy who will not work but will fish, is half as large as some would have us believe, would it not be wise for the state to create an industry by which this large body of its citizens might with certainty benefit themselves and the whole community?[9]

My angling mentor: Uncle Gordon Hines

My Uncle Gordon had a reputation of being one of the best bass anglers on the Lake. He would take my cousin, Bill, and me to his secret spots, only if we vowed never to tell anyone. He threatened to disown us and never take us fishing again if we told of certain submerged boulders and structure off the deep side of which, large bass invariably lurked. I recall fishing in one of these secret spots and after successfully catching several big bass, a boat pulled up to us and asked, "Any luck?" And Gordon answered, casually, "Nothing biting...." I even taught my own children to tell the same "white lie," to protect our favorite fishing spots. Ed Zern was right: "Fishermen are born honest ...but they get over it."

Brown's Boat Basin in 1939

My uncle had an ongoing rivalry with Shep Brown, owner of Brown's Boat Basin on Meredith Neck, for catching big bass. I recall Uncle Gordon, in his white "Laker" boat "PUT-PUTTIN" across the lake toward home with a granddaddy 5-pounder attached to his stringer, stopping every few minutes to keep the monster revived, just so he could show it off to Shep Brown, before releasing it. Bragging may not bring about happiness, but no angler, having caught a trophy fish, sneaks home quietly with it! These monsters would invariably live with dignity under Brown's Boat Basin docks where Bill and I would ardently fish, hoping to hook one of these giants. I recall once when I was ten or eleven, hooking into "Ol'

Methuselah," a giant bass who was often seen from Brown's dock, but never caught. As he took off on his second run on my dead hellgrammite (the price of helgies being what they were, Gordon allowed us to use only his dead ones), I couldn't feed out line fast enough. He just kept running toward Bear Island …and never stopped.

Author as a boy with small mouth bass, circa 1949

My line broke when it ran out and there was no stopping him. Everyone knew that the big ones, which hung around under the docks, were bass released by my Uncle Gordon. In the late 1940's when I was a teenager working in summer pumping gas at Brown's, I had the opportunity to scuba dive beneath the docks. I was awed, and a bit frightened, by the huge bass, swimming fearlessly toward me, opening and closing their huge mouths, like bullies, warning me that I was in their turf. Watching my uncle was my first experience of seeing the practice of catch and release, and I knew of no others doing it at that time. Everyone we knew, including me, was practicing catch-and-eat back then.

Let Them Run:

Letting bass run before setting the hook was an important bit of angling knowledge Uncle Gordon passed on to me. If you set the hook as soon as the bass takes your bait, as many children and some tourists do, 8 times out of 10, you would lose him. Later we were to discover more about this process as well as the discovery of diving down to stir up their anger, curiosity, or appetites.

One late afternoon in July in the 1960s, I was fishing with my sons, Eric and Gregg, then 7 and 6 years old. The fish weren't feeding and I put on my mask and flippers and noisily jumped overboard. After swimming around the rocks we had just been fishing, I spotted two huge bass, just off the side of a large ledge. They curiously eyed me from a distance of about ten feet. Bass are not afraid if you're under the water with them. This is what makes them so vulnerable to the illegal spear fishermen, who sometimes poach them in Lake Winni. It's a sacrilege to shoot a spear into the side of a beautiful bass and haul him in half dead with a heavy cord, when the fish could give such a noble fight on a light line.

I surfaced and hollered to Eric to cast out a frog. We use small green frogs when we can get them. We hooked them through the thigh with a # 1 hook and no weight, so they swim freely on the surface. Eric let fly with the frog. The frog splashed several yards from me and began to kick around on the surface. One of the big bass took off like a rocket toward the frog from his lair, 15 feet below the surface! Never stopping, he engulfed the frog with a splash, and took off on a deliberate run toward open water, away from smaller, bothersome fish, to savor his dinner. I followed with mask and flippers as Eric fed him slack line, to run unimpeded. I noticed that the bass carried the frog by one leg, almost daintily in his lips. After running about 10 yards toward deeper water, I watched the bass stop, spit out the frog, and then gulp it down headfirst. He took off on a second, faster run, this time visibly opening his mouth, presumably to allow the force of the water to flush the frog deep down into his stomach.

Daughter, Laural Collier's 4.7 pound bass caught on a helgi in 1970

On this second run, Eric set the hook. The unique spectacle of watching a 4-pound bass from under water was not only instructive, but exciting. To watch from under water, while the big bruiser raced toward the surface and disappeared, as he jumped, was a rare sight! That same year, I watched from under water as my sons caught other bass on helgies, crawfish and frogs. All these fish were deeply hooked in the stomach, which makes it difficult to catch and release. Whenever we accidentally set the hook too early, before the second run, in most cases, the bait was pulled from the bass' lips. Only on rare occasions would we lip hook and land such a bass. Needless to say, with a fly or other artificial lure, one does not have this problem as the fish strikes the lure and is either instantly hooked or missed.

That same year, at age 7, my son, Eric, caught a big bass on a live frog in that same spot which won a first prize gold badge in the Junior Division of the *Field & Stream Magazine* fishing contest. Two years later, my son, Gregg, at age eight caught its identical match, pound for pound, and a year later, our daughter, Laural, age 15, caught one, almost the replica of Eric's and Gregg's.

Fish Dogging

Our trick of going into the water to stir up the bass corroborated a practice my Uncle Gordon used years before. When he had no luck fishing in one of his favorite spots, he would pull in his anchor and repeatedly throw it out again, four or five times, making big splashes and dragging it back to the boat each time. He claimed that this would attract the bass' curiosity and they would come in and begin feeding. We have now developed this into an <u>almost</u> fool proof method, using either an anchor, or substituting a human diver for the anchor. The anchor, dragging on the bottom, dislodges rocks and crawfish, which attract the bass. And the commotion of the splashes also attracts, rather than scares bass. So our children became our "fish dogs" - excellent at holding a point and with great "noses" for bass! When we arrived at one of our secret spots, the kids, usually led by Laural, would dive into the water in mask, snorkel, and flippers and go hunting for bass, even before I could get the anchor out.

Left: Little son, Eric, holds big bass he caught

Laural would swim off the rocks, diving down to 10 or 15 feet from time to time until she spotted a big one. She would then signal to us, how many and what size, using hand and arm signals, holding up 3 fingers for a 3-pounder. Once she'd attracted and discovered the fish, she'd remain holding "on point" until I cast a helgy, crawfish, or frog. If a smaller bass beat the large one to the bait (not usual, as the dominant fish will usually attack the bait first), she would tell me, so I would not let him swallow the bait and get hooked. Once when I was tied to a 4-pounder, our daughter swam between the fish and a buoy, around which the fish was threatening to wrap my line, warding him off with outstretched hands and feet, every time he charged that way!

Hand and Arm Signals

We anglers have our own hand and arm signals to communicate with passing anglers about the fishing, a kind of a semaphore communication system between anglers. As I pass another boat trolling, I hold my hands upward palms toward the sky, asking: "Had any luck?" The other angler answers with thumbs up for positive response, and fingers for one, two, three or more fish. Or if no luck, he holds thumb down. I then point into the water asking, "How deep?" He answers with five fingers (5') four times for 20' deep. I ask, again, "How big?" by holding my hands apart, palms facing each other. He answers by holding his hands widely apart for big, or close together for small. I don't know the origin of this, but I have been doing it for over 50 years, and always took it for granted that it is the way to communicate silently to another passer-by angler.

Impressing an Angler Father

Son Dan with catch for dinner

One August a young man from our church approached me and explained that his father, from whom he had been estranged for several years, was going to pay him a visit. His father loved to fish and his son wanted to show him a good time on his visit. However, the boy was not a fisherman. He asked if I would be willing to take his father out for a fishing trip. In spite of the fact that his father was a lawyer, I agreed. When the son and his father arrived at the dock, I was there to meet them in my boat. I took him to some nice structure near Six-Mile Island and put a crawfish on his hook and a helgy on mine.

No luck. After several fruitless casts, I decided to use our old trick of going in the water with mask and snorkel. As I swam around a ledge, there, watching me, was a huge bass. I surfaced and told the father to cast the crawfish to me, which he did. I took the bait and dived down, actually tossing the crawfish out to the bass and then pulling back to watch. He eyed it and watched as it slowly sank. Just as it neared bottom, he swam forward, grabbed the bait and began swimming out to open water. I surfaced and told the lawyer to give him slack to run — that he had a good fish taking his bait. He was excited, letting line out fast now, as the bass swam out toward open water. I instructed him to wait until the fish stopped and began on a second run.

Granddaughter, Crystal Gosnell with her first Bass caught on a night crawler

As the line began to run out again, I told him to take up the slack and strike hard...but not too hard as the line was light. He was soon fast to a leaping bass. 10 minutes later, we slipped the net under a 5-pound Lake Winni smallmouth. This was one excited father ... and son! His father had the fish mounted and the young man was very grateful for having significantly impressed his father for the first time he could remember, which was sad, but true.

In August the bass are often down about 15 to 40 feet in cold water, just off the drop-offs, large ledges and boulders. This doesn't stop them from racing to the surface after a kicking frog or a slowly drifting helgy or crawfish - especially in the late afternoon or evening.

Catching Them on the Beds in Spring Time

Some of the other Master Anglers only fish for bass in the spring spawning season when they are "on the beds." They are very easy to catch then, attacking any lure which comes near their spawning bed. I enjoy going out in a canoe with my fly rod and a bass bug and casting into shore and their beds in early June. The spawning season usually runs from mid May to June 15, and is triggered when the water reaches 59°.

The male is the star of this activity, doing most of the work. Males come into water 2-10 feet deep and with their tails sweep clean a sandy bed from 2-4 feet, depending on the size of the bass. Loyally the male guards the nest until the female, fat with eggs, appears for a few brief minutes, laying her eggs in a cloud of the male's milt (sperm). She is then finished with the entire process, never to see her young again — the inverse of what occurs with us humans! The male faithfully guards the eggs from hungry predator fish, like sunfish, horned pout, and perch. When the eggs hatch 2-10 days later, depending on water temperature, he carefully guards the fry from predators and attacks anything that comes near the bed including lures, flies, or swimmers. On several occasions, I have had them charge and attack me – courageous fathers! The male remains with the bed for another week until the small fry make their way from nest into the shallows and rocks to fend for themselves. Fishing bass on the "beds" in spring is definitely a catch and release time. Not only is it illegal to keep them then, but if you take a bass off of a bed, you may be preventing the opportunity for a thousand new bass fry to begin their lives. You may legally keep 2 bass from June 15–July 1, when the limit becomes 4. Still, I prefer to carefully release them to return to their beds.

A numbered brick study

The New Hampshire Fish & Game biologists did an interesting study using University of New Hampshire students to help. They placed numbered bricks along a hundred visible sandy bass beds. They waited until the bass had completed their spawning ritual and then caught the male bass from each of the beds. Half were immediately released and returned to guard their beds; the other half were transported a half mile away and then released. The numbered beds were observed daily. Very few of the beds where the bass were taken away, became occupied again by that bass or another. The implications of this study are important. Bass do not swim far from their habitat like salmon or trout and catching them at this time is not good for the propagation.

Gourmet bass food

Close up of the hellgrammite, the gourmet food for bass and one of the best baits. The helgy is the larvae of the Dobson Fly which spends several years in cold rivers under rocks in the larvae stages before hatching into the Dobson Fly.

Hellgrammites, which are the larvae of a Dobson Fly, are mean and ugly critters — especially to a child. But I recall my granddaughter, Miranda, proudly holding her own helgies and crawfish, much to her mother's distraction. Helgies can bite hard enough to draw blood from a tough working man's hand. I taught our children and grand children to pick up helgies and crawfish just behind the head or the collar to avoid getting pinched. I hook them very shallowly just under the collar, passing the hook from front to rear, being careful not to penetrate deeply, which shortens the life of the insect. A good lively helgy, wriggling freely in the water, will attract far more bass than a dead one. Helgies are gourmet food for bass.

When I was a boy in the 1940s and '50s, we bought bait at John Week's place, an old family house and bait business in Meredith. Bill Hines and I would catch and sell crawfish for a penny apiece to old Mrs. Weeks, a retired schoolteacher who ran the family business. I was always impressed by how this tough lady could put her callused fingers into the helgy box and pull her hand out with several ferocious helgies holding onto her fingers with their mean pincers. That was 58 years ago! Mrs. Weeks always had the biggest and most desired red headed helgies which always seemed to catch the most bass. I sometimes paint a bit of red nail polish on the helgies collar to simulate the naturally red ones, and it works!

The "Community Rod"

When fishing, I usually rig up an extra rod, which we called "the community rod." Whoever has not yet caught a fish (or the smallest child aboard) can take whatever hits the "community" rod. We often fish helgies, crawfish, or live frogs on the community rod, a long spinning rod with 6-pound test line. I usually cast out the "community rod" and leave the bale of the spinning rod cocked open so a bass hitting the bait can run unimpeded. Each angler can fish up to two rods at one time in New Hampshire.

Rigging for Bass

I use a # 1 or 2 unsnelled Eagle Claw hook, which seems large to some people. However, fishing primarily for large bass, I want a hook, which when set, has little chance of slipping out. It is curious that few of the New Hampshire sporting goods stores used to sell hooks that large and I often had to order them from elsewhere. I attach my hook to about 7 feet of 4-pound test monofiliment leader, attached to my fly line.

Using a fly rod, I strip cast the helgy 2 or 3 times from one side of the boat to the other, until I have the line out where I want it. I learned this awkward procedure from my Uncle Gordon when I was a boy. You must be careful not to cast off the bait or beat it to death during these back and forth strip casts. With a light spinning rod, it is an easier process to just cast the bait out. I never use any weight, but allow the helgy to drift downward slowly and naturally. Sometimes a bass will rush up and take it as soon as it hits the water or as it begins its descent. On other occasions, they will wait until the bait reaches bottom, at 15 or 20 feet, and watch it for movement before picking it up and running with it. Small bass will usually run toward the shelter of the rocks and I know when it is small, as their runs are usually short and jerky, compared to the steady, fast run of a large bass who usually heads toward open water and knows where he is going.

Granddaughter, Tiiersten admiring big string of bass and looking for the one she caught

If you allow a helgy or crawfish to sink all the way down to bottom, you will be losing hooks as well as helgies. They'll quickly crawl into crevices in the rocks and hold on tightly with the tiny but tenacious hooks on their tails. I never leave them out for longer than the three minutes it takes for the bait to slowly drift to the bottom. Often, while gently and slowly stripping my line back in, a bass will grab my bait. The important thing is to immediately release the line for the bass to run, hoping he didn't feel any resistance. Another trick is to break off one of the two claws on your crawfish bait, which reduces his probability of getting hung up in the rocks. You can also clip off the tiny twin hooks on the helgy's tail with nail clippers to prevent him from holding to the rocks.

In teaching my young grandchildren to fish, I usually bait with night crawlers on their rods. It is quite easy for them to learn to bait them themselves, and they are cheaper than the expensive crawfish and helgies. But they catch nice bass, from time to time.

French kissing a frog

Years ago we had a city slicker guest, a flat-lander who had never fished before. We were using frogs for bait, and he complained that his kept sinking. It was clear to me that his frog was obviously dead from his not so gentle casting.

"How do you keep your frog floating?" he asked.

Without looking up at him from my fishing, I replied, "From time to time, you have to blow air into his mouth."

In my peripheral vision, I could see him wince. "How do you do it?" he asked, not wanting to appear as naïve as he was.

"You have to kinda French kiss him," I replied, trying not to smile and give the fun away. "Just thrust your tongue into his mouth and give a quick burst of air."

By now my kids were about to laugh and give my joke away. We all turned to watch him holding the frog up to his face, and we doubled over in laughter when he inserted his tongue into the dead frog's mouth. His eyes were closed and he had a painfully disgusted look on his face.

"I can't do this!" he cried.

It took him some time to forgive me from making him the butt of our bass fishing joke.

Catch & Release ... or cooking an occasional bass

We release far more fish than we keep. However, while we always release bass two pounds or under, we keep some for eating. My wife and I love fresh lake fish. I usually scale most fish, except for perch and horned pout, which I skin. When I prepare a large bass for baking, I leave the head on, as I do with trout and salmon, out of respect. After cleaning it, I stuff and bake it. I also do this with lakers, which taste great baked, stuffed, and sprinkled with grated cheese. The cheese melts into the Corn Flake Crumbs and it makes some fine eating.

Hal's Baked Fish Recipe

It is a simple but gourmet recipe:
- Wipe olive oil over a 3 to 5-pound fish and salt it inside and out.
- Stuff the fish with Pepperidge Farm herb stuffing.
- Sprinkle the fish with seasoned Corn Flake crumbs and lemon juice, and then cover with grated cheddar cheese.
- Garnish fish with lemon slices and sweet basil.
- Cover fish with foil and bake it at 450° for the first 10 minutes, turning down the heat to 375° for an additional 30 minutes. (Remove the foil for the last 15 minutes.)

Hal's Fried Fish Recipe

I also fry bass filets, my wife's favorite fish dish. This is another simple recipe:
- Combine one egg and a cup of milk in a small bowl. Dip the bass filets in this mixture, then coat them in a mixture of equal parts of Corn Flake crumbs and flour.
- Fry the filets in hot olive oil until golden and serve with lemon slices.

These fried bass filets are best served with grits. We enjoy them mostly for big breakfasts, which we eat late on summer mornings by candlelight after angling. Our summer meals are always timed to avoid prime fishing hours - fresh fish breakfasts at 11 AM after fishing, and late dinners at 9 PM after angling. Both my wife and my mother were from Florida and brought to us this fish & grits southern tradition along with homemade coffeecake. This meal is always a great surprise for our summer guests.

But keep in mind what Ed Zern says about eating fish:

> "Roughly two-thirds of all fishermen never eat fish. This should surprise nobody. Fish is brain food. People who eat fish have large, well-developed brains. People with large, well-developed brains don't fish."

Buoy Hopping

Since all bass love structure, especially the granite rock ledges that abound in Lake Winni, even when a novice angler comes to fish, he or she can do well just by fishing the structure. And how is structure found? Simply fish the buoys. We call this practice "buoy hopping." Go to a buoy, drop anchor and fish it for 15 minutes or so. If you are using helgies or crawfish and a good bass is there, he will often take your bait. And the biggest bass will usually be the first one you catch, as he is the dominant champ of that piece of structure. If I have no luck in the first 15 minutes or so, I don't waste my time fishing that spot; I go on to another buoy and give it a try. This way I cover a lot of water and also eventually find a spot where the bass have ascended from deeper water to feed ... and they will take my offering. I never stay and fish a spot for longer than a half-hour. If I stayed there for several hours, yes, some bass might eventually come up from the deeper waters to feed. But I'd have to wait around for them, and I am eager to get into fish, rather than wait them out.

Are you a "Tortoise" or a "Greyhound?"

My brother, Robert Lyon, a fly fishing writer and guide from Washington State, labels me a "greyhound" and the guy who waits in one spot for the fish as a "tortoise." On a river the greyhound covers miles of water, fishing the best water and then getting on to the next. The tortoise, on the other hand, carefully covers every square foot of the stretch of water, changing flies often to entice fish. A tortoise and greyhound might catch an equal number of fish over a given period of time with their different strategies, but the greyhound sees much more structure and scenery. I'm definitely a greyhound! Being a greyhound is kind of like "triaging" the fish, taking the best ones first. If you have time, you can always come back and fish in more detail for the more finicky stragglers.

Chapter 3

LANDLOCKED ATLANTIC SALMON
SALMO SALAR LINNAEUS

Sparkling fresh caught salmon caught on a Maynard Marvel streamer fly on surface in May

THE LANDLOCKED ATLANTIC SALMON is one of the most beautiful and spectacular fish in the lake. The name *Salmo* comes from the latin word *salire* meaning to leap, and leap it does, especially when hooked on a light line! It is known for its spectacular cartwheels, and high jumps when hooked near the surface, as it often is in the spring, when the salmon are pursuing smelt near the surface.

A salmon takes to the air just after being hooked.

Of our Master Anglers in this book, the majority of them have listed the landlocked salmon as the fish they think is the best fighter. These silver fish are characterized by small black "x" pixel-like spots on their upper body. Though once an ocean-going fish, which migrated, into major rivers only to spawn, landlocked salmon are now common in northeastern America and Canada. Originally there were plentiful runs of Atlantic salmon from the ocean up the Connecticut and Merrimack Rivers all the way through what is now the Pemigewasset River.

Jack Noon in a note to me states, "I have yet to find a verifiable account of them [salmon] in the Winnipesauke River," which leads to Lake Winnipesaukee. There are many tales in the 19th and 20th centuries including of the Abenaki Indians catching salmon by the thousands as they passed through the narrows at the Weirs, (an Indian name for fish trap). Some say that the salmon stayed in the Lake when passage back to the sea became difficult, but that is not the case. "By 1847 dams outside of New Hampshire had completely blocked Atlantic Salmon from the state. Landlocked salmon, genetically identical to Atlantic salmon, were enthusiastically welcomed into New Hampshire because they were unaffected by dams. They seemed to promise a simple solution to the complicated problem of salmon restoration."[10] But simple it is not, as you will learn!

There are salmon this big in Lake Winni! This one is from the 1970's.

A 10.5 pound, 30" salmon caught by George Hunt in Lake Winni on a fluorescant Mooselook Wobbler in 1946

I can remember catching landlocked salmon with my uncle 60 years ago in Lake Winnipesaukee. They were first introduced into New Hampshire lakes in 1866. They were brought to Newfound Lake from the St. Croix River of New Brunswick and a year later they were stocked in Winnipesaukee, Squam and Sunapee Lakes. 13 New Hampshire Lakes now have the Landlocked salmon.[11] Salmon thrive in cold, clear, deep and well-oxygenated water. In the spring this means they will be found on the surface from just after ice-out until early June. This is a fly fisherman's delight! They thrive in 55° F water, but you will catch them wherever the smelt are.

The salmon spawn in the fall, beginning in early October and lasting through November. They approach the shore, guided from imprinted memories, seeking familiar swift streams where they travel up-current to gravel nesting sites near where they were spawned. The female clears a bed with her tail while the waiting male wards off other competitors. When the female is ready to lay her eggs, she settles into her bed with the male beside her. They are modest creatures, spawning under the cover of darkness. "At the climax both fish open their mouths, stiffen their fins, and quiver, as the eggs fall to the bottom of the egg pit in a cloud of milt."[12] The female then moves upstream and digs more gravel which washes down to cover the nest. Both parents-to-be then head back to the Lake, leaving the eggs to hatch on their own in early spring. The naturally spawned young will remain in the stream for two-three years before migrating to the Lake where they will grow fast. Stocked salmon grow even faster. When there is ample food, 6-7" stocked yearlings grow to an average of 18.8" by the end of their second year; 22.2" by the end of their third year; 23.2" by the end of their fourth year; 23.7" by fifth year; and 24" or larger by end of sixth year according to Fish & Game studies of netted salmon by big lakes biologist Don Miller from the fall spawning netting. But, all of this size data is dependent on the smelt population and the numbers of salmon to forage on the smelt.

The Delicate Balance Between Forage Fish and Salmon

P.H. Killelea with a 16.5 lbs. landlocked salmon taken in Pleasant Lake, New London, exact date unknown

The yearly size of our salmon varies, of course, depending upon the salmon's food source, which is mainly smelt supplemented by terrestrial insects. Salmon are very dependent upon a healthy smelt population. In 1988 and 1989 the Fish and Game overstocked salmon in Lake Winnipesaukee, given the small smelt population, stocking 45,000 salmon. I remember how elongated and thin the salmon were that next spring, looking almost as lean as pickerel. There was considerable concern expressed by fishermen. Steps were taken to curtail commercial smelting in the Lake, by establishing a two-quart limit of smelt per day. Smelt eggs were purchased also from Canada in an attempt to replenish the population.

A 6-pound male from the 2003 fall netting.

Rick Davis, one of our Master Anglers, organized an effort back then to bring smelt eggs from Canada and the Great Lakes. However, the most effective solution was to cut back on the stocking to 16,000 in 1990, 20,000 in 1991, and later in the 1990s to between 24,000 to 27,000 yearlings per year. This final number was based upon acoustic and electronic studies, as well as the size and health of the Salmon during the fall netting survey at Melvin Village, when the fish run up the river to spawn. This reduction in numbers of salmon stocked the previous year, had a dramatic effect on salmon size the next spring. We became excited by 4 to 5-pound fish when 3-pounders were about as large as we were catching a few years before.

In 2002, we had one of those fertile years with large 20-24 inch salmon weighing 3.5 to 5 pounds being quite common. In 2003, many of us on the Lake Winni Angler site: **http://www.fishlakewinni.com/** (click on "Message Board") found that we were catching mostly some very large salmon and lots of small ones. But we did not seem to be catching the most common fish — those between 18-21".

Left: nice lake Winni salmon ready for my smoker
Right: Edith Lyon with spring catch of salmon caught on a Lake Winni Smelt streamer fly, created by Master Angler, Jim Warner, and trolled on top with a fly rod.

In 2003, I sent an email to Steve Perry, one of our Master Anglers, who is the New Hampshire Chief of Inland Fisheries for the State, who sent my email to the Big Lake fish biologist, Don Miller. Here is Don's email to me explaining our discovery of the missing class of salmon:

> We do indeed have a weak year class of salmon in Winnipesaukee [in 2003] and for that matter in all our salmon lakes that are stocked by our Powder Mill hatchery. The year class in question is from the 2001 stocking of landlocked salmon that were smaller (11.3 fish/lb. in size compared to our management target size of 8 fish/lb. in size). I stocked 28,000 of these salmon yearlings into Winnipesaukee in 2001 and our netting results from the fall of 2002 revealed the lower than normal numbers of this age-class. The breakdown of our (fall 2002) trap net catch shows only 30% of our catch consisted of age 2 fish (these are now age 3 fish and are the missing 18-21 inch fish). Typically the age 2-year class constitutes 50-60 % of our fall trap net catch.
>
> The reasons for the lower survival are due to the poor condition of the salmon yearlings and a touch of furunculosis that they acquired in the months prior to stocking in 2001. Cold water temperatures in the winter of 2000-2001 were probably a causative factor in the reduced size and vigor of these salmon. We consistently produce a superior landlocked salmon yearling for stocking in our big lakes and I commend the staff at Powder Mill Hatchery for their efforts in raising a difficult species of fish. I started my career as a fish culturist and know well that this job is a tough one with a lot of variables that are not under the control of the hatchery system. On the other hand, our year class of age 4 fish is larger than normal and will produce the bulk of 3.5-5 lb. fish this open water season. I feel that the excellent fishing in the spring of 2002 was aided by the near total lack of ice-fishing pressure in the previous ice-less winter that we experienced. Anytime a fishery has a closed season or length limits for that matter, mortality through catch and release does occur. It is imperative that when we release a fish, it is done in a manner that will benefit the future of a fishery.
>
> — Don Miller , Region 2 Fisheries Biologist —

Don Miller, fisheries biologist holds two prime salmon from the fall netting, a roe-filled female (left side) and a milt-filled male (right side) ready to be stripped and mated with help from the biologist team.

Here is more info from biologist Don Miller which is a bit more hopeful for the 2004 salmon season as the fish stocked in 2002 will grow more from lack of competition from the missing year group, stocked in 2001:

"I expect the '02 year class of salmon to be very good, primarily because they will have less competition from the weak '01 year class and the fact that they were good sized fish when stocked (8.2 fish/lb., 22,500 stocked). We have seen age 2 fish in the fall that have been up to 4.5 lbs. and 22 inches in length! I also like the wet spring we are experiencing, primarily for the nutrient influx that helps to drive our smelt populations."

For some more real insight into the delicacy of this balance, read biologist, Steve Perry's, account in his Master Angler section toward the end of the book.

Trolling — How It Started Here

Jack Noon quotes old records stating that:

Major E.E. Bedee, an experienced fisherman tried trolling in the spring of 1886. He was eminently successful, and there was in consequence great excitement among fishermen. This was the commencement of trolling ...here. As many as 400 pounds have been caught in one day. It is seldom that a trout is taken by trolling that weighs less than five pounds, while the larger number weigh from eight to fifteen pounds." He quotes a report stating that, "Major Bedee caught eighteen trout and landlocked salmon, weighing 189 3/4 pounds, in four days one of the salmon weighing 15 1/4 pounds.[13]

Those days are gone forever!

How Deep to Fish?

Some of us Master Anglers have kept fishing journals over the past years. In Chapter 14, I present a "Chart of Secrets" showing average depths and colors of leadcore line, lures, and trolling speeds month by month from all Master Anglers of their angling for salmon in Lake Winni. This is a synthesis of the past six decades – and a significant piece of angling intelligence. Though this was carefully held secret information, it is now available in this book for the first time. Later in the book, the Master Anglers present their own favorite depths, lures, tips, and techniques. Also in Chapter 14, I share the hottest salmon flies and lures currently being used by the Master Anglers.

Later in the summer, I often catch Salmon between 30-65 feet near the thermocline, depending on the time of the day and the weather. The thermocline is a variable threshold plane in the lake below which both temperature and oxygen content drop off dramatically and just below where the smelt like to hang out, optimizing both the amount of oxygenated water and the colder temperature. From July through mid-September, depending upon where in the lake you are, the average depth of the thermocline is about 40 feet. That is exactly why Master Angler Mario DeCarolis uses 40 feet as his default summer fishing depth. But the depth of the thermocline varies. I tend to experiment with depths ranging from 30-65 feet. I sometimes "chase" salmon by moving my downriggers up or down to where I see fish and bait fish on the electronic fish-finder. But you can't argue with success, and Mario is one of the most successful salmon anglers on the Lake. So if you want an easy to remember consistent number, fish in summer (July and August) at 40 feet, like Master Angler Mario.

Actually, very few salmon will go to the 100-foot depths where lake trout often venture. Even in mid summer if you get up very early at 4:30 or 5 on one of those glorious calm mornings you can often see fish swirling on the surface. These are usually salmon, rainbow trout or sometimes white perch. If they are salmon, they are after smelt which they round up like sheep dogs after sheep. They chase them from underneath gradually to the surface while the sun is still low and boat traffic is at a minimum. The smelt naturally move toward the surface at night to consume plankton, which rise in darkness and go deeper in the light. This is the reason why salmon fishing is best in very early morning or late evening as they are after those smelt.

Casting to the Early Morning Swirls

I love to be out on the lake early watching the beauty of the sunrise unfolding in the Great Spirit's Smile. On rare occasions, I have caught salmon and rainbows by drifting in my boat quietly and casting to the swirls with a fly or spoon. Most often in early morning I troll for them at various depths from 10-50 feet with flies or spoons. In the spring, I often troll very slowly on the surface with a fly or a live smelt, hooked with a # 10 hook and four-pound test line using a simple line release on my rod handle. This allows the fish to run freely while swallowing the smelt, once he has taken it and popped the line free from the release. You can merely use a rubber band around the rod handle and just tuck a loop of line under it with spinning reel bale open, or you can purchase a small release device with an adjustable tension screw. I troll slowly with a very light line, which enables the smelt to swim naturally behind the boat as well as to enhance the thrill that a salmon might break the line if I fail to play him carefully.

Trolling Speed

I am often asked how fast I troll. I never knew for sure in miles per hour before my friend Mario got his new boat which tracked our speed. Now I know it is between 1.5 and 2.2 MPH with the slower speed best for lake trout and the faster for salmon. Trolling speed is something I have gotten used to over the years when I had no accurate gauge for it. My best gauge was the 10 to 15 degree angle my downrigger cable makes with the horizontal, which are a few degrees slanted to the rear. When using a boat which does not idle down slow enough, I sometimes drag behind the boat two old plastic buckets tied together with a 10' piece of heavy rope. I place both buckets over at the same time, one on each side of the stern, with the rope in each of the two side cleats so it drags in a balanced manner, slowing the boat down to proper trolling speed. I now take my small portable GPS that I use for hunting and it accurately gives me my speed. Among our Master Anglers the average trolling sped is 1.8 MPH. Some troll faster (up to 3-4 MPH) and some slower. But one, Ted St. Onge, trolls at .5 MPH!

Salmon and Lake Trout Lures

Of course I use salmon flies in the spring when the fish are on top. My favorites are a "pumpkin head" with weighted head tied by Master Angler Alan Nute, owner of AJ's Bait & Tackle in Meredith. Another favorite is Master Angler Jim Warner's "Winni-Smelt," a small sparsely-tied smelt imitation. Running a close second with the "Winni-Smelt" is the Maynard's Marvel. Alan Nute also ties a Meredith or Winni Fire Smelt that I like without the weighted-head but with pearl beads, which works well in spring for me. I also use the old standbys, a red or orange sparsely tied Maribou streamer, smaller than normal smelt imitations with heavy tinsel on the hook and a bit of red, and the Grey Ghost. In the summer when I fish deeper (between 25-50 feet), I usually troll with spoons. Many spoons will catch fish, but I have several favorites. I dress the silver ones up by putting a thin stripe of florescent red on the spoon.

The all time favorites from my fishing experience are as follows in order of preference and success:

1) Sutton spoon, # 61, (the thinner one is better because it will maintain its action even at the slowest speeds which the heavier ones will not).
2) DB Smelt, a thin smelt-like lure which is new to the Lake Winni scene, but which is a great consistent producer, designed by Dave Broder. Master Angler Jay Parent has designed his own secret version with special colors and dots, which is a big hit.
3) Top Guns in various colors, dark for low light and bright for sun
4) Needlefish, the silver with red tip.
5) Mooselook in brass, 1/6 oz size.
6) Kent's Hippy Tad, my secret lure, a small lure which wobbles which is no longer in existence which came from the old timer who sent me Lake Winni's first downrigger from Michigan, Kent Bishionette, but that's a story for later. After reading a controlled research study which found that fish will attack a lure which has visible eyes on it, more than lures without eyes, I started putting small paste-on eyes on all my lures. Why not? It's fun and sometimes practical to experiment!

"Bean Counter's" Compulsive Research on Two Sides of the Boat

Our late angling friend Paul Philippe, whom we knew on the CB as "Bean Counter," was an accountant and he kept fishing data like one! The word was that for twelve years he supposedly conducted carefully controlled empirical studies on various trolling techniques. Many of our practices, such as trolling speed, depth, lines, and especially lures have been reinforced by Bean Counter's famous studies.

Brass versus Copper Mooselooks

On one side of his boat (the right side was for the "experimental variables" and the left for the "controlled variables"), he was supposed to have compared for five years the fish catching results of copper versus brass Mooselook lures, which my humble eyes are incapable of distinguishing! He found that he caught 8% more fish on the copper, and from then on, only used them. I offer no hypothesis for this since I can't believe the fish can tell the difference. But I'm colorblind!

Bean Counter is also purported to have compared silver Sutton # 61 spoons (on left side of the boat), used without any color added, to those on the right side which had a small red strip of tape. After 12 years the data supposedly showed a 23% increase in fish caught with the red, so we now add red to our Suttons. My hypothesis is that it might look like red gills and, hence, more realistic. It could be that, like a bull, red irritates and angers the fish into striking.

For years, without the empirical design of Bean Counter, I compared various lures, which led me to my list of preferred lures. I also experimented with 10-pound test lines compared with 6 and 4-pound test for the portion of my leader connected between the in-line swivel and the lure (lighter by several pound-test than the line on my reel to insure any break will take place below the swivel). I caught more fish with lighter lines. This is especially true in spring when trolling a live smelt on the surface behind the boat as the lure or smelt can have more natural action with a lighter line. And it is much more sport and fun on light lines.

Swivels Snapped Directly to Lure versus Inline Swivel a Rod-Length Away

Paul Philippe is said to have compared a swivel with snap connected directly to the lure (left side of his boat) with lures tied directly to the monofiliment (right side of the boat) and concluded that he caught 9% more fish with the lures tied directly to the line than with the snap swivel. To prevent twist, I use an in-line swivel 8 to 10 feet from the lure. My hypothesis is that the lure has better action tied directly to the line and is, perhaps, more realistic looking. Most of us who heard about Bean Counter's study have taken it as gospel and are doing the same. This is how fables develop! It is interesting how much of what we do as anglers comes from such research, either our own, or that of others like Bean Counter.

Leadcore vrs. Downriggers

I have made the observation over the past few decades that I catch 20% to 30% more fish on my lead core lines than I do on my downriggers. Bean Counter is said to have gathered data on this as well, comparing over ten years fish strikes on lead core versus downrigger presented lures. This data is said to have shown significant differences with 17% more strikes on the lead core than the downrigger. This diagram shows how a downrigger operates.

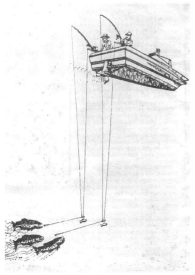

The fishermen in the boat have put their lures out 10-100 feet behind the boat. Then they have hitched the line to release devices just behind the balls (lead fish shaped weights in this picture), lowered the balls using either an electric or hand crank small wench mounted on the side or back of the trolling boat. When a fish hits the lure, he pulls it free of the release on the ball, hooking himself and then being on a light line from the rod. Some anglers also use side outriggers or planers, to get the lines and lures out to the side, away from the boat, because in very clear water and, especially in spring when salmon are near the surface, the boat will often spook the fish to the side away from the boat, where the lure is away from the prop wash of the boat.

So why do I continue to use the downriggers? First, I enjoy fighting a fish on light lines which the downrigger enables me to do once the fish has pulled the line free from the release on the heavy ball. Battling a fish on eight colors of lead core wears both the fish and me out! Second, it is easier and faster to get line out and down with the downrigger than it is with lead core. Finally, fewer tangled lines result when the downrigger takes it directly down vertically to 40 feet instead of the gradual angle of the lead core.

When fishing alone, I have one line out with lead core and the other on the downrigger. This results in fewer tangles behind the boat and allows me to have one line at a definite 40 feet or so with the other at 7 or 8 colors. At my ideal trolling speed of 1.8 MPH, I have calculated that lead core drops about 3-5 feet per color. So with 8 colors I expect that I am about at 24 to 40 feet deep. This depends on both how heavy your lead core line is and your trolling speed. One of our Master Anglers, Travis Williams, estimates his leadcore lines go deeper – 6 to 7 feet per color - than mine. I have judged this only imprecisely by watching my downrigger ball hit bottom at 35 feet while 8 colors (8 colors X 4 feet = 32 feet deep) of leadcore never touches, indicating it must be higher than 30 feet. Travis may be using heavier lead core.

3 generations of Lyon Anglers, Me with my son, Gregg, his wife, Brenda, and my granddaughter, Taylor at age 7, holding her first salmon. 2002

How Far Behind the Boat?

I like to use at least 50 feet of 4-6 pound test leader behind the leadcore. This provides the hooked salmon with enough light leader to surface and entertain me with his spectacular aerial cartwheels and leaps. The lake trout, of course, will never do this and I know within minutes whether I have hooked a salmon or a trout. The trout will always bulldog it down in the depths while the salmon almost always takes to the surface.

But when I hook a large bass, it feels heavier than either an equivalent salmon or trout.

This begs the question, why do we catch more on lead core than on the lighter lines on the downriggers? I have my own theory to explain this. The downrigger line is solidly fixed behind the 8 or 10 pound downrigger ball and even in waves, this will not produce any action back where the lure is being dragged behind the ball. On the other hand, the lead core rod (and I like to use a long and flexible rod for lead core) is in a rod holder on the boat, which with every wave creates action in the rod that is transmitted down the non-stretchable lead core line directly to the lure. This gives the lure some extra action that I believe attracts more fish to the lure. I have seen some old Winnipesaukee anglers rig up with a windshield wiper motor rod holder that gives back-and-forth action to their rods. One of our Master Anglers, Jason Parent, manufactures his own jigging machines, which he sells which I describe in the next chapter.

Creative Ways to Overcome the Action-less Disadvantage of Downriggers

In 1966, I first saw the "DownJigger" at the Kittery Trading Post in Maine. This device was created by a New Hampshire inventor to overcome the disadvantage of the downrigger's lack of action. I thought this was very clever.

A downrigger ball is connected under a large hollow plastic fish. There is a propeller in front that uses the water flow to drive it. A set of worm gears pulls the lure attached to the release device at its rear in and then back out via a small parachute dragging behind in the water. This provides some action to the lure, even on a downrigger. I tested the DownJigger for a couple of years. Theoretically, it seemed to make sense, as long as the big plastic fish doesn't spook the salmon. However, I found that during my tests, which were not conducted with Bean Counter's empirical preciseness, that it seemed to catch as many fish as the leadcore—more than a plain downrigger. It is a more complex set up, which is getting a bit too high tech for this old angler who believes that simpler is often better!

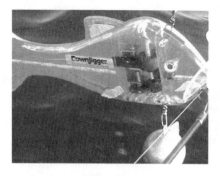 

Left: This shows the Downjigger close up. The ball hangs below it; a cord is connected to a small parachute which pulls in the water and on which is attached a release device holding the fishing line with lure behind that. As the parachute pulls out line, giving back & forth action to the lure, when it reaches a certain point, the propeller on the front of the Downjigger, cranks the gears inside to pull the parachute (and lure) back up.

Right: Here's a picture of the Downjigger suspended to the downrigger boom about to be lowered into the water. The line behind it is attached to a small parachute which has a release device on the back of it to which the fishing line is attached with lure at the end.

But technology will keep advancing, even if I and some of the other older Master Anglers remain with our old ways. My friend Vince Giuliano is talking about making plans for a whole new generation of digital fishing lures. His secret plans are to place a tiny microprocessor chip in a lure that will receive its power through a thin conductor inside the line all the way from a battery in the angler's reel. This tiny chip will imitate a fractal simulation of a real fish swimming which will give the lure its action. It will also emit sounds and smells simulating the physiological responses of a real smelt. So that's a glimpse of my friend's vision into the future — one I will refrain from taking!

An Attractor on the Downrigger Ball

The "cable flashers" used as an attractor above the downrigger ball, simulate a school of fish.

Master Angler, Travis Williams, catches many fish by using a series of Dave Davis spinners which simulate a school of fish attached directly to the downrigger ball as an attractor. He places the release device about 2 feet above the Davis rig, dragging a Sutton or other lure about 4 feet behind the Davis rig. The fish see the "school" of fish and come up to look and then attack the lure just behind it. Moosalamoo, a family business from Burlington, Vermont make an interesting "Cable Flasher" which hooks to the downrigger ball, as an attractor. It can be used horizontally or in line, parallel with the surface. Many other anglers use a shinny dodger on their line just ahead of their lure, which also attracts the fish to the lure and gives a fly great action, whipping it back and forth. I don't care for using dodgers as they create considerable resistance in the water on my line and one does not feel the fish's struggles as vividly on their rod.

Angler Radio and CB Culture...and "Mighty MO" (aka"Donald Duck")

Bill Whall. aka The Duck

During the 1970s through the 90s, most fishermen had CB radios tuned to channel 13. However, now fewer and fewer still use CBs, having converted to more reliable and expensive VHF Marine radios. On any morning on the CB, one could hear humorous patter back and forth among names like: "Angler" (our Master Angler, Mario DeCarolis), "Bean Counter" (the late Paul Philippe), "Chicken of the Sea" (Bruce Hack), "Sky King (an angler now in his 80s who built his own light aircraft and who sometimes buzzes my boat or dock, just off the deck), "Whoa Joe," "Winni-Guinea" (an angler who passed on several years ago), "Cool Waters" (Master Angler Travis Williams), "Legal Eagle," "Salmonitus" (AJ who started the very helpful Internet site for Lake Winni Anglers: http://www.fishlakewinni.com/ Click on "message Board,) "Aardvark,"(that's me!), and the indomitable, "Donald Duck" or "Mighty MO 2" (Bill Whall, a blind navy vet, whose CB is still the ears of Lake Winni.) The Duck, who lives in Melvin Village in Moultonboro, was awarded a medal several years ago by a team of dignitaries sent up from Washington in recognition of his service in saving the lives of many on Lake Winni.

For years, Bean Counter acted somewhat coolly toward the Duck. He suspected the Duck was reporting secret angling information—information that Bean Counter felt should be kept top secret—to other anglers. Bean Counter had the courage to invite this blind hero fishing with him, a story that will be told later in this book as well as in person by the Duck in the DVD/video which supplements this book.

After this fishing trip, The Duck came to hold Bean Counter in the highest respect. The Duck had difficulty knowing how many colors of lead core to let out while trolling. To assist him, Bean Counter efficiently tied a knot at the magic 6-color mark where fish were hitting; The Duck could feel that knot between his sensitive fingers. The Duck still tells the story of catching his first salmon on Bean Counter's boat. He was understandably excited and was reeling up the salmon so fast, according to the Duck, that he reeled it through the tip guide and ended extruding a 20" salmon to twice its length but now only a bloody quarter inch thick! Well, at least he impaled it on the rod tip.

The Duck was "a dyed in the wool" navy man, and therefore is unmerciful and quite successful in his attempts to humiliate me, since I am a West Point graduate. My wife, known as "Gypsy" on the radio, for some reason trusts the Duck in matters of the lake much more than me—even after 60 years of boating on this lake. She always radios The Duck in questionable weather before we leave our dock at Fay's Boat Yard on our way to our Bear Island home. His reply is always the same.

"Do not go out in a boat in this weather with Aardvark! He's a 'ring knocker' who went to 'Hudson on High,' where he never learned a clue about boats! And in weather like tonight, I would not advise anyone to be out in a boat with him," he invariably tells her.

Too often, he reinforces enough lingering doubts in Gypsy's mind to cause her to boycott our trip to the Island! I often find him gloating on the radio about that landlubber Aardvark, who, even with an engineering degree from West Point, cannot even get his island pump primed. He shares all of these stories and the ones that my granddaughter Miranda gleefully leaks to him, on the radio, like the one about the time I screwed my boat seats in so well that the big screws went all the way through the bottom of my boat, sinking it.

I would sometimes ask Bean Counter or Angler on the radio where or how deep they were catching fish. They often answered in cryptic code. To decode their transmission, I had to know a secret key that they carefully gave only to special anglers. This code was used to throw off the tourist flat-lander anglers who were always monitoring the radio to learn our secrets. For example, if Bean Counter said, "20' deep on Suttons," I knew to add 15' and change the lure to Flash Kings.

The CB and now the marine radios unite us anglers in a special community. "Community" does not necessarily mean being physically together. We can live in "community" while being physically alone. Because of the bond that unites us with other anglers, even when time and place separate us from one another, we are a community. The "community of anglers" stretches out, not only beyond the boundaries of lakes, towns, countries, and continents, but also beyond the boundaries of decades and centuries. Not only the awareness of those who are far away, like my living children and grandchildren, but also the memory of those who lived in the past like my Uncle Gordon, my father, and anglers like Bean Counter, who left us last year, can lead us into a healing, sustaining, and guiding community. The space for God or the Great Spirit in community transcends all limits of time and place.

In our Master Angler DVD-Video, (you can order it at **DeepWatersPress.com**), Donald Duck narrates much of it and openly tells many funny but embarrassing stories on some of us Master Anglers. But this is not the time to air dirty linen, so I will not repeat them here! (Get the Master Angler DVD to hear and see more!) The Duck is an important current and historical fixture among anglers on Lake Winni! And he can still be found out there "seeing" and reporting on all that is happening on Lake Winni via his trusty 20-20 radio-vision. My advice is NEVER try to outwit him. You will lose. Donald Duck reigns over our radio community of anglers.

The Catch & Release Nazis

FILLET and RELEASE

One morning while trolling I hooked a nice Laker who literally swallowed the Needlefish lure. While trying in vain to save him as I extracted the hooks from deep in his gullet, a large boat with several anglers approached my boat (too close for my own comfort since I still had another rod out). One red-faced man in the back repeatedly yelled in an insistent voice, "Catch & Release! Catch & Release!" Now I do my share of catching and releasing, a practice that I respect and which ensures that there remain in the lake plenty of fish for other anglers. However, I also like to keep a fish or two once in awhile to smoke or broil to the delight of my hungry family and guests. The law allows me two per day. This was too much, this man forcing his values down my throat, particularly since he had no clue that this fish would never survive my surgical extraction of the lure. I shouted back, "I'd rather eat him!"

Another good fisherman, Bruce Hack ("Chicken of the Sea" on the radio) tells me: "I am a master in this catch and release effort. In fact, I have gone way beyond catch and release to *no catch, no release....* I am now considering removing all hooks from my lures to promote even greater efficiency at no catch, no release!"

Recently a NH fish biologist shared with me that though he has difficulty promoting this because of the suggested restrictions on fish consumption warnings, we seem to have learned "Catch and Release" too well, and now we need to practice more selective harvest, keeping and eating, not the biggest trophy fish, but some of the medium-sized ones. This is good news to me!

Bear Donuts

My angling begins the night before when I prepare the coffeepot and my thermos bottle for early morning auto-brewed coffee. I also get some frozen "bear donuts" from the freezer to thaw, wrap them in foil and place them in the toaster oven, ready to be turned on when I awaken. What are "bear donuts," you ask? It's a long story. Just understand that a few years ago when I was helping a friend put out bait for bears, I went to the local donut shop and they offered me their day-old donuts, muffins, and sweet rolls which they threw away each evening. My picking up 50-60 pounds of them 2 to 4 nights each week saved the donut people having to cart them to the dumpster. I would take them to my friend Bill, for bear bait. Sometimes, when I failed to drop them off to Bill, my car would be filled with a hundred pounds of juicy sweets and their aroma. I would pick out 4 to 5 dozen of my favorite jelly or maple frosted ones that would end up in my freezer, to be thawed for fishing goodies. They tasted delicious with a steaming cup of coffee in the early morning. But I never let anyone in my boat have one until all our lines are out and we are underway trolling! This became a tradition and my children and grandchildren, as well as my neighbor, Vince, always ask for "bear donuts." When one fishes with Angler (Mario Decarolis), another small ritual takes place. He always reminds us that, "First, biggest, and most (cold water fish), earn $1 each from the others...." By "cold water fish," Mario means salmon, rainbows, or lakers.

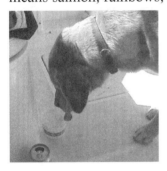

Tag drinking . . . beer.

Angling is never dull with Mario. At some time during the day, he will give his excellent Golden Lab retriever, Tag her daily beer. Mario will pour out a full can of beer into her bowl and she will eagerly lap it all up. Her taste in beer is not very good, as she prefers Budweiser, which I consider junk beer having spent many years teaching in Germany where I was spoiled by good rich German beer. On one occasion when Tag was watching Mario bring in a nice salmon after her beer, the fish made a big cartwheeling leap beside the boat. Tag, with her eyes glued to the leaping salmon, leaped over board, and grabbed the salmon in her jaws demonstrating her excellent duck retrieving expertise. After a beer, Tag becomes an interesting diversion when the fish are not hitting - a salmon retrieving-beer-drinking hunting dog!

Dr. Paine Was Still Angling in Lake Winni at 94

One of the colorful anglers who passed on some 20 years ago was Dr. Paine from Meredith Neck, who had worked for many years at the famous Menninger Clinic in Kansas.

Old Dr. Paine, with whom I fished up until he was 94, triangulated to find his grandfather's "underwater meadow" where he caught all species of fish, except salmon, from his little rowboat. Unfortunately this spot was directly in the path of the Mount Washington Ship's cruise route. The Mount insisted making its morning run just where and when Dr. Paine fished. Worried that the Mount might swamp the old man, the captain called water safety and complained. The next day, just before the Mount came by, the water safety patrol came and warned Dr. Paine that he was in the path of the Mount and might be hurt. The crusty old man's stern response was that his grandfather taught him about this secret fishing spot long before the Mount decided to run there so "... the Mount could damn well change its path, as he had every right to fish where he wished!" The next day when the Mount came by, veering to the starboard to avoid hitting Dr. Paine, he let fly with a huge deep sea casting rod with 4 ounces of lead weight attached to his line. It made a loud, satisfying "clank" as it hit the side of the big ship. Dr. Paine held his ground.

Dr. Paine at 93 with a nice catch! He had never in 70 years of fishing Lake Winni caught a land-locked salmon, and asked me to take him out which I did. He caught a nice one and we became friends, scheming about how we'd create an inflatable "sea monster" to rise in front of the Mt. Washington with a load of impressionable tourists on board.

The year before he died, he tried to enlist me in a scheme to shock the tourists on the Mount as it cruised by. He wanted me to help him rig up a huge 20-foot auto-inflatable dragon-like sea monster - a Lake Winni Monster - which he would trigger with CO_2 cartridges to rise up from the depths, just in front of the Mount. I feel I failed him by not assisting him in this task before he passed on.

I don't fully understand why, but Dr. Paine had never in his angling life caught a land locked salmon. It was probably because he hardly ever trolled and mainly fished his secret spot with night crawlers and crawfish. He had heard reports of me catching some salmon and approached me to take him out. On our first trip out together when he was 92 years old, he a caught a 4 pound salmon and was ever grateful to me for helping him to add this fine fish to his angling history.

Shortly after that, he asked if I would be willing to take out a friend of his, a world famous artist and sculptor who had bought all the wrong tackle. I agreed and with uncanny luck, during his first half-hour, he hooked and landed a 5-pound salmon. After taking pictures and thanking me back at his house, I asked if my wife and I could view some of his art. He wrote down the name of the curator at the Smithsonian Hirschhorn Museum and told me when I returned home to Washington, to visit the curator and ask him to show us his work. My wife did just that and when the curator heard that we were friends, he said in awesome tones that this man was one "…of the greatest living American artists."

We viewed the very impressive massive cast iron sculptures, many of which were over 1000 pounds with holes cut out of them with welding torches. All I could think of was what great bass structure they would make under Lake Winni! I was crass enough to write our new artist acquaintance after our visit to the sculpture garden with an unconventional suggestion. I wrote that perhaps he might stage an unusual art event. He could put one of these massive structures on the barge which was used to take them to shore from the island where he lived, video the loading. Then in 20 feet of good bass water, the barge would tip over in a secret spot known only to the artist and me, depositing the sculpture on the bottom of Lake Winni.

Within a few months, the bass would find it and an underwater team could video the bass swimming in and out of the holes in this new artistic structure which would provide excellent bass fishing for him and me. I even suggested that the video be shown at one of his exhibits as "the secret underwater sculpture."

I thought my new fishing buddy would get a chuckle out of my creative new way of presenting his art. Not so. After sending him a letter about it, I received a curt note to the effect that he took a dim view of such "art events." He and I never went fishing together again, though I did call and invite him the next year. One man's $200,000 art is another man's fishing structure.

Two men, Don Miller, big lake fisheries biologist, and John Viar, (photo overleaf) fisheries technician have worked hard to keep the smelt-salmon populations in balance to give us anglers the optimal sized salmon in Lake Winnipesaukee. They deserve our salute!

Fall-netted Winnipesaukee landlocked salmon held by Don Miller, big lake fisheries biologist, and John Viar, biology technician, two men we all salute for their great work which has helped make Lake Winni the prime angling water it is today!

Chapter 4

LAKE TROUT
SALVELINUS NAMAYCUSH

15 lbs. male lake trout with gorgeous fins; captured in gill net in fall netting operations (measured, weighed, and released)

THE LAKE TROUT is the largest native fish in these northern lakes. Originally it was in seven New Hampshire lakes including the two Connecticut Lakes, Winnipesaukee, Squam, Winnisquam, Newfound, and Crystal Lakes. It has since been stocked in many other deep lakes, which are cold (below 60-65° degrees) and have high enough oxygen content in the summer. Lake trout thrive at around 50° degrees, which is a bit colder and bit deeper than salmon. Sometimes when we lower our downrigger lines 10 to 20 feet, we will begin catching lakers.

Some big trout hanging outside of Martel's Bait shop circa 1945.

Around the last week in October, lake trout will begin spawning on shallow shoals and reefs in about one to six feet of water, depending upon the weather conditions. Because of these shallow spawning grounds, if the water level drops unusually low in October, it can have serious consequences on the next year's hatch. But in the old days, according to Jack Noon:

Lake trout were most vulnerable during the fall, when they congregated in shoal areas of lakes for spawning — the same areas every year. At night they were less wary or else dazzled by torchlight and were readily speared. To the extent that early native Abenakis needed a late-fall supply of fish, they would have hung their birchbark or pine-knot torches over the sides of canoes or dugouts, paddled to the spawning shoals, and speared the fish, much as they reportedly had done for sturgeon in the brackish waters by the coast.[14]

Gregg Lyon with large male Laker

Windy, stormy, cold nights are the chosen times for the lake trout to spawn — the very nights when we'd prefer to be before our fireplaces with a good book! Like the bass, the male trout arrive on the spawning scene first to clean the site, though no clear beds are chosen, removing debris and algae from the bottom area with their bodies, tails, and fins. Actual mating lasts only a few seconds in the evening between sunset and midnight, with two males usually sandwiching a female between them, while she drops her eggs to the bottom to be mingled with the male milt.[15] The fertilized eggs drop into the cracks between rocks and are not attended by either parent, as contrasted with the diligent parenting of the male bass. The spawners leave and then return each night for approximately two weeks, promiscuously mating with others. The eggs hatch in late winter or early spring and the fry, which survive, retreat to the depths to slowly grow stronger and larger, eating small crustaceans and insects. As they grow larger they will eat perch, smelt, shiners, minnows, insects, and other fish, dead or alive.[16]

We catch Lakers between 2-5 pounds fairly regularly in Lake Winnipesaukee in the summer, but much larger ones thrive in the depths and they grow very slowly. A keeper (18') is about 5 years old and weighs about 2 pounds. They will continue to grow about 2-3 inches a year until mature. After their first spawning, which occurs somewhere around the 5th-6th year for males and 6th-7th year for females, they grow very slowly. A 5-pounder will be about 24 inches long, while a 3-foot trout will be about 18 pounds.

Some of the old timers who fish with large 6-8" suckers for bait sometimes catch 10 to 15-pounders. And each winter or two, we learn of a 14 to 18-pounder being caught through the ice. But in truth, there are much larger lakers lurking in these depths. Why aren't the 20+ pounders caught, which sometimes show up on fish finders or in the Fish & Game nettings? They seemed to catch them in the old days:

George (Count) Zarynoff, former wrestler of Springfield MA with 15lb 12oz, laker caught in Lake Winni, 1936.

The early catches of lake trout must have been impressive. Lake trout can live a long time and grow to enormous weights, but in modern-day New Hampshire, they are almost always caught and kept long before they have a chance to reach their potential. The lake trout spearers of a century and a half ago would likely have snorted in derision at the sizes of the lake trout that now win fishing tournaments.... However, these old-timers today would fare no better than we do; we, back in their era, would have done as well as they did and with our fishing rods would likely have had a lot more fun than they had with their spears.[17]

Two old codgers holding stringer of trout -- supper for a few families during the great depression. Note the sign, "We are for the Farmers"

With the railroad lines in place tourism and sportfishing developed quickly at Lake Winnipesaukee. Meader reported in his book that lake trout and pickerel were the most important fish, that some people highly prized cusk, and that even inexperienced fishermen could catch quantities of yellow perch and horned pout. By the end of the 1860s, lake trout were smaller and less abundant than in earlier years. (Overfishing was beginning to show its effects.) ...Sportsmen trying to catch lake trout would hire an "oarsman" and then fish with bait in deep water.[18]

The Hidden Monsters of Lake Winni

The NH State Record Laker, weighing 28 pounds 8 oz, caught on April 24, 1958 by Albert Staples

Big trout sometimes feed on large fish and when they do, they feed only once every week or two. Most fishermen don't catch these enormous trout since they fish with small bait. In 1996-97 two 14 to 16 pound trout were caught in Lake Winnipeasukee which had 14" and 16" salmon in their stomachs! If one consistently fished with 12" bait, I believe much larger trout would be caught, but no one seems to do it. The New Hampshire record lake trout was caught in Newfound Lake in 1958 and weighed 28 and a half pounds and was nearly 40" long. According to Master angler Rick Davis, a larger laker was reportedly caught and witnessed by Tom Clow and Captain Lavalle off Ship Island on Lake Winni which weighed 29+ pounds. It was mounted but never entered as a State record. The largest caught with a hook and line was from Lake Superior in 1952 and it weighed just over 63 pounds and was 51 inches long. The world record was 102 pounds caught in a net in Canada in 1961.

Bean Counter and Angler's Encounter with the Shark

Nice laker caught by author using the first downrigger on Lake Winni.

My friends, Angler and Bean Counter, had an interesting encounter with one of these monsters in Lake Winni during the Salmon Derby several years ago. While bringing a struggling 18" salmon into their boat, a huge V- shaped shark-like wake came from nowhere attempting to eat their hooked salmon! One of my friends happened to be videotaping the action and recorded what appeared to be at least a 4-foot monster attempting to eat the hooked salmon! They estimated the fish to be at least 50 pounds! Ironically, this situation repeated itself the next day in the very same spot and was again recorded on tape! Angler and Bean Counter have spent many hours during every fishing derby since, trolling through this same spot. I discussed this with one of the New Hampshire fish biologists and he felt certain that this was a monster lake trout, which was after his biweekly meal of a struggling salmon. He assured me that there are many huge 20-pound+ lakers in Lake Winni, but that most anglers just do not use large enough bait to tempt them.

An antique pearl wobbler (lower part of picture), is my favorite laker lure.

The lake trout is a bulldog fighter, hardly ever coming to the surface when hooked and often making deep sounding power dives. I know when I have hooked a laker, by its deep power pulls. You cannot troll slowly enough for lakers - the slower the better. Sometimes when trolling very slowly and catching a trout, I will speed up and catch a salmon, or vice versa. My favorite old lake trout lure, the Pearl Wobbler, made from mother of pearl, is no longer manufactured and is now an antique dating back to before the turn of the century, and difficult to find. I am always looking for one at yard sales. Here's what it looks like.

If you happen to find any, contact me and I will buy them from you, not to display as a collectable, but to use fishing!

In the Old Days of Real Hardware

My Uncle Gordon loved to fish for lake trout in his old wooden laker boat in the 1930s-50s. He used Monel wire line on his heavy trolling rods, dragging multi-spoon Dave Davis Spinners. He sewed a fresh 6" shiner on a snelled hook so it slowly turned behind the long column of copper spoons as he slowly trolled. Catching one on this heavy tackle was more like weight lifting than fishing! Other old timers used hand lines with the same Davis rigs or with a sewn sucker, holding the line over the side in their work-glove-protected hand, bouncing the lures off the bottom with a pendulum action which had to lead to bursitis.

I watched with satisfied wonder one early morning, before the lake became alive with tourists, as an old man in a red and black checked mackinaw smoked his corncob pipe in a modest 14-foot boat and 1950's 5 HP-motor. He worked his hand line with great success while a young man in a $100,000 boat equipped with every manner of electronic high tech fish finders, electric downriggers, and side planers trolled in the old man's tracks, without success. This sight makes an old man feel good!

Lake Winnipesaukee's First Downrigger

I believe that I hold the dubious distinction of bringing to Lake Winnipesaukee the first downrigger in 1972. I still fish with this old Luhr Jenson hand crank machine! The story is a bit of an odd one.

An old vintage photo of a man in a fancy over coat holding a nice laker. Strange the way men dressed up for their fish photos back then...and even wore ties for angling!

At the time, I was serving in Washington in the Federal Government as Director of Education for the Gifted & Talented. A patent attorney called on me to discuss a curriculum he had designed to teach creative young inventors how to invent. After confirming with me that our most creative years are likely between 18-30 years old, he then asked me to guess the age when an inventor takes out his first patent. I guessed about 25. He told me that I was way off and that creative inventors averaged age 42 before having their first patent! The reason for this, he explained, was that people don't know the simple process of how to patent their ideas. What a waste of their earlier and most creative years! So he had invented a curriculum for gifted young people to teach them how to invent and get their inventions protected and into the market where they are needed.

He asked if I knew how to do a patent search. When I responded negatively, he asked me to think of a problem for which I sought a solution. I knew already what the problem was. I wanted to fish for lakers and salmon during my annual august summer vacation on Lake Winnipesaukee with light lines. But the fish were too deep to reach without using my uncle's heavy line. He asked if I had thought of a solution. I said that I had thought of using a hand crank winch which could lower a lead weight down to depths were the fish were and which would have a close-pin type of release, dragging the lure behind it until a fish struck the lure and caused it to release. I drew him a sketch of my idea.

The author sitting on his old 140 HP Johnson which blew up in 2003 holding a string of Lakers....To my right is the oldest Downrigger on Lake Winni, an old black Luhr Jensen, which was sent to me by a friend on lake Michigan in 1972 and which when I took it around to the sporting goods shops, no one knew what it was! I began using it to get my light lines down deep in summer where the lakers and salmon were. It worked...and still works! My friend's name who sent it was Kent Bishionette, a remarkable man who had several patents on downriggers and releases. In fact I found him at the U.S, Patent Office in Washington, DC which began a fruitful friendship.

"Good! Let's go do a patent search." He drove me a mile away to the U.S. Patent Office and showed me how to search my idea. Sure enough, there were about 6 on file not very different from my sketch! We looked them all up and I wrote down the phone numbers of the inventors hoping I could purchase a device that would accomplish my task. The patent that looked most interesting was on file by Kent Bishonette from Michigan and I called him. This began a fascinating relationship with a 78 year old man who sent me literally hundreds of pages of hand written notes about trout, salmon, down riggers, and other angling lore. He invited me to visit him for personal hands-on demonstrations of his inventions. It was time for me to accept the invitation of the Michigan Association for the Gifted to speak at their summer conference. Afterwards, I joined Kent Bishionette for some amazing fishing on Lake Michigan! We drove to the Northern Peninsula, put his fishing boat (equipped with four electric downriggers) into the water, and trolled with his unique equipment and salmon and trout flies all tied on Swedish steel hooks. We caught Coho salmon one after another, lowering our lines with downriggers equipped with his patented release devices, flashers, and flies. Boats pulled up to us when they the saw the "Kent Fishing Team" emblem on the side of Kent's boat, asking to buy his "chartreuse fly" and offering deeply inflated prices of $25 or more for one. After being begged, Kent would throw them one for free, obviously enjoying the power of his position. After catching salmon until my arms ached, he then took me to small streams where he showed me how to antagonize large native brook trout into striking by repeatedly slapping a fly noisily beside undercut banks. When a stranger happened by, my septuagenarian host insisted on pretending we were catching nothing, propping his fly rod against a branch like cane pole fishermen southern style. "Nuthin biting," he muttered to the intruder, after cautioning me to be quiet and let him do the talking.

He showed me how to catch large spawning brown trout on flies which were finding their ways through the shallows of a bay and up through beaver dam clogged streams. He instructed me that this had to be accomplished between 1-3 AM in a small boat under the cover of darkness, quietly. I was lectured to paddle without noise and make no splashing while lowering the anchor. We went out in a rowboat while still daylight and he had me rehearse lowering the anchor at least 20 times until I got it perfect! At 1 AM, after hours of Kent tying flies while I fought against sleep, we finally made our approach in the small boat under cover of darkness. Silently presenting his fly, Kent proceeded to catch 4-8 pound browns in the shallows in an unorthodox manner by not putting any pressure on the hooked fish. Once the trout took the fly, he gradually guided the large trout toward the boat and his landing net with no struggle as if the trout did not know he was hooked! He dispatched the trout silently, reminding me of my Army Ranger missions, by quickly inserting the blade of his penknife into their brains to prevent noisy struggles in the boat.

By the time I arrived home from this amazing experience, a package with Lake Winnipesaukee's first downrigger was already awaiting me. Inside was a black Luhr Jensen hand crank which I have used until this year, when I finally got some new Big Jons, plus a slew of flies, "Hippy Tad" lures, and release devices he had invented. I took the equipment to local angler stores and no one had seen anything like it. I tested it and it worked! Most of the high tech fishermen, and even some of the low-tech fishermen, like me, use downriggers, which got their start on the Great Lakes. The second one he sent me in 1972 was an old silver Riviera hand-crank that I also use. (If there is someone out there on Lake Winnipesaukee who had a downrigger on the lake before 1972, write me so we can exchange stories.)

Many anglers use the process of triangulation to fish in the exact spot where they have had luck in the past. I always use this to find my favorite bass spot, an unmarked spot in open water where a huge bolder rises from 30 feet to within 5 feet of the surface. Now that we have GPS satellite guided hand-helds, or boat mounted GPS devices, it is much easier to find those secret places, as did Bean Counter in his last angling years.

The older Master Anglers seem happier with the old technology but, understandably, the younger ones who grew up with computers and digital gadgets are quick to change over to high tech gear. And the technology keeps getting more sophisticated. In some cases, like with my old hand crank downriggers and the new electronic ones, the new technology is a refinement of the old gear. Boats have been using clunky sonar fish-finders for many decades, but now there's an electronic sonar gizmo so small it can be attached to the fisherman's release down in the water, or even to the lure. It's a fishfinder that beams an image of fish to a wireless receiver connected to the angler's watch-like device! And a Japanese company makes a reel with a microchip controlled spool that can lengthen a cast from 200 feet to 300 by automatically adjusting the speed of the spool while the lure flies through the air! And you know they are not making this technology for Japanese anglers! What's next? A device which reaches out and grabs the fish?

A Jigging Machine to give action to the lures

This device was created by Master Angler Jason Parent. It gives action to the lure by jigging with its windshield wiper motor which excites salmon into striking.

Outdoor writer, Bob Harris told me about a highly respected angler and outdoor writer named Harry Kenerson, who was "The Little Fisherman" on the radio and was one of the early successful users of the "jigging box." Harry was one of those anglers who was definitely a Master Angler. Some say he invented the "jigger box" and took all winter to custom make them, delivering them in the spring to a select group of anglers who swear by them. Others say that wherever he got them, he proved time and time again that the action given a lure or fly with a "jigger box" caught significantly more salmon than merely dragging a passive fly. Harry, who had Parkinson's Disease, passed on December 24, 2003. Angling guide Pete Grasso ("Dr. Hook") wrote a wonderful tribute to Harry Kenerson in the *Weirs Times*:

> Harry spent a lot of time teaching me the finer points of salmon fishing and operation of the "jigger boxes." Of course our bait was limited to the two special flies that were Harry's secret weapons and DID we catch some fish. We caught over 20 salmon in a bit less than three hours. Tony, who was 16 and had fished with me since he was big enough to walk, caught the biggest salmon he had ever gotten hold of. Now that was not good advertising with me being a guide and all. When we got back at the dock Harry asked me, "Now what do you think of the jigger boxes?" Needless to say, I placed my order and a year later I had two of them rigged up on my boat. I am still using the same ones and have NEVER had a problem with either of them. Also I don't think I have run the fly-dodger combinations since I put those boxes on board.... The grand old man of salmon fishing is finally at rest.... He will be sadly missed by all. "TIGHT LINES, HARRY!"[19]

One of our Master Anglers, Jason Parent has also invented a jigging device to give action to flies and lures. He calls it the Jigging Machine. Jason's Jigging machine is a nifty device enclosed in a water proof aluminum box with a back-and-forth arm which has three settings, a long jig, a medium and a short jig in which is inserted a pressure release device to hold various thicknesses of line. It also has a fast and slow jig setting activated by a lever, running off your battery. 60 years ago, my Uncle Gordon would jig his fly rod back and forth and he swore the action it generated resulted in significantly more fish. I used my new Jigging Machine last year and it did produce results once I got it mounted in the right spot, which is to the rear of the boat. I am now using mine with considerable success — particularly to give a jigging action to a fly on my fly rod. It also works well with lead core. In the summer of 2003, I found I caught many more fish using the action of the jigging machine than without it. Of course, it is impossible to use it on the downrigger. Jason will custom make one of his Jigging Machines for you for a modest cost of about $229. You can find Jason Parent's web site to book him as a guide or to contact him to buy one of his inventions at this site: www.NHGuideservices.com

Author's granddaughter, Miranda Collier with her first laker.

Talking about low tech, or maybe I should say,"New Age," I can remember during the 60's, we use to meditate while trolling deep for lakers, focusing on transmitting our energy and "vibes" out through our hands, to the rod, then sending it out through the line all the way down 50 yards to the lure, and then radiating the energy out to a waiting trout, attracting him to the lure. What a thrill it was for us when, in such angling meditation, a trout would suddenly strike our lure and we'd be fast to a powerful fish from the deep! It reinforced all the holistic powers we had — or thought we had. But now, a lot older, a bit wiser and more seasoned, I much prefer to pay attention to what pseudo-scientific research, like Bean Counter's, plus hundreds of years of Master Angler wisdom suggests for the best lures and techniques. But as a kind of carry over from the old days, when nothing else works, I do still find myself telling my grand children, to pray for or "Think fish!"

Chapter 5

RAINBOW TROUT

SALMO GAIRDNERI

OR ONCORHYNCHUS MYKISS

"I stared at that unexpected bouquet of orange and green and white as if I had been hypnotized. I was suddenly a kid again, and if I had been struck dead at that very moment I probably would have said 'brook trout' the way Orson Welles said 'Rosebud' in Citizen Kane." — E. Donnall Thomas, Jr.

4 lb rainbow trap netted fall 2003 Lake Winnipesaukee; note weighing scale, pan, and tripod in background - length and weight data is critical in fisheries management

I CAN REMEMBER the first trout I ever caught as a young boy. It was the most beautiful creature I had ever seen ...even to a color-blind boy. My hands trembled uncontrollably as I fondly cradled the fish in my hands. What a beauty God created in the trout!

The rainbow trout is distinguished from the landlocked salmon by its profusion of black spots on its body and dorsal fins. But as a fighting fish, it matches the salmon, taking to the air in spectacular leaps. The rainbow was introduced into Lake Winni in the early 1990s as a kind of "fail-safe" mechanism for anglers — insurance in case the sensitive salmon population declined. The rainbow was selected by Fish & Game biologists because it would not directly compete with the salmon since it also eats terrestrial insects as avidly as it eats other forage fish, such as smelt. Like other trout, it prefers cold water and grows very fast when introduced into the Lake. It has replaced the lake trout as the main ice fishing game fish for the Winter Ice Derby at the request of Fish & Game biologists to allow the much slower growing lake trout to have a break from angling pressure to reach maturity and larger sizes. Rainbows have a strong migratory urge, which drives them into the rivers entering Lake Winni in spring as the waters warm, as contrasted to salmon and other trout that go into the rivers in fall, as temperatures drop. The fish biologists tell me there is also a fall-spawning variety of rainbow. Rainbows are able to survive higher temperatures than our native brook trout.

Author with nice 5 pound rainbow caught while trolling for salmon. The rainbows in Lake Winni , which were stocked for the first time in the early 1990s, thrive here and grow large in a short time. The rivers going in and out of Lake Winni, however, are too acidic to support natural spawning of the trout in the spring, so it is a put and take fishery, which adds a nice bonus to salmon fishing. The rainbows, which consume terrestrial insects, as well as small fish, do not threaten the delicate balance of the smelt- salmon population, and so do not compete enough for available food to create a problem. They are fun to catch and match the salmon in fighting ability.

However, rainbows are a put-and-take fish in Lake Winni since the pH of streams in our area is too low (too acidic) for them to reproduce naturally; hence 10,000 8-10" yearling rainbows are stocked each year by Fish & Game. The rainbows eat all food (omnivorous) including insects, ostracods, water mites, larvae, and worms. They grow from spring to fall into 18-20" fish weighing 3-4 pounds. The Lake Winni stocking program began in 1991. In the old days rainbows were caught, but they were the rare ones entering Lake Winni via streams like this big one from the 1940's (illustration on the next page).

I enjoy catching rainbows as a bonus fish throughout the year while angling for salmon. The methods of angling for them are similar, though I find small sparsely tied smelt imitation flies work best. The Barbara Cotton Special tied by Master Angler Jim Warner is an excellent rainbow fly. And I do not have to go as deep for them as I do in summer for salmon. I have caught rainbows up to 5 pounds these past few years.

Large rainbow trout caught in Lake Winni, 1949, probably from a local stream.

They seem very healthy and in the next decade, I thought we'd be catching holdovers up to 10 pounds and larger as they thrive and grow fast in the lake. But fisheries biologist Don Miller tells me that this is not likely as the rainbows in the lake not caught by anglers are drawn to migrate down river from the lake as far as the dams will allow. For some reason, some are bright silver colored while others are almost black. The rainbows which won money in the 2002–2004 Rotary Ice Fishing Derbies were in the 4-6 pound range, and they seem to be getting bigger each year.

Need We Worry About Acid Rain?

I recommend a small book entitled, *The Atlas of New Hampshire Trout Ponds* for an interesting discussion of acid rain in New Hampshire. Most of us have read about the dead lakes of New York's Adirondacks where acid rain has left behind barren fishless lakes. New Hampshire also receives acid precipitation, enough to threaten our more sensitive ponds and small lakes. In over half of New Hampshire's smaller lakes and ponds acid rain already "...suggests stressful conditions and impacts on the food chains of trout."[20]

3.75 lbs female rainbow trap netted in Lake Winnipesaukee fall 2003

Where does acid rain come from? The combustion of fossil fuels in coal and oil fired electric generating plants, smelting, auto exhaust, and other industrial operations generate oxides of nitrogen and sulfur dioxide which become airborne and are delivered by prevailing winds to us from Canada and our own industrialized Ohio River valley. The acid rain drops on our lakes in rain, snow, and fog. Acid in rain is measured on a scale from 1-14 — a logarithmic pH scale, 7 being neutral. Below 7 is acidic and above is basic. "For example, a pH of 4 is 10 times more acidic than a pH of 6. It also means that the amount of acid rain required to reduce pH increases tenfold for each unit decrease in pH.[21]" "Normal" rain has a pH of 5.6 but where some acid rain exists, like here in the Northeast, our normal rain has a pH of between 5.9 and 5.2. This has been monitored since 1963 by State and Federal scientists. The median annual pH for precipitation in New Hampshire was 4.2 to 4.4. [22] This amounts to 10 times more acidic than normal rain, which gradually has a devastating effect on smaller ponds and lakes, especially in the higher elevations where greater rainfall, snow and fog exist. As of 1993, the State Fish & Game Department released data on 592 New Hampshire lakes and ponds which shows 14 lakes (with pH less than 5) already acidified, 27 lakes (with pH 5–5.4) critical, 76 lakes endangered (with pH 5.5–6.0), 474 lakes (with pH greater than 6) satisfactory. What does this mean? First, high acidity reduces the amount of food available to fish. Secondly, the acid can directly harm the fish.

What About Lake Winni and Acid Rain?

Fortunately this huge body of water is not as quickly affected by acid rain as smaller bodies of water. Lake Winni has a pH of about 6.7 and is currently in good condition, though still too acidic (not high enough pH) for our stocked rainbow trout to naturally reproduce in the spring in the Lake Winni rivers. "At pH 6, some of the freshwater mussels begin to disappear. At a pH of 5.5, there are fewer Mayflies. Below 5.5, crustaceans die. No snails are found in water below pH 6.0."[23]

Cleaning a nice catch of rainbow trout for breakfast

Certainly in our remote small ponds, where 95% are at least highly sensitive and two thirds are already endangered, we face a crisis. If our children and grandchildren are to have the wonderful fishery we now have, political action to stem both auto and industrial pollution will have to be initiated at the local, regional, national and international level. Some of this is already underway... but not enough. Though this is a gradual process which might not effect us in our lifetimes, it is important for each of us to dialogue with our elected representatives to insure that pH levels continue to be monitored and legislation is beefed up to reduce both auto and industrial pollution, if our great grandchildren are to enjoy the pristine waters of New Hampshire.

> **Milfoil:** Another concern in our lakes is the proliferation of Variable Milfoil, which grows very rapidly, threatening bays and coves of Lake Winni. It is very difficult to eradicate. Attempts at harvesting it for eventual use as fertilizer have been tried, as have attempts at poisoning it. But so far, no ideal answer has been created. The best we can do as anglers is to make certain we do not help spread it on our boats and trailers as we move from lake to lake. We need creative minds to tackle these problems. For example, my granddaughter, Miranda, did a school project on Milfoil when she was only 10 years old. She found, by accident, as many discoveries are made, that the Milfoil plants in one of her tanks disappeared, which happened to contain Mayfly larvae. The Milfoil flourished in the other tank without the larvae. Could the introduction of more Mayflies into Milfoil congested waters both help us with this problem, while also providing more food for the fish? Or are we, once again, messing with Mother Nature, as we did when we brought Milfoil to our waters in the first place? Though Miranda won first prize in her school science fair, this was certainly not a definitive study. But it is an example of the kind of creative research less rigid minds than we old Master Anglers have, which is much needed to one-day tackle and solve this problem!

The Myth of the Perfect Anglers Who Have No Dog Days

At least this Master Angler will confess that he has dog days when, no matter how hard I try, I fail to hook fish. Sometimes after a week or two of bad luck, I begin to believe that most of the other Master Anglers, who may be catching fish, are better fishermen than I am. It is true. Master Angler Ted St. Onge says he never gets skunked. And I do believe him. Mario DeCarolis will catch many more fish than I will over the long haul. At times I will follow Mario imitating what he does to break my spell of bad luck. I can fish along side him fishless, while Mario's rod is bent double with excitement. How does he do it? He taunts me, encouragingly, on the radio, "Fish 40' down with a #61 Sutton at 1.8 MPH." I imitate him precisely as I can. He hooks salmon. I drag water. But then, I rationalize, he spends many more hours on the lake than I do. Besides, he has an unfair advantage in his amazing retriever dog, Tag, who leads him to the best fishing ground and gives him luck. But I usually get up earlier and fish the earliest and latest hours - prime times for salmon and trout. In desperation, I go out with him and catch salmon in his boat! My boat must be jinxed! I am only rarely encouraged when he calls to tell me that he spent all day on the Lake and caught nothing. There is a lot of luck in this sport, like in deer hunting. But once you have learned the techniques offered in this book for the first time by the Master Anglers, it is a combination of hours put in on the lake and pure luck!

Author's granddaughters, Amanda and Crystal Gosnell holding a rainbow they just caught with their grand father. (Note the oldest downrigger on Lake Winni to the right).

On the message board of the anglers' web site, (http://www.fish-lakewinni.com/), partly to justify it to myself, partly to encourage others in a slump, I urge fellow anglers to share when they have bad luck as well as their successes. It helps us all to be humble, though I often feel a bit inadequate when some anglers, who never seem to have a bad day, report catching 12-25 salmon on a morning when I have not caught one! I hear them on the radio, "Just caught another 4-pounder....Whoops! Gotta go! Another fish on!" I sometimes console myself by thinking, "They are just acting this scene out to fool the rest of us. They are lying. They are doing this to feel superior ...and make the rest of us feel inadequate...." It works. Then I wonder if I am transmitting my pessimism down through the fishing line to the fish? There are others out there who get discouraged. At the salmon derby last year, I heard a frustrated angler say over the radio in dispair, "I haven't had a strike all day. There are no salmon left in this lake! The Fish & Game propaganda is just that, to make us come up here and spend our money."

Uncle Gordon Hines, cooling it, with a big string of lake trout, circa 1929

The author smiling after a successful day on the Lake whether or not catching fish.

Colonel Harold Lyon with his son, the author, 1979

My great love —Lake Winni

My sons, Eric, Gregg and I with bass (1968)

Sunrise from Bear Island

My old friend, Bill Beetham, holding a nice laker. Bill did some of the photography in this book.

Eric Lyon, age 7, won 1st prize in the Junior Divison of Field and Stream Magazine's annual fishing contest with this beauty—a 4.5 lb small mouth caught on a live frog at Old South Ledge.

Ed Mosher's 41.5 inch 24.97 lb lake trout, caught while ice fishing, Winnisquam Lake, in March 2000. Ed passed away at the early age of 45 on November 18, 2003. He was considered by many as the best lake trout angler in the Lakes Region, catching many large trout mostly by dedicated jigging with a small piece of sucker on his jigs. He had won numerous New Hampshire Fish & Game sanctioned trophy fish awards. He was also the subject of a feature article in "Hawkeye," When he landed this trout, the second largest laker ever landed in New Hampshire history." (Photo, courtesy of John A. Viar, NH F&G Dept.)

A hellgrammite, larvae of the Dobson Fly, which is one of the best baits for smallmouth bass.

In 2003, at the fall salmon netting and stripping, this 7 pound female salmon was netted, stripped of her roe, and released. The salmon will be healthy in 2004!

My granddaughter, Crystal Gosnell, with her first big salmon.

Tony DeCarolis with 5-pound salmon which won 2nd place in the 2003 junior Division of the Salmon Derby.

Gregg Lyon with large male laker

Author holds nice laker in sun

Side view of laker in the sun showing the beautiful colors.

The author sitting on his old 140 HP Johnson

4-pound rainbow trap netted fall 2003 Lake Winnipesaukee

Andy French, cover artist for this book and son of Master Angler Chuck French with large mouth bass caught in local marina

My granddaughter, Taylor Lyon with her first large mouth bass — a 7-pounder!

15-pound male trout with gorgeous fins, captured in gill net in fall netting operations (measured, weighed, and released) by Don Miller's team of fish biologists.

The author-mentor's wife, Edith, daughter, Laural, and son, John with Laural's first salmon, late 1970's.

Top left: An assortment of the hot new Lake Winni salmon lures, the Top Gun, from the Moosalamoo Shoe-Horn Co. out of Rutland, VT.

Top right: More hot new lures, the DB Smelt, created by Dave Broder from Berlin, New Hampshire. This lure and the Top Gun have emerged as 2 of the 3 top lures for salmon on Lake Winni in the past few years.

The Master Anglers' 6 most popular salmon streamer flies (all tied by Master Angler Alan Nute), from left: the Lake Winni Smelt (created by Master Angler Jim Warner); the Maynard Golden Marvel, the Pumpkin Head, the Red Marabou, the Fire Smelt (created by Alan Nute); and the Grey Ghost.

Ice fish with Mario and his family and you will eat well! (Chops, steaks, chickens, soups, pasta, veal, and deep-fried turkey, all out on the ice!)

Mario in his well-equipped bob house

The tip up is up!

Mario in fine form

Aprés ice fishing derby gathering of DeCarolis family and friends for pasta and wine.

The Rotary Derby Board

Chapter 6

LAKE WHITEFISH, PICKEREL, AND LARGE MOUTH BASS

White fish: (Coregonus clupeaformis)

THE WHITEFISH LIVES IN DEEP, cold water, coming into shallows on reefs and ledges in early December to spawn when the water cools down to between 40°-50° F. They also visit these reefs in the late winter as well as early spring where they can sometimes be caught near the surface on flies.

The whitefish is one of the few real natives to Lake Winnipesaukee and is found in only three New Hampshire lakes: Lake Winni, Squam, and Wentworth. Though they have reached 20 pounds in the Great Lakes, in the New Hampshire lakes, they normally go from 1-4 pounds. They are called "shad" locally. They spawn up on the surface where they let their eggs and milt drop to the crevices in rocks below. Unlike bass, the eggs go unguarded and are on their own to hatch in later winter. This may be one reason for the decline in their numbers, as the eggs are vulnerable to predator fish as they drop unguarded to the bottom.

I remember in the 70s catching my first whitefish while trolling for salmon. At first I thought it was a "roach" or fallfish, until I noticed that it had an adipose fin, like a member of the trout or salmon family, and much smaller scales. Many years ago, the old timers will tell you that they caught 10-pound "shad" usually through the ice, chumming with cut up pieces of smelt in baited spots where the chum was left several days earlier. A light sinker with a small hook was used, baited with a small piece of cut fish or a tiny mealworm. Overexploitation has caused a sharp decline in shad. I used to catch 2-3 per year while trolling for salmon. Though the whitefish is normally a bottom feeder, feeding on small insect larvae and crustaceans, and on animal plankton in deeper water, it also feeds on small smelts, especially in winter. The fish biologists tell me that they still net an occasional whitefish in their sampling runs, but it has been at least ten years since I have caught one.

A large lake whitefish, caught by Master Angler Steve Perry

In my opinion, there is no better eating fish than the sweet, firm white meat of the whitefish. There are two subspecies. Though locals call both "shad," one is the lake whitefish and the other, the round whitefish, which likes shallower waters than its cousin. There are more round whitefish in Newfound Lake than in Lake Winni. The whitefish seems to be joining the other species that are disappearing in the Lake, either from over exploitation, over competition with white perch for food, or because of their fragility and the fact that they are at the southern limit of their preferred habitat. Each of the Master Anglers shares his opinion about what has happened to the "shad" in that section of the book. Angler-author historian, Jack Noon, tells me that our DVD interviews with the 14 Master Anglers might also serve to correct some of the considerable and persistent historical fisheries misinformation — often quoted — such as in Benjamin Franklin Parker's *History of Wolfeborough*, where he claimed that the "shad" the ice fishermen were fishing for were descendants of the anadromous shad, when in fact they were the local misnomer for whitefish. Whitefish, though locally called "shad", are not really shad at all!

Chain Pickerel: (Esox niger)

The pickerel likes shallow, warmer muddy areas, usually in small coves, which have an abundance of water vegetation. When I was a boy on Lake Winni, my cousin, Bill Hines, and I loved to take our rowboat to quiet coves like Salmon Meadows in the northern part of the lake and fish the lilypads for pickerel with a red and white Dare Devil spoon. We also caught them around the pilings of Brown's Boat Basin docks on occasion, as well as through the ice. The pickerel is a thin streamlined fish that attacks its prey, or Dare Devils when we were lucky, with a vengeance, ambushing them from a concealed stationary position. It will take the bait sideways and then run to swallow it head-first. For this reason, when ice fishing for pickerel, like with bass, it is best to let them run until they have swallowed the bait. Pickerel have sharp teeth, which can cause nasty wounds. On rare occasions we have caught them trolling in deeper water.

Holding a string of large pickerel, circa. 1926.

The pickerel spawns just after ice out in shallow weedy areas and the young are hatched in time to begin their voracious appetite for other species of small fish when they hatch out a few months later. A 20" pickerel weighs about 2 pounds and is about 5-6 years old. The world's record was caught in Georgia in 1961 and was 31" long, weighing 9 pounds, 6 ounces. The NH record was caught in Plummer Pond in 1966 and was 26" weighing 8 pounds. Jack Noon tells us:

> Before black bass were introduced into New Hampshire, pickerel were the most popular warmwater fish among sportsmen, subsistence fishermen, and commercial freshwater fishermen. Their original range in the state was a good deal more restricted than it is today.[24]

The pickerel is a fun fish to catch and to eat and has tasty sweet flesh. The primary problem when eating pickerel is the numerous small "Y"shaped bones. I learned as a boy to score the pickerel filets with a sharp knife and then to either fry or broil them so the heat will penetrate the flesh and dissolve these pesky bones.

The story of my largest pickerel in Lake Winni is a rather unorthodox one from back in the early 1940's. My cousin, Bill Hines, and I were out on our dock one summer day on Meredith Neck, when I was 6 years old. A huge pickerel happened to come swimming slowly by the dock just under the surface - a rare occurrence! Not having my rod with me, I made a quick decision and leaped into the water on top of this monster, thrusting my hand up into its gills to hold him. The water was a foot or so over my head and a struggle between boy and fish erupted amidst much splashing. I struggled to the dock, not letting go of this monster, while coughing and sputtering water from my nose and throat. Bill reached down and helped me hoist the fish up and onto the dock, where he leaped upon the struggling fish like he was recovering a fumbled football. This pickerel was 25" long and weighed over 5 pounds, the largest I have ever caught in Lake Winni and it was caught by hand! My right hand was dripping blood from the monster's sharp teeth but it was worth it!

I love to paddle in a canoe in a small cove and cast to the lily pads for them in summer. It has been some time since I have fished for pickerel, but I always enjoy the experience. Just have a pair of long-nose pliers handy to free your hook from those sharp teeth!

Jack Noon writes about how the pickerel came to many New Hampshire lakes:

> In a very common pattern throughout the state's waters, but particularly in lakes and ponds with narrow inlet brooks easily straddled by fishermen, the brook trout were over-fished during their fall spawning runs. When settlers could no longer catch trout in the quantities they once had, they often introduced new species — particularly pickerel. Pickerel were readily caught through the ice in winter and had the additional advantage of spawning right after ice-out in splashing groups of adult fish in shallow water, where they could be speared from quietly paddled canoes or boats. They seemed a clever supplement to the over-fished trout. Thus the pickerel and occasionally

yellow perch and horned pout began to be moved from what had probably been their original range near the coast and in the major rivers and in a few ponds and lakes with easy access to rivers. They were stocked into waters of the interior they hadn't been able to reach earlier because of impassable falls, distance, or other restricting factors.[25]

Noon reports that fishermen angling for pickerel in the 1860s used a long cane pole and a "hook, baited with a frog's leg peeled and skittered along the edges of weed beds."[26]

John McPhee in his foreword to Jack Noon's scholarly book, *Fishing in New Hampshire — a History,* writes elegantly about fly fishing for pickerel:

Now for twenty-four consecutive years I have fly-fished for chain pickerel in the autumn in Lake Winnipesaukee.... I share this habit with George Hackl, of Center Tuftonboro, each of us in his own canoe. In the big lake we see a lot of bass fishermen. They appear out of nowhere and in less than fifteen seconds have cut their outboards, turned on their electric trolling motors, and begun to heave their hardware. To them we are really weird — standing up in our canoes and flailing with fly lines — and even weirder after they learn what we are fishing for: "Pickerel? You have to be kidding? Who would want to fish for pickerel? Anyone who would do that is crazy!" Pickerel — ubiquitous pickerel, freshwater barracudas — irritate bass fishermen because they frequently beat bass to the hardware and as they are reeled in are looked upon as intrusive, interfering, time-wasting trash. Odd as we may seem to bass fishermen, they like what we are doing. They even thank us.

In the Northeastern arm of the big lake, Ann Hackl, George's wife, owns an eleven-acre forested island on which the only roof covers a very small shack heated by a tin stove. Some mornings, ice has been very thick in the water buckets. Fly lines, as they arc stripped in, carry water to the rod guides, which gradually fill with ice until the line is frozen tight and won't move. Guide by guide, you punch out the ice with your thumb. Your numb red thumb. You eat the pickerel for breakfast — delicious sweet white fish. This is the reverse of big-fish fishing. We catch some good-sized pickerel — George caught one nearly two feet long — but the smaller pickerel are the tastier pickerel.

In Fishing with Hook and Line; a Manual for Amateur Anglers (New York, 1858), Henry William Herbert, whose pen name was Frank Forester, said that pickerel feed on almost nothing in summer, the colors of their skin go dull, and they are in such torpor that small fish fearlessly swim around them — a set of facts we would come to know empirically.

Very large pickerel, circa. 1929. The largest I caught was when I was 7 years old. I jumped on its back as it swam by my dock!

Pickerel are in much better condition in the fall, he noted, as their voracity rekindles with the approach of winter. Forester described what happened when a nineteenth-century chain pickerel was let loose in a pond of various fish. It ate the entire pond "except a carp weighing nine pounds, and it had bitten a piece out of him!"

The way pickerel hit a fly is less a take than an explosion. Keep them high or you will loose them. After the first big swirl, they sound. They tie two half hitches around the stem of an aquatic plant, chew through the line, and what you recently held throbbing is now a dead snag. For the most part, we use large, heavy flies, size 4 — white zonkers, natural zonkers, yellow muddlers, white muddlers, skunk muddlers, white wooly buggers, Alaskabous. Lay them at the edge of lily pads. Inspect them after every catch.

Pickerel teeth are sharper than concertina wire and will cut into the leader. Seven feet of flat twelve-pound test is plenty for length and strength. I once used a braided metallic tippet, but it was too clumsy.

On a shelf in my house in New Jersey, between Herman Melville and Izaak Walton, is a slender book right up there with Moby Dick and The Compleat Angler. I pack it in my gear and always take it with me to the island in New Hampshire in the fall. Eighty-one pages long, densely packed with hundreds of titles, it is E.J. Crossman and G.E. Lewis's An Annotated Bibliography of Chain Pickerel. The bass fishermen may have a point.[27]

Largemouth Bass: (Micropterus salmoides)

My granddaughter, Taylor Lyon with her first large mouth bass—a 7 Pounder! Poor little girl can hardly hold it up for the camera!

The largemouth bass is also not a native to New Hampshire and was introduced into our Lakes in the 1894.[28] "In the late 1940s and 1950s Fish and Game stocked largemouth bass throughout New Hampshire. This species ... was found in only eleven bodies of water during the watershed biological surveys of the late 1930s."[29] The largemouth bass is found in much warmer and dirtier water than the smallmouth. It is a more sluggish fish than its energetic smallmouth cousin. It prefers warmer, muddy, weedy areas in coves and around marinas. It seldom ventures out into open water. It is probably for that reason that I never caught a largemouth bass as a young angler in Lake Winni. The spawning habits are very similar to those of the smallmouth and anglers enjoy casting to them while they are visible on their beds in springtime. Though growing much larger than its cousin, the largemouth bass is not nearly the fighter the smallmouth is. It is also not as good an eating fish, as it often tastes muddy. It is best distinguished from the smallmouth by its dark horizontal stripe running along its side, whereas the smallmouth has a series of vertical bands on its side. It feeds like its cousin, mostly in early morning or late evening. The world record largemouth was caught in Georgia in 1932 and was 32.5" long, weighing 22 pounds, 4 ounces. The New Hampshire record is a 10.5-pounder, caught in Potanipo Pond in 1967.

During the past 50 years, largemouth bass have become available throughout New Hampshire in shallower lakes or in the coves and less clean portions of larger lakes like Lake Winnipesaukee. We smallmouth bass anglers often arrogantly think of largemouth bass as second class, warm water "hick" fish, except when it was caught by my granddaughter Taylor at age 7 and was a 7-pounder!

Andy French, who designed the cover of this book and is the son of Master Angler, Chuck French, is an angler who specializes in fishing for Lake Winni largemouth bass. He has established a tradition of always releasing the bass he catches...after kissing them on the mouth! Here he is about to release a large one he caught under the docks of a Lake Winni marina

Master Angler Chuck French's son, Andy, is an excellent largemouth bass fisherman. Maybe he is good at largemouth bass fishing because of his somewhat bizarre tradition of kissing each large bass he catches.

Chuck French takes pride in passing his skills on to his children like Andy, who has become one of the most skilled Lake Winni largemouth bass anglers I know. Since I am not a largemouth bass angler, I asked Chuck French if his son would tell a story of fishing for largemouth bass in Lake Winni. Here's Andy's story:

Two Perspectives On Fishing (or..."What to Do with a Fish")

By C. Andrew French (son of Master Angler Chuck French)

It was a beautiful warm summer day and I was at one of my favorite fishing spots on Lake Winnipesaukee, the docks of a popular local marina. It is a place where I can always expect to find excellent shallow water fishing that includes a tremendous diversity of warm water species, especially largemouth bass, pickerel, horned pout, yellow & white perch, and a variety of pan fish. The "bigmouth" is my preferred quarry in these waters because of its potential size and very aggressive territorial behavior.

After a fairly productive afternoon of four good bass in the three-pound category and a huge pickerel that snapped my line, I decided to move to a new section of the marina. On the way I passed by a boat slip that held a nice new red-speckled Ranger Classic fishing machine. While being temporarily distracted in order to admire this beauty I happened to spy a momentary dark flash in the murky water just to one side of the Ranger's prop. Not being able to resist such an opportunity I quickly decided to switch from a quarter-ounce blue and black jig to a plastic chartreuse crawdad. I didn't use any extra weight because I wanted the lure to undergo a slow, angled descent to the suspected territory of whatever had caused that flash below the dock.

But just prior to my initial cast my concentration was interrupted by a very young voice behind me asking,"Whatcha doin'?" Turning to my left I was surprised to learn that I had an audience of two cute youngsters, one a girl of about nine years of age, and her little brother of three or four. "I'm trying to catch a big fish", I replied. "Oh, are there any in there?" the girl queried. "Well I'm just about to find out. Just keep your eyes on this plastic crawfish." As I made my highly anticipated cast I explained that you have to be very patient and give the fish a chance to grab the lure.

As I turned my head back toward the water a notice-able quivering of the line gave the three of us hope that something was going on "down there". Then all of a sudden the line took off under the dock and I responded by slowly lowering my rod tip, pausing briefly, and then thrusting it upward in order to set the hook into the fish's jaw. When the rod abruptly stopped its upward motion two feet above the water I knew I'd hooked a good one. By this time, of course, I could feel my elevated pulse rate and when the humungous largemouth showed itself at the surface things simply went into "overdrive".

I yelled to my long-time angling buddy who was fishing about three docks away, "Hey Wilson, I've got a beauty! It's a boot!" Ed was there in an instant to offer whatever assistance I needed. And the two kids were having a great time watching all of the commotion. Their screams of encouragement must have been heard all throughout the marina. After all they were witnessing the classic battle between two very different and determined earthly creatures, that of "man vs. beast". The fish naturally tried every possible avenue of escape available under the dock, including weeds, branches, and of course the pilings themselves. But the hundreds of past encounters that Ed and I had logged in on those docks were now paying off. The spectacular action lasted for several minutes before my opponent showed signs of battle fatigue. As my partner carefully lifted that big tired "lunker" out of the water it was plain to see we had a real trophy-sized fish to be proud of. We agreed that it was easily within the seven-pound weight category, a personal record. In the midst of getting some quick photographic proof of our success the two little spectators proceeded to call out to their father who was not too far away. By the time he arrived I was in the process of preparing to release our prized specimen back into the lake. This was our standard practice. Neither Ed nor I have ever considered any alternative. We believe a creature that has given so much enjoyment during the battle has "earned" its return to freedom. It is our contention that a great game fish like a bass is much more valuable alive in its natural habitat than it is on someone's wall. We are more than gratified by a photograph of the fish as opposed to a lifeless replica of it. This doesn't mean, however, that we don't understand that an occasional fish taken home for supper is entirely acceptable. But what followed the father's arrival on the scene could only be described as a bizarre ending to our whole fishing experience.

When the little girl sensed that we were about to release our catch back into the water she became very insistent that she be given the fish so her family could make a meal of it. And her father only compounded the situation by supporting her desire to not "waste" such a great meal. He even tried to claim ownership of the fish by stating that it was caught under "his" dock. It now apparent that we were possibly headed toward a physical confrontation over that fish. This is when I realized just how quickly the situation was deteriorating and I, therefore, decided there would be no more discussion of the matter.

As I hastily eased our incredible specimen back into its home environment I couldn't help but think of the totally opposite viewpoints on the natural order of things that had been played out right there during that otherwise pleasant summer day on Lake Winnipesaukee, under the "Smile of the Great Spirit".

The father has learned much from his son, Andy - a sure sign of a good teacher, when the pupils surpass the teacher! Here's a large mouth bass Andy's father, Chuck, caught on a fly

Master Angler Chuck French
lands a large mouth bass on a fly

Chapter 7

YELLOW PERCH AND WHITE PERCH

Yellow Perch (Perca flavescens)

Yellow Perch

THE YELLOW PERCH was native to New Hampshire but was found mostly in the larger rivers and coastal waters with access to the large rivers. In the 1920s and 1930s, the Fish & Game was actively stocking yellow perch along with horned pout, white perch, and smelt, "introducing them into many waters. The activity with horned pout and yellow perch may come as a surprise to us because of the pest status these two species have achieved today in many waters where they are overcrowded and stunted."[30]

The yellow perch was a very popular fish to us as boys learning to angle in Lake Winni. We would catch them on worms, night crawlers, and small spoons and spinners in abundance from docks, where they school up in cool waters. The spawning season is in April or early May in coves and shallows when the water is in the mid 40s. The yellow perch is a slow grower, taking 6 years to reach 6". A very large yellow perch is less than 2 pounds. I will always remember catching yellow perch by the bucket-full in the 1940s and 50s from the old Bear Island Mail Dock on the northern end of the Island in the fall when they schooled up off the deep drop off 30 feet out from the dock. And we boys learned how to skin and clean them for frying, along with stabbing our hands too often on their sharp dorsal fins. They are an excellent tasting, sweet, white fleshed fish.

Master Angler Chuck french teaches his grand children how to catch yellow perch. He is a Master Angler as well as a Master mentor, passing the skills down to children and grand children, his most important role.

Up until 1992, we caught many more yellow perch than we wished while trolling for salmon. They became a nuisance fish, causing us to have to reel in a hundred feet of lead-core line just to release a yellow perch on our salmon lure. But that has changed. I am not sure why, but it has been almost ten years since I have caught a yellow perch while trolling for salmon.

Where have all the yellow perch gone? This was a question I asked our Master Anglers while compiling the material for this book. They have different theories. One suggests that they are still here but have left the open waters and moved into the warmer coves where the lake is more fertile. I do get reports of people catching them in small bays and coves. Some speculate that this is because our new septic system laws have been enforced more recently, causing the lake to become less fertile which the yellow perch do not like, as the young consume plankton, small crawfish, and insects. It is also true that we catch fewer crawfish at our clean-water lakefront on Bear Island than we use to. I could put a fish head in a crawfish trap and catch a dozen in a night in the 60s and 70s. Now I hardly ever catch but one or two in a week. Is this because we have cleaned up our lake too much for the crawfish and yellow perch to thrive, except in the bays and coves? And so we trade clean water for fewer perch, which isn't bad. One Master Angler speculates that the increase in salmon, white perch and rainbow trout in the Lake, which forage on young perch, has diminished the population. Fish biologist Don Miller has a theory. He believes that the healthier the smelt population, the fewer the yellow perch and white fish. I was amazed to learn from him that the smelt - especially the big jack smelt are ferocious predators which eat the small perch, whitefish and other fry. If you have ever looked at a large jack smelt's teeth, they look like a pickerel's. Maybe this is the answer to this puzzler.

Perhaps it is better having too few than too many yellow perch as when they become over-abundant, they also compete for the smelt and forage fish we need for the trout and salmon. It's a jungle of survival out there in the lake's food chain! And too many fish leads to stunted fish.

Master Angler, Chuck French, shows off a "trophy" yellow perch, caught through the ice! The yellow perch population in Lake Winni seems to have been drastically reduced in the past decade. There are still many in the coves and near marinas, but their numbers have diminished in open waters where a decade ago I caught them much more than I wanted while trolling for salmon. Some speculate that the white perch have pushed them out, competing more aggressively for smelt and other forage food.

The world's record yellow perch was caught in the Delaware River in 1865 and weighed 4 pounds, 3.5 ounces. The New Hampshire record was caught in 1969 in Heads Pond and weighed 2 pounds, 6 ounces. It was 15.5 " long.

White Perch: Morone americana

A cooler filled with nice white perch and bass. Lake Winni holds the State record for white perch, 3.7 pounds! They are getting bigger every year and some fear that they will force other species out of the lake. When you get into a school of them they will hit anything you throw at them from spoons and spinners to worms and crawlers!

The white perch is now an abundant and important fish in Lake Winni, though I never caught one in my youth. They seem to somewhat resemble in shape the yellow perch, and bass, but are silver-green in color. They spawn at age 3 in the spring up on the surface when the water reaches the upper 50s°. It is curious to watch hundreds of them in coves in the shallows as they float vulnerably on the surface up side down. They are easy prey to sea gulls, ospreys, or boys with landing nets. Their eggs settle to the bottom where they hatch unattended in 4-6 days, depending on the water temperature. But I learned from Don Miller and John Viar that this is not a normal situation. These fish experts believe that the white perch in Lake Winni are record sized and that they keep growing larger every year until they have outgrown their natural genetic maximum size. Don Miller postulates that their egg sacks have grown too large for their bodies and are now too large for the fish to naturally spawn. Nature's way of culling them out is to make the females struggle on the surface when engorged with too many eggs thereby being very vulnerable to sea gulls, osprey, eagles, and other prey. I have seen people in small boats scooping them up in nets while they float helplessly on the surface in the spring spawning season. Don Miller's is an interesting theory and who am I to question the biologists?

This picture from 1939 was proof to me that white perch were in Lake Winni back when I was a boy, though I never caught one! My mother, Toni Lyon holds what is unmistakably a white perch, caught while wearing her dress?! What was the matter with our old relatives, having to dress up to fish?

When I was a boy, I never remember anyone catching a white perch. But I have evidence that they must have been here as I have an old photo of my mother, Toni Lyon holding up a white perch in the late 1930s on our dock on Meredith Neck while wearing a dress and heels!

White perch sometimes live up to 10 years. It is not uncommon to catch 1.5 to 2 pounders. They cruise the shores in schools, feeding on smaller fish. White perch seem to have grown in population and to have largely replaced the yellow perch. I now catch them through the ice as well as while trolling. Here's the 2004 Rotary Derby winning white perch well over 2 pounds.

This white perch won the 2004 Great Rotary Ice fishing Derby on Lake Winni and weighed close to 2.5 pounds.

You can catch them on worms, minnows, smelt, and small shiny lures and flies. Once in awhile, while fishing for bass, I will encounter a school swimming through and can cast a shiny spoon and have fun catching a stringer full. Once while swimming with mask and snorkel off my dock on the east side of Bear Island, a huge school of thousands of white perch came foraging through where I was swimming. The upper ones in the school were smaller and toward the bottom I could see larger ones - 2+ pounders. One of my fears is that white perch will become over-crowded, competing with other more important game fish for the available food.

So no need to catch and release white perch, as there may be too many already! This is already happening in some other New Hampshire lakes.

Here's our son, Dan, with his daughters Amanda and Crystal with a nice mixed string of white perch and bass ready for cleaning and a fish fry!

Left: Son, Dan, and granddaughter, Amanda, caught bass and white perch one afternoon as fast as they could cast out a night crawler. They caught 25 in two hours, releasing many of them but bringing home enough for a fish fry. White perch, skinned and filleted, and then breaded and fried in olive oil, make a delicious meal!

Right: Granddaughter Tiirsten, looks proudly at a big string of white perch and bass which contains her first white perch!

Below: Nice white perch which will be eaten later.

The white firm flesh of this fish, filleted, is a delight when lightly breaded and fried in olive oil. Master Angler Mario DeCarolis catches them through the ice and after filleting them, cuts them in small pieces, grills them quickly, and serves them up with sauce and cocktails out on the ice as "Poor Man's Shrimp."

The New Hampshire record white perch was caught in Lake Winni and was 17" and weighed 3 pounds, 11.5 ounces in 1986. The world record weighed 4 pounds, 12 ounces, and was 19.5" and was caught in Maine in 1949.

Chapter 8

CUSK, HORNED POUT (BULL HEADS), BLACK CRAPPIE, AND OTHER FISH

The Cusk (Lota lota)

The only cusk I have ever caught while trolliing in summer -- in fact the only cusk I have ever caught in the summer anyway of fishing! The cusk is very inactive in summer, almost hibernating, while they become highly active in winter — the only time we usualy catch them.

Jack Noon describes some interesting history of cusk in Lake Winni:

John Wentworth, the last Royal Governor of New Hampshire, had Jotham Rindge haul "saltwater cusk to the governor's estate in Wolfeboro in the early 1770s," where they were dumped into what is now Lake Wentworth. "If the cusk had survived their adventure, it would have been a short jaunt for them down through the outlet and into Lake Winnipesaukee, where cusk can be found today.
This introduction of saltwater cusk achieved ambiguous results. About sixty years after it had taken place, a traveler named Nathan Hale claimed with misplaced enthusiasm that Governor Wentworth's stocking experiment "proved beyond a doubt, that saltwater fish will live and breed and thrive on fresh inland waters."[31] However, the Winnipesaukee cusk Hale was aware of then were the freshwater cusk (Lota lota) that are there today rather than the saltwater species (Brosmius brosme) and were not descendants of the ones Rindge had hauled from the coast for Governor Wentworth. There's a good chance that later Hale might have regretted his all-too-public rhapsody about the many benefits to be gained by stocking New Hampshire's lakes and ponds with saltwater fish, clams and oysters, and lobsters and shrimp. J.W. Meader in his 1869 book about the Merrimack watershed reported, "A variety of salt-water fish were

some years since placed in this lake [Winnipesaukee] by experimenting parties; but ... nothing was seen or known of them afterwards."[32]

Here's a cusk which was another first for me -- the first and only one I have ever caught in summer while trolling for salmon or lakers! I must have been down deep and trolling slowly!

The cusk is a strange looking fish, with a single barbel beneath the lower jaw. I frequently catch them through the ice. Cusk are found only in cold, deep lakes. In summer cusk become inactive actually hibernating, while, in winter, they become very active, especially at night. Other names for the cusk are burbot, ling, eelpout, freshwater cod, and lawyer. The cusk is a night feeder. Spawning takes place in winter from December to March in the shallows. The eggs are dropped and abandoned.[33]

As a boy, I never caught a cusk, even through the ice, but the old timers tell tales of catching them up to and over 10 pounds. They are voracious feeders, consuming mainly crawfish, rough fish and perch. Though they may live as long as 20 years, attaining a length of 4 feet and 75 pounds, the NH record is a 11 pounds, 2.2 ounce cusk, 34.25" caught in Sunapee Lake in 1984. But the old timers, like our Master Angler Bill Martel tell of much larger cusk.

My largest was a 9-pound cusk, which I caught through the ice from one of my cusk lines off Bear Island in 1982. I also caught a 6-pounder that same morning. I didn't think I could get the 9-pounder through the 8" hole I had drilled in the ice, but once he was on the ice, out from his gullet came a 12" cusk, which had my hook in it! The 6-pounder had also swallowed a 10" cusk, which had taken my bait! Neither of these fish had a hook in it, but had swallowed a smaller one, which had been hooked. So they are definitely cannibalistic! From that time on, whenever I have a small cusk on my line, I just leave it out as bait for a larger one.

One may have up to 6 cusk lines out over night, which is when you will usually catch cusk. But they must have at least a one-ounce weight, not farther than 6" from the hook, which must sit on the bottom. The line must be tied in a stationary manner to the cusk trap, which is usually a stout stick, which must have the name and address of the owner on it.

It is placed across the hole, so the fish cannot run, but only swallow the bait. This is to avoid catching a salmon or trout on a cusk line, as they will not usually pick up a static bait from the bottom with a heavy weight. But if you should bring in a laker on your cusk line, you must release it immediately. (Only two trout lines or fish traps can be used at one time by one ice fisherman.)

One February while fishing through the ice, I went out to tend my cusk lines. I had something huge on one line and finally worked it slowly up to the hole, which I feared was not large enough for the big head I saw looking up at me. I finally squeezed it through the hole and it was the biggest cusk I had ever caught -- a nine-pounder. But the most interesting part of the story is that out of its mouth came a 12" cusk which had my hook in it, which the bigger one had swallowed! The next cusk hole contained a similar adventure. A six pound cusk had swallowed a 10" one which was on my line! Learning that cusk are cannibalistic, I started leaving small ones on my line as bait for bigger ones!

Cusk is a delicacy for gourmet anglers, either cooked in a chowder, or skinned, filleted, and fried in a light batter like Tempura and served with a squeeze of lemon. The meat is white, firm and tasty. Some call it fresh water "scallops." The cusk is easy to skin with pliers, and, like a horned pout, it has no scales. If you make a chowder, skin the cusk, cut off the head, take out the intestines, and boil the whole fish, backbone and all, so as not to waste any of the flesh, which is easy to take off the skeleton after boiling. After removing the meat from the backbone sift out by hand and discard the bones. Add a couple of boiled chopped onions, a diced potato, some sliced carrots, a little salt and freshly ground pepper, and a cup of cream or milk. Simmer for another 15 minutes and serve with a dash of Tabasco, fresh lemon, and fresh pepper. Ummm, delicious after a cold day out on the ice! I used to fry the liver, like cod liver and it is full of vitamins A and D. But after reading studies of the mercury levels in fish, much of which ends up in the liver, I have stopped eating this delicacy.

Horned Pout (Bull Heads): *Ictalurus nebulosus*

One of the sweetest eating fish in the Lake, caught mainly at night with a worm or crawler off docks or other structure.

Though there are several members of the catfish family in NH, the horned pout or brown bullhead is the most common. Though they look almost black from above, they are often mottled and range from olive to dark brown. The underside is whitish. The whiskers or barbels are black and they contain taste buds, which the horned pout uses to sniff its food. The horned pout is a bottom feeder that feeds primarily at night. Worms threaded on a large long-shanked hook are the best bait. The long shank enables one to extract the hook, which the pout invariable swallows, inhaling its food like a child sucking in spaghetti. The horned pout prefers a mud bottom in coves or under docks and it is fun to fish for them with a light suspended above the water illuminating the depths. I have seen old timers catch them under light using only white rubber bands tied to their hooks, which simulate worms, I suppose.

Beware of the top and side fins, which conceal sharp barbed spikes that can easily penetrate your hand. These fins are flexed when the fish struggles. I will always remember learning my lesson about holding horned pout when I was about 9 years old. I carelessly picked up one I had just caught and its dorsal spine penetrated my palm, resulting in a painful wound and a nasty infection. The preferred way to hold one is to carefully position the fish to enable these 3 fins to emerge in the space between 3 fingers.

My father taught me a painless way to skin a horned pout in one easy step. He made a deep cut with his knife from just behind the dorsal horn slanting toward the head and downward about halfway through the fish. He then stood on the fish's head while peeling off the thin scaleless skin which he held by pliers, leaving a skinless horned pout with tail (which, by the way, you should never cut off as when fried, it is crisp and delicious) and head ready to finish severing. The horned pout has a firm dark red flesh, which, when from clean water, is the sweetest tasting fish in all the northern lakes.

The horned pout is an omnivorous scavenger, eating almost anything including worms, crawfish, snails, small fish, plants, garbage, and dead fish. I once learned a new technique from people fishing at night from the public dock at Brown's Boat Basin. They fished under the all-night street lamp, which is at the end of the dock. They had a bucket full of horned pout, and were catching more as I docked my boat and came to see how they were doing it. Instead of bait, they had a small piece of white string on the hook, which they rubbed on each fish they caught. And the horned pout would come and suck in the string with the hook! No worms needed!

The average horned pout is between 6-14" weighing less than a pound. Although horned pout up to 18" and 4 pounds are on record. [34]

The sweet, firm red meat of the horned pout is my wife's favorite eating fish. Other old anglers will testify that it is the tastiest fish in the Lake. We need to go out at night, like when we were children, and catch a mess of pout!

The Black Crappie: (Pomoxis nigromaculatus)

A new fish has appeared on the scene in Lake Winnipesauke, the black crappie. I have never fished for them in Lake Winni, though I did many years ago when in the military in the southern states. My friend and outdoor writer Bob Harris, who enjoys fishing for crappie volunteered to write about this fish.

The Black Crappie —by Bob Harris

The black crappie is a beautiful and popular panfish, fun to catch and excellent tablefare. The delicious meat is firm and may be cooked using various methods. Adult crappie vary from 5 to 12 inches and weigh less than a pound. But a large specimen may weigh two pounds or more and measure 15 to 16 inches. The old New Hampshire State record (2 lbs. 8 oz.) was caught in Lovewell Pond, Nashua. Tom Noyes caught the current record (2 lbs. 12.8 oz. and 17.25 in.) on February 9, 2000 at the Bellamy Reservoir, in Madbury, New Hampshire.

Not native to New Hampshire waters, crappie were illegally introduced into the southern tier waters of the Granite State many years ago. Over time, its popularity rose causing the New Hampshire Fish and

Game Department to begin a program of transplanting crappie to other suitable waters in the early 1990s. But, Lake Winnipesaukee was not among the waters stocked. According to Fisheries Biologist Don Miller, "It was definitely illegally introduced and had already appeared at Lees Mill in Lake Winnipesaukee in the 1980s." In recent years, spotty catches have occurred in Moultonboro Bay, Back Bay (Smith River at Wolfeboro), the bandstand area of Alton Bay, and in various coves containing preferable habitat.

two nice black crappie -- a new pan fish in Lake Winni along with the small marabou jigs which caught them. (Photo by Bob Harris)

Black crappie prefer the clearer, cooler waters of lakes and ponds. They congregate in coves, bays, around old stumps, logs, brush, sunken trees, lily pads, hyacinths, bulrushes, weeds and vegetation. Rivers and streams entering a lake can be hot spots. Crappie will bite most of the day, but do not like bright sunlight. During the middle of the day, unless cloudy, they seek shady spots and deeper water. They lurk in shady areas under overhanging tree branches, bridges, piers, docks, rafts and anchored boats. They will not dive down for their meal. They prefer that a lure, jig or bait be presented at their exact depth or slightly above. A variety of popular crappie jigs, flies and live baits (nightcrawlers, small shiners, smelt) can be used successfully by anglers.

OTHER LAKE FISH

Rainbow Smelt (Osmerus mordax)

rainbow smelt (what anglers call "pin" smelt) caught trawl netting in Lake Winnipesaukee; this along with hydroacoustic (sonar) sampling allows biologists to estimate forage fish abundance.

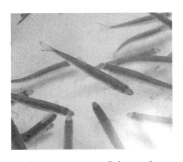

These tiny sweet fish are the staple upon which the entire salmon population in Lake Winni is very dependent! One bad year for these delicate litle fish, and the salmon will suffer significantly!

In some ways, this slender, almost transparent delicate fish is one of the most important fish in this book. It is the staple forage food for our landlocked salmon. As the smelt go, so go the next year's salmon, which are totally dependent on the population of smelt in the Lake. We now manage the smelt population to manage the salmon. On those years when there are too many salmon for the smelt population, the smelt get wiped out and the salmon are inferior in size and quality. The smelt live only in cold, clear, deep lakes, several dozen of which are in New Hampshire. Lake Winni, Squam, and Winnisquam are the ones with natural smelt populations.

In early spring, just after ice-out, smelt move up into the rivers and streams to spawn and the salmon and trout follow them there. They head up the streams usually just after sunset and return from their spawning run the next morning. On rare occasions when the water and streams are overly high, the smelt eggs will become stranded before they hatch after the streams recede. This causes their numbers to diminish which, in turn, severely effects the salmon that are so dependent upon them. This occurred in 1985, when all our docks in the lake were underwater in the spring and the rivers were flooded.

The smelt is important not only as such an important forage fish for salmon, but also as an eating fish. I remember eating huge messes of them deep fried as a boy, heads, guts, and all. They were very sweet and delicious! But to protect them as a forage fish, limits were established for "dipping smelt" with nets to 2 quarts per person.

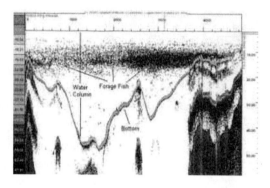

This is a cross section of a portion of the Lake viewed by the acustic study equipment used annually to estimate the health of Lake Winni's smelt population.
The top of the chart is the surface and the irregular line in the middle is the contour of the lake's bottom. The black cloud near the top is a cloud of forage fish, more than likely smelt. If the population is down, the Fish and Game biologists will stock fewer salmon. If up, they will stock more. Stocking too many will result in insufficient smelt for the number of salmon resulting in smaller stunted salmon the next season

To ensure adequate smelt populations, the Fish & Game used to introduce millions of smelt eggs into tributary streams of salmon lakes, like Lake Winni, but they no longer do this. They also do fall acoustic studies with sophisticated new technology with is very accurate in estimating the size and health of the Lake's vitally important smelt population. This illustration is from one of those studies. The black cloud in the upper portion of the read-out is smelt.

Large lake fisheries biologist Don Miller, and biological technician John Viar, are two professionals to whom all Lake Winni anglers owe a huge debt of gratitude for their tireless work in behalf of the salmon we are now blessed to catch. They tell me that smelt numbers were up in 2003 and that means good-sized salmon for the 2004 season. Don Miller shared that when yellow perch and whitefish numbers are up, it is an indication that smelt numbers are down. And when the smelt population is up, the larger jack smelt actually forage as predators on the yellow perch, white fish, rainbows, salmon and lake trout fry! This is another answer to my question of why so few yellow perch and whitefish seem to be in

Lake Winni. According to Don Miller, in Maine, they are not fond of the big jack smelt, since they are such ferocious predators of game fish fry. This illustration of 4 class-years of smelt (age 1-4) shows how large they grow each year...and this is not just from eating plankton!

Four age classes of rainbow smelt from top (age 4) to bottom (age 1)

Read Master Angler Steve Perry's section of this book on the Smelt Studies for more information on smelt.

White Sucker (Catostomus commersoni)

This photo shows (in the shadow) a dull colored large egg laying female being crowded by smaller males with a horizontal stripe on each side.

The sucker is a bottom feeder, but an important one as a forage fish, for lake trout, especially. They make an excellent live bait or can be used as a cut bait in winter when you place a small strip on a jig for lakers. Some of the old timers use a large (6-10") sucker fished live ...and patiently, for big lakers. They grow even larger than 2 feet and 5 pounds. Every spring, a strange event takes place exactly on the same spot to the right of my dock right up next to the shore. The suckers come into this place to spawn. The males have a reddish horizontal line on their sides, and the much larger females will be sandwiched between two males while laying their eggs for the males to squirt with their milt. Hundreds of these suckers will gather waiting their turn to spawn, in the same spot. They must have imprinted on this specific place on shore where they were spawned, as they spawn here year after year. Egg-laden females, twice the size of the males, get washed right up on shore, at times, but this does not interrupt their mating.

Fall Fish (Roach, Lake Chub, Stone Roller) *(Semotilus corporalis)*

This is a picture of a roach or small fish, which seems to have been also crowded out by the white perch — a much more desirable eating fish.

The roach or fallfish is a silver fish, which we learned to dislike as boys, as they were very prevalent then and would steal our expensive hellgrammites when we were bass fishing. They were strong fighting fish, and yet, we were always disappointed to find we had hooked a roach! It is the largest minnow in New Hampshire, reaching a length of 16" and up to 2-3 pounds. It is good, used as a strip bait or a sewed-on trolling bait for big lakers. But the large fallfish we used to catch seem to have disappeared, and I have not caught a big one in over 10 years. The big ones are known to be highly predatory on small game fish like bass and salmon, so this is not bad that they seem to have diminished in numbers.

Pumpkin Seed Sunfish (Lepomis gibbosus)

These are the small sunfish that we called "bait snatchers," kibbees, or kivvers. They hardly ever get large enough to eat and they always provide for my young grandchildren their initial sport as they learn to catch their first fish from the dock, which whets their appetites for more. They spawn in early June into August and you will see small gravel beds close to shore into which the female drops her eggs. If not too numerous, they are nice angling teaching fodder.

Crawfish

Good sized crawfish with hand showing perspective. Good bass and cusk bait!

The crawfish population on the east side of Bear Island has greatly diminished over the past few decades. At night, you could always see them crawling around on the bottom. As a boy you could put your line with a worm over the edge of dock, and within minutes, crawfish would come out of the cribbing and rocks and begin to eat your worm. Now I cannot catch but 1 or 2 in a month, compared to catching a dozen in a few days in the old days. I could always catch all we needed for bass bait by putting a fish head in a crawfish trap off the cribbing of my dock; but not any more, though they are present in bays and not-so-clean water. I thought for awhile that the mink that live in our dock cribbing were catching them all, but others have also reported this change. Is this an indication of poorer water quality or higher? The scientists tell me that this is more likely a result of tighter septic system control rules in the past decades. The lake is getting cleaner, but the crawfish (and the perch, it seems) seem to like it more fertile. I have even tried stocking them at my dock by purchasing them at the bait store and then releasing them at the dock.

The crawfish is the main food for bass and if the crawfish disappear, what will the bass eat? My fear is that they will start to forage more on other small fish like young salmon, perch, bass, smelt. The food chain in the lake is in delicate balance…or imbalance! So, as most of the Master Anglers say, "Don't mess with Mother Nature!"

Fresh Water Mussels

The lake abounds with fresh water mussels who help filter and clean the lake. I do not see as many as I did as a child. For some time, I blamed this on the mink, which live in our dock cribbings who would hunt them at night, and leave all their opened shells in the back of my boat! My brother, Bob, always curious about food, visited us one time and decided to make a supper of steamed freshwater mussels. They didn't kill him, but they were extremely tough and flavorless, even with a little hot sauce.

Chapter 9

ICE FISHING

A lonely ice fisherman jigging for a big trout

ICE FISHING IS ALMOST A separate culture of hearty men and women who gather on Lake Winni as soon as the ice will support them and their bob houses. On Meredith Bay and other spots around the lake, communities of bob houses appear shortly after ice reaches a depth of 6-8", and sometimes earlier much to the misfortune of some who go through the ice!

Ice fishing is often a social event, with fishermen like Angler bringing food and beverage to share with those others who drop by to see how the fish are biting.

Master Angler Mario DeCarolis has all the comforts of a small home in his bob house. I fish out near my island cottage without a bob house, but those who have bob houses enjoy the comforts of home ...almost.

Mario drilling a hole with his power augur. Having learned the hard way, it is MUCH easier to drill through 18" of hard ice with power, than it is with a hand powered Swedish ice drill!

Above: A natural ice highway of serious ice fishermen
Below: A village of bob houses at the annual Great Lake Winni Ice Derby sponsored by the Rotary Club of Meredith. They have raised over a $1 million from the derbies over the years which they have donated to worthy causes, built much needed and appreciated community projects, and helped needy children from the area.

The big event of the ice fishing season is the annual Rotary Ice Fishing Derby, where over 6,000 ice fishermen compete for over $50,000 in prizes. There are virtual villages of bob houses on Lake Winni for the Derby and entire social communities as well.

This antique 100-year-old tip-up still works just as well as a new one.

There are several ways to fish for lakers, rainbows, pickerel, white perch, and cusk, the main quarries for the ice angler. The main technique is to use tip ups, a wonderful antique piece of New England ingenuity — two sticks situated in a cross which straddles the hole in the ice and a third vertical stick which supports a reel of line under the water in the hole and which has a pop-up flag which pops when a fish triggers it by taking the smelt on the hook, and pulling out line. Though there are some plastic modern versions of the tip up, most are simple but effective devices.

Mario rigging this great piece of New England ingenuity, the tip up

I prefer to fish for lakers beside drop-offs or on underwater plateaus about 15-40 feet down in 40-60 feet of water. I hook my smelt just behind the dorsal fin with a #5 hook and add a small steel split shot about 3 feet above the hook. Each angler is allowed only two trout lines. If I am fishing for rainbows, then I fish in shallow water 4-10' just under the ice using small smelt or a night crawler. Salmon will take your bait and must be immediately released if caught. I never take them from the water, but instead cut the line. I leave the hook in them as it will rust out eventually and there is less chance of injuring them than if you attempt to remove the hook on the ice. It is perch, pickerel, and lakers that most Lake Winni ice fishermen are after.

Left: Phil DeCarolis catches a nice lake trout.   Right: Mario's brother Phil with nice laker caught through the ice.

Left: A trout emerges from the ice hole.   Right: A nice bass up through the ice

Unfortunately many salmon are killed each year through the ice. White perch come in schools and are bonus fish when I can catch them. But if a school is around your hole, then be ready for great fast action using small smelt or night crawlers for bait. We even catch a bass occasionally through the ice.

New Hi-tech Ice Fishing Jigging Box

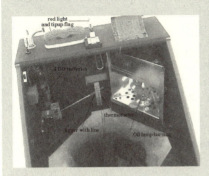

This is another piece of new technology for creative ice fishermen, from the creative Finicky Fish Factory. This photo shows inside the tip-up jigging box showing the DD battery powered jigging arm and motor, the oil lamp to prevent the ice-hole and line from freezing (also good hand warming device), the red light and flag on top, and the release device which pulls off the jigging arm leaving the fish free to pull line from the under-water spool, and the thermometer to tell how cold it is. This device resulted in quite a few hits in the 2004 Derby.

In Alan Nute's store, (AJ's Bait & Tackle in Meredith, New Hampshire) you can buy for about $100 an ingenious device, as shown and described in the picture here. It covers your hole in the ice, heating the space enough to keep the ice from freezing over it, has a battery powered jigging arm to give your lure or live bait action, and has a red light and flag to indicate a hit. It was invented and made by Jerry Sanderfoot, an experienced ice fisherman from Wisconsin. Jerry, who founded the Fincky Fish Factory, has been working on his invention for over 10 years. At first he wanted a machine that would jig to give the bait the needed action down in the depths but also be efficient enough to run for 8 weeks on 4 DD batteries, which he finally developed. Then he needed to solve the problem of the ice freezing over the hole and the line going down through it. He finally created an oil lamp with reflector that runs on highly refined lamp oil. He fastened this heat source inside the box along with the batteries and motor connected to a jigging arm with release. In a fishing contest test of the device in Wisconsin, Jerry faced off his ice jigging box against a team of other anglers and ended up catching 70% of the fish caught in that contest! The picture here shows this ingenious device called the Finicky Fish Factory, which I tested with considerable success in February 2004 at the Great Lake Winni Ice Fishing Derby. (The device is available from Maverick Mfg., 8190 S. Wolf River Rd, Fremont, WI, 54940)

If you fish in coves near weedbeds, you are likely to catch pickerel through the ice on your shiners or smelt. Jack Noon quotes a report from the 1860s:

> "... two fishermen could cut thirty to fifty holes in the ice, suspend live shiners just above the bottom, and then tend to their tip-ups.... Five thousand lines are the average of the daily set.... Many of the inhabitants about the lake have shanties constructed on a sort of sled, provided with comfort and accommodations for sleeping and cooking, and when the ice is sufficiently strong, oxen and horses are attached, and they are hauled upon the lake to the fishing-ground, and rented to parties, affording a considerable revenue to the enterprising proprietors.[35]

Master Angler Mario DeCarolis jigging on the ice for trout and white perch.

One can fish for cusk using up to 6 cusk lines, leaving them out over night and tending them the next morning. Cusk lines must be tended at least once every 24 hours. And your cusk device must have the name and address of the owner on it. A cusk fishing device is, to quote the New Hampshire Fish & Game regulations:

"A device for storing line in a manner which is not free-running and is securely attached to the device and to which is attached a sinker, weighing at least one ounce, not more than 6 inches above, and independent of, an attached single hook for bait, The weight must rest on the bottom of the lake."

It is not free-running and sits on the bottom with heavy weight to discourage trout from taking the bait and running with it. I use a large #03 -04 hook as a cusk will inhale the bait. Bobbing or jigging or any other movement of the bait to attract fish is prohibited. And if you catch any fish other than a cusk, you must cut the line without removing the fish from the water.

Hal pulls in a fish slowly and carefully after having let it run 10-20 yards to swallow the live smelt which is hooked just below the dorsal fin. And Tag is ready to pounce and retrieve.

What's the best bait for cusk? Most will use a live shiner or smelt or a piece of cut bait. But from my experience, the best bait for cusk is a live cusk! I shared earlier how I caught a 9-pound cusk and a 6-pound cusk the same morning both of which had swallowed 10-12" smaller cusks who were on my line, having already taken my bait! Ice fishing is discussed further on in the Ice Derby section and in some detail in Master Angler, Mario DeCarolis' chapter where you will even find how to make "poor man's shrimp" from white perch. His trusty dog, Tag is always there with him, ready for the fish to come up out of that hole.

It is great fun and a hearty sport for those who enjoy the outdoors in the winter!

Laker caught through the ice

I have to tell a political ice-fishing story. Once upon a time, long, long ago there was a Presidential Election that was too close to call. Neither the Republican presidential candidate nor the Democratic presidential candidate had enough votes to win the election. It was decided that there should be an ice-fishing contest between the 2 candidates to determine the final winner. There was much talk about ballot recounting, court challenges, etc. But a week-long ice-fishing competition seemed the fairest way to settle things. The candidate who caught the most fish at the end of the week would win.

After a lot of back and forth discussion, it was decided that the contest would take place on a remote and cold lake in New Hampshire. There were to be no observers present since both men were to be sent out on this remote lake and return daily with their catch for counting and verification. At the end of the first day, George W. Bush returned to the starting line and he had 10 fish. Al Gore returned and had zero fish. Well, everyone assumed Al is just having another bad hair day or something and hopefully he would catch up the next day. At the end of the 2nd day, George W. came in with 20 fish and Al Gore came in again with none. That evening, Bill Clinton gets together secretly with Al Gore and said; "Al, I think George W. is a lowlife cheatin' son-of-a-gun. I'm a gonna dress up this good ole' Southern Boy, James Carville, as a jackass (now some folks say this wouldn't be too hard to do) and send him out on the lake to act as a spy."

The next night (after George W. came back with 50 fish and Al Gore with none), Bill got Carville and Al Gore together and said to Carville: "Well, what about it boy, is George W. cheatin'?"

"He sure is, Bill, he's cuttin' holes in the ice!"

CHAPTER 10

THE FISHING DERBIES AND TOURNAMENTS

The Spring Winni Salmon Derby

A History by Master Angler Rick Davis

IN THE MID TO LATE 1970S, Lake Winnipesaukee had been overstocked with landlocked salmon; at the same time, the forage base, or smelt, were in a rapid decline. This created a problem of too many fish competing for too few smelts. The result was that salmon were 6 and 7 years old and only 14-15 inches long. Reports of salmon hitting surface lures of the bass fishermen in shallow water were commonplace. There were also rumors about the legal minimum length being dropped to 14 inches or even, possibly, 12 inches to rid the lake of so many fish as a result of the overstock. There was also talk about raising the limit from two to a higher number.

A group of concerned fishermen, along with representatives from the Chambers of Commerce, marine dealers, guides, tackle reps, retail operators, and representatives from the New Hampshire Fish & Game Department, met and discussed the possibility of holding a fishing derby to help remove some of the surplus fish rather than go through the legislature to change the legal limit or minimum size. With everyone agreeing to the idea, the annual Winni Derby was born in the spring of 1980.

The first Derby was to be held the first weekend of May 1981. Planning this may have been a mistake for that weekend because the ice was still in parts of the lake until Thursday of that week. A decision was made at that time to move the date later by a week. Without realizing what we had done, the Derby landed on Mother's Day, another major politically incorrect mistake that we soon put behind us. We moved it to where it is now which is the weekend after Mother's Day. Our first Derby saw 600 registered participants, and over the years we have seen a high of nearly 3,500.

For a while, the Derby Committee purchased adult Atlantic salmon and released them into the Lake, usually during the fall. After a couple of years doing this, we realized that these great fish, some up to 14 pounds, were not making it through the winter months. We then started to look at the forage base situation, and decided to try and do something about that.

A bill was presented and passed by the legislature which, in effect, shut down all salmon lakes to the commercial harvesting of smelt. The Committee then went to work with biologists trying to gather smelt eggs or smelts for transfer to Lake Winnipesaukee. From several locations in New Hampshire and alder swamps in Maine, nothing seemed to produce the volume of eggs needed to make an impact on the forage base.

Through a friendship with a senior biologist in New York, we obtained permission to do a live transfer of smelts from one of their lakes that had an abundance of smelt. On our first overnight trip, we brought back hundreds of thousands, of smelt to spawn on burlap in a controlled situation in New Hampshire. With female smelt dropping approximately 50,000 eggs on average, this would give our lake a much-needed boost.

The eggs were placed in a hatchery until such time as they "eyed up" or you could see their eyes with a 100x microscope. When this happened, the eggs were placed in the lake, and their life cycle began. Under ideal conditions, a smelt-spawn in the wild would have a success rate of 3%. In the controlled environment, that rate of hatch was about 80%. So, after a couple of years of trips to New York, the lake began to hold its own.

In the fall, the Fish & Game Biologists do a survey of the smelt population through the eyes of a side-planer sonar. When this information is tabulated, they adjust the stocking rate of game fish accordingly. The results of this planning are that the lake is now having 50 year highs in the quality of fish for the last 10-12 years (1993-2005).

The Derby Grand and Major Prizes have evolved since the beginning from a 12-foot boat with a 6-HP motor to four boats and motors with a 19-foot boat and a 90-HP high-lighting the list of prizes. In addition, there is a 14-foot boat and motor as prizes in the Junior Division for anglers 15 years or younger.

O.M.C. and Evinrude have been sponsors from our second derby and they continue to this day. Their participation has been unequaled, and, most surely, greatly appreciated. Princecraft Boats came aboard in the early

90s and have provided us with beautiful products for prizes. Lowrance has been a part of the Derby for 15 of the 20 years, and were a major part of the formation of the Derby. These companies are the major sponsors of the event and along with them are several others that are big contributors to our event. Over the years, the Winni Derby, has had participants from every state as well as Europe and Canada. It is known as a family event nationally, and many families plan their vacations around the Derby dates.

If you want to enter, be sure to read the rules and regulations, download the application form and send in to join us this coming spring in May for the spring's most prestigious event on Lake Winnipesaukee in New Hampshire.

Also, take a peek at our Derby photo album posted here where we show most of the winners from 1986 to 2002. You may see yourself here, or see a friend! If you have comments and/or questions, we hope you'll email the Derby headquarters at mail@winniderby.com

PICTURE GALLERY OF WINNI DERBY WINNERS

Grand prize winners from 1986, 1987, and 1988

1990 winners   *1992 winners*

1993 winners

1995 winners

1996 winners

1997 winners

1997 Junior Division winner

1998 winners

1998 Grand Prize winner

1998 Junior prize winner

1998 ladies winner

1999 winners

1999 Grand Prize Winner

1999 Junior Winner

1999 Ladies Winner

Winner of Lady's division in 2000 with her nice salmon

Rick Davis awarding prizes to the winners in 2000.

Anthony DeCarolis, with his 4.94 pound salmon which won 2nd place in the Junior Division of the 2003 Derby

The Annual Great Rotary Ice Fishing Derby

An ice sculpture commemorating the 25th anniversary of the Great Rotary Ice Fishing Derby in 2004.

The first Rotary Derby Chairman, Peter Hall in front of the 1980 board.

The tagged rainbows caught at the 2004 Great Winni Derby. The biggest tagged rainbow, 3.18 pounds, caught by John Piragis, won the Grand Prize of a $31,000 truck.

The Great Rotary Ice Fishing Derby attracts over 6,000 ice fishermen each winter, while awarding over $50,000 in prizes, donating, since its beginning 25 years ago, over 1 million dollars back to the local Meredith community and other good causes such as fish research and quality of water studies while also contributing significantly to the local economy. This derby is the largest non-profit fishing derby in the entire United States. It is usually held in early February, depending on the ice thickness.

The first Rotary Ice Derby was held in 1980 under the Meredith Presidency of John Breault who recruited John Sherman and Bruce Sanderson to help run it. Peter Hall was the Derby Chairman. Here he is at the first Great Rotary Derby in 1980 with the fishing board full of prize-competing fish behind him. The Derby has had rotating chairmen since then, to prevent burn out. 2004 was the 25th anniversary of the Great Rotary Ice Fishing Derby.

I received most of my information from Jim Wallace, a Rotarian who has played a key role in the Derby. He still does, standing out in the cold for most of the day, almost as long as us ice fishermen, cheerfully showing the fish on the boards and explaining the rules to the thousands of tourists and anglers who come by.

Left: Rotarian and Derby organizer, Jim Wallace, holds the day's largest pickerel at the 2004 Derby
Right: Charles Pinkham, of Franklin, Maine proudly holds the 2nd day's largest pickerel, a 5.65-pounder, which he caught in his grandfather's secret pickerel hole near Long Island on Lake Winni entered in the 2004 Derby.

In the early years, one had to catch a certain tagged lake trout whose number was drawn from among those tagged fish stocked by the Fish & Game to win the grand prize which for eight years, was never won. In 1983, Pepsi Cola became a sponsor and guaranteed a $2500 prize for the largest laker.

Ice derby board with cusk and lakers

In the early years, celebrity Curt Goudy angling sports caster, became the honorary host of the Rotary Derby and the news media began to take notice, including national coverage on "Good Morning America" and other national shows. In 1989, a major change guaranteed prizes, including a boat and trailer, for the biggest laker, tagged or not tagged, plus prizes for the biggest rainbows, yellow perch, white perch, pickerel, cusk, and bass. In election years, politicians, wanting the crowds and coverage, come to the Derby for exposure. The Ice Derby has paid for such projects as a Center Harbor grandstand, a basketball court, Christmas Children's Fund, services to the disabled, medical support, scholarships for needy students, fish stocking programs, and a long list of other worthy community programs.

The entire Rotary Great Ice Fishing Derby board

This home on the ice was assembled by an enterprising man complete with kitchen, living and bed room, out door patio with full furnishings so he could live there 24/7 and not miss any good ice fishing time!

An entire village of bob houses and food and other concessions appears on the ice on Meredith Bay just before the Derby begins. In 2003 and 2004 a man somehow dragged a 3 room house with patio and sliding glass doors out onto Meredith bay, living most of the winter there in his home on the ice!

I have enjoyed the community of the ice derby, where one can socially stroll from one bob house to the next, being offered anglers' hospitality from ginger brandy to steaks and burgers on the grill. One year, I caught a large 6+ pound laker 14 minutes before the Derby ended. Having heard that no large lakers had been entered I threw the laker into my snow mobile basket and sped off from the east side of Bear Island to Meredith Bay to check in my catch. I was flying when I hit an ice fault and went soaring through the air. Lucky my snowmobile did not tip over and I set off again, but looked over my shoulder to discover that my trout had bounced out! I wheeled around to retrace my tracks, finally finding the fish on the ice about a quarter mile behind me. I put it in my lap and sped off again. Upon arriving in Meredith at the check-in station, a large crowd had assembled for the final count-down, and I pushed my way through holding the still fresh trout in my arms. People said, "Clear the way! Here comes a big fish — maybe a winner!" When I finally pushed my way into the Rotary scale, the man looked at his watch and said, "You missed it by 30 seconds!" So much for my lack of Derby success!

The Great Rotary Ice Fishing Derby Winners from 1994 to 2004

Grand Prize winners for largest tagged rainbow trout:
2004: **John Piragis**, 3.10-pounds, 19.5"
2003: **Ryan Bonner** 3.95-pounds, 20.75"
2002: **Weymouth Sargent, Jr.** 3.25-pounds, 20"
2001: **Mark Posson**, 4.77-pounds, 21.5"
2000: **Perry Davidson**, 2.25-pounds, 17.75"
1999: **James Feeney**. 3.13-pounds, 19.75"
1998: **Grant Conley**, 2.46-pounds, 18.5"
1997: **Scott Carbone**, 2.43-pounds, 19"
1996: no record available
1995: **Robert Brooks**, 3.2-pounds, 18.5"
1994: **Michael Richards**, 2.5-pounds, 18"

Left: Alton's Ryan Bonner holds up his winning catch in front of the new board at the 24th annual Great Rotary Fishing Derby in 2003. Bonner reeled in the largest tagged rainbow trout (3.95 pounds, 20.75 inches) to win the event. (Laconia Citizen Photo by Caryl Carlson). He won a boat and motor.

Right: John Piragis of Orange Massachusetts won the 2004 Grand Prize, at the 25th Annual Great Rotary Ice Fishing Derby. His prize was a new GMC $31,000 truck which he won from catching a tagged 3.18-pound, 19.5" rainbow trout.

Large Notable Fish caught:
2004: **Dan Davies**, 7.13-pound, 27.5" pickerel
2003: **Greg Chapman**, 6.52-pound, 23.5" rainbow trout
2002: **Jason Bickerton**, 11.02-pound, 34.25" cusk
2001: **Gregory Trefethen**, 9.85-pound, 30" lake trout
2000: **Charlie Benson,** 7.65-pound, 30.25" lake trout
1999: **Emory Tobin**, 10.53-pound, 28.25" rainbow trout
1998: **Daniel Handrehan**, 13.34-pound, 32.75" lake trout
1997: **Keith Mongeau**, 3-pound, 16" white perch
1996: no record available
1995: **Larry Mayer**, 3.12-pound, 16" white perch
1994: **Brad Bonneau**, 9.36-pound, 31.5" lake trout

Bass Tournaments: Good for the economy; but bad for the bass?

I have a big concern about the large number of professional bass tournaments our lakes host each summer week. These commercial tournaments are about money. Big money...both for the contestants and also for the lake's region economy. Do you have a guess just how many bass tournaments there were on Lake Winni in the 2002 fishing season, for example? Well, get ready for a startling figure. According to an eight-page list of NH bass tournaments, given me by New Hampshire Fish & Game, there were 78 tournaments on Lake Winni in 2002, involving 2,268 boats! That's about a tournament every other spring and summer day on Lake Winni. There were another 57 on Lake Winnisquam for a total of 135 tournaments in one year. In the entire state, there were 358 bass tournaments in 2002 - that's 3 to 4 bass tournaments per day during the season! No wonder it is more difficult to catch a big bass now than it was before these pro tournaments began competing with us amateur anglers!

Each boat speeds out to catch as many big bass as they can in a given time, culling out the largest, and releasing the smallest. They put them in live wells, and go back to marinas where they check in their large plastic bag full of fish to see who caught the most pounds of bass. The fish are then released in the much dirtier water of the marinas, never to return to their natural habitat from which they were taken. One fish biologist estimated that 40% of all released fish will die. Steve Perry's studies (see Master Angler Chapter 12) on mortality of Bass caught in tournaments seems very conservative compared to this. Certainly many more transported in live wells back to the much dirtier waters of marinas die either enroute or after weigh-in and release. And these fishermen are most often structure fishermen who "buoy hop," taking most of the dominant bass from these spots. I'm a good bass angler and I used to catch three or four 4-5 pound-bass in a summer of bass fishing. I have caught almost no bass that large since the pro Bass Tournaments began. And I have wondered where the big bass have gone. My theory is that they are constantly being culled from their natural habitat and transported to marinas where a small percentage of them survive, but never return to their natural homes. How damaging the current practice may be is still an unknown.

There has been some recent talk about having an official judge on-board each boat to witness the weighing of bass which could then be immediately released back in their home habitat. I'd certainly be in favor of this practice. I know that these tournaments bring big bucks into the region. Take a small percentage of that money to hire the on-board official for each boat. It would certainly be worth whatever it cost to leave our bass alive in their natural habitat. John W. Corrigan, who writes the "Angler's Journal," for *The Concord Monitor,* reported in his October 26, 2003 column, the good news that hearings were held by the NH Fish & Game Department to address some of these issues to help insure the survival of bass caught in tournaments. Among the rules established is a prohibition of culling bass kept on stringers, a practice used by some of the contestants who do not have live wells with fresh water continuously being pumped through the holding tanks. Another regulation is that bass "...entered for a weigh-in be released unharmed into the same body of water, no less than 300 feet from shoreline...." But this will still not address my concern that they are being released in areas that are not their original habitat — usually near marinas where the water is not as clean as the place, perhaps miles from there, where they may have been caught. But at least enough concern has been voiced to generate some changes!

Take the time to learn more about these tournaments on our lakes. This will confirm why you see so many bass boats speeding around the lake on any give summer day...and it may indicate why you are catching so few big bass.

Chapter 11

THE MASTER ANGLERS OF LAKE WINNIPESAUKEE

The Senior Master Anglers: Barbara Cotton, Bill Martel, Jim Warner, Al Stewart, Mario DeCarolis, Ted St. Onge and, in Memoriam, the late Paul Philippe)

> Fishing seemed to be the one sport which best gratified that innate craving for an intimacy with those forces of which I knew so little."
> — Ray Bergman —

THROUGHOUT THIS BOOK, I refer to "Master Anglers" instead of "THE Master Anglers." Though the 15 together have over 600 years of Lake Winnipesaukee angling experience, there are other Lake Winni fishermen who could be called Master Anglers who aren't featured. Some of them seem to catch fish when no one else does; others I haven't met. Not all want to share their secrets. I've selected this group of 14 others because of their years of successful angling, their support of other anglers, and their gracious willingness to "pass on" their secrets of success. Each Master Angler completed a questionnaire gathering a history of their Lake Winni angling, their top tips, favorite stories, and some opinions on issues.

Each was asked the ubiquitous question, "Why do you fish?" The chapters which follow contain each one's answers to this questionnaire. I have presented them by age seniority, the oldest first. As unique individuals their responses are different and varied. But thanks to AJ ("Salmonitis") we have a Web site where one can find daily reports of what our angling community members are catching (or not catching, as negative reports are not only also helpful, but humbling and tend to make others feel better when we are not having the luck of some) and information on hot lures and depths. Here's the Web site for daily fishing reports: **http://www.fishlakewinni.com/** (Click on "Message Board.")

Bill Whall aka "Donald Duck" or "Mighty MO 2"

Bill Wahll, aka "The Duck" a blind USNavy Vet who's radios are the eyes and ears of anglers on Lake Winni. Bill is known to all oon the Lake as the man to call for help, if needed. He monitors several radios from his Moultonboro home about Lake Winni and has been credited with saving many lives. He was decorated by the US Coast Guard for his life-saving on Lake Winni.

I must say a word about "The Duck." Bill Whall, known to most anglers on the Lake is a blind friend, who is omnipresent on the Lake if you need help in any kind of emergency (except when he is asleep before 0800 in the mornings since he is an ex-navy man and, as such, used to sleeping in late!) Though he is not always physically out there in a boat with us anglers, he is out there using his radio on which he has perfect 20-20 vision. I am listing him here, since he belongs here with the rest of us Master Anglers as he, like others, has served and saved many anglers on the Lake by answering emergency calls and by directing Water Safety craft where they might be needed. Monitoring his radios from 0800 to 2400 hours every day, he also knows all about where, on what, and how deep the fish are hitting and who is catching what, when, and where. "The Duck" as he used to be called on the CB radios when we all had them, is now "Mighty Mo 2" on the Marine radio. (This call sign is because Bill Whall once proudly served on the Battle Ship Missouri.) One time he went fishing with Paul Philippe, and that one fishing trip has generated many stories including the one about him reeling a salmon in so fast he impaled it on his rod tip! In May, 2000, he was twelfth recipient of the Bunzel Award at the State House in Concord, for his life-saving work here on the Lake. Coverage appeared in the national news media, *Readers Digest*, including being on the Paul Harvey Radio Show and a proclamation from the Governor of New Hampshire. Captain Moyer, U.S. Navy (ret), came up from Washington, D.C. to decorate Bill. In the DVDs series "The Master Anglers of Lake Winni," "The Duck" serves as its colorful narrator. (You may order the DVDs at this web site: www.deepwaterspress.com)

HONORARY MASTER ANGLER PAUL PHILIPPE
In Memoriam...Paul was a victim of esophageal cancer in 2001 (22 Years angling in Lake Winni)

"The fisherman fishes as the urchin eats a cream bun — from lust."
— T.H. White —

Left: A picture of the late Paul Philippe with a rainbow trout caught through the ice with his friend, Mario DeCarolis, on a cold winters day. Right: A wreath in Paul Philippe's memory floats over his favorite fishing spot on Lake Winni

Paul Philippe, a successful accountant, with a call sign of "Bean Counter," came to Lake Winni later than most of the older Master Anglers. He began fishing with a determination which would not be denied! Paul had a significant influence on many others whose lives he touched either in-person, or on the radio on Lake Winni. He was known for his generosity, good heart, and his accountant-like empirical studies of the best lures, depth, speeds, and colors of lures. As the story goes, Paul would designate one side of his boat as the "experimental" side, the other being the "control" side. He'd only use Sutton #61 lures with a small red stripe on the left and plain Sutton #61 lures without the red on the other side of his boat. He gathered data on hits on the red versus the plain lures for 5 years. He'd then compare the results and reach conclusions like, "The Sutton #61 with the red tape caught 23% more fish over a 5 year period than the one without the red." This research influenced many of us to swear by the results of his studies. When Paul told us that the copper Mooselook caught 9% more salmon than the brass one (being color-blind, I can't tell the difference and had doubts that the fish can...), we all automatically shifted to copper, knowing that the data leading to this conclusion was sound coming from Paul. But you had to be careful listening to Paul over the marine radio. He was known to broadcast fictitious data to throw off flat-landers. Some of us in the know, like his good friend, Master Angler Mario DeCarolis, when he heard "Bean Counter" report that he, "Caught a salmon on copper Mooselooks at 30 feet," knew, by pre-arrangement, to add 20 feet to this coded report and conclude, that he actually caught 3 salmon at 50 feet on a #61 Sutton with red stripe. This kind of cryptic deception still goes on in the derbies when people are reluctant to give away valuable information to the competition. Pictures here show a moving tribute to a great Master Angler Paul Philippe when his family and friends, aboard boats over his favorite fishing spot (determined exactly by GPS to be the spot where he caught his 16.5 pound laker!), floated a wreath in his memory, drank a toast to our angler friend, and threw over-board some of his favorite lures.

*Left: Mario DeCarolis, family and friends of Paul Philippe,
bid a tearful farewell to our angling buddy out over his favorite fishing spot
(found by GPS where Paul caught his 14 pound laker).
Right: Friends and family of Paul Philippe, celebrating his life on Lake Winni.
A wreath was floated and his favorite lures were dropped over board
in honor of this good man and Master Angler.*

We miss Paul. "Paul, we know you're smiling down on us as we fish in your favorite spot with your proven lures!" Mario DeCarolis swears that every time he trolls through Paul's favorite spot, he gets a fish, as a gift from Paul.

"God does not deduct from a man's time on earth the hours he spends fishing." — George X. Sand —

MASTER ANGLER BARBARA COTTON — The Grand Dame of Lake Winni Anglers (71 years of Lake Winni angling)

Barbara smiling

When I began working on this book, asking others who they thought were Master Anglers of Lake Winni, the name Barbara Cotton, kept coming up. One Master Angler, Chuck French, told me that every opening day would find him at her place, where he'd launch his boat after being treated by Barbara to a cup of coffee. Barbara Cotton, with her late husband, Mert, founded a small landmark called the Opechee Trading Post on the shore at the end of Lake Opechee where the Winnipesaukee River begins.

Left: The Opechee Trading Post of Barbara Cotton, the oldest Orvis Fly Shop owner in America as it looked then...and now! Right: Barbara Cotton and her angler son, John

When Barbara Cotton goes to the Orvis Dealer annual meetings in Manchester, Vermont, they have her stand for recognition as the oldest living Orvis Dealer in America. This 94-year young lady was gracious when we met to talk about this project. She would politely interrupt me from time to time to tell me an angling story. She knows all the old timers *well as she supplied them with their tackle. She had not been well, and after several visits to her place by the lake, she finally consented to being videotaped if her son, John, also an experienced angler, would help with her questionnaire. Just before Christmas 2003, Barbara had a stroke and was hospitalized. I visited her at the St. Francis Home in Laconia in early 2004 where she is recovering. She announced that I had it all wrong, listing her as a Master Angler. She feared some of the anglers would be upset to find that she was listed as a "Master Angler." I told her that was nothing to fear. Master Anglers Jim Warner, Bill Martel, Chuck French, and Carl Gephardt had said, "If you're writing about Master Anglers of Lake Winni, you must have Barbara Cotton in your book!" Her response was that she needed to get on home to open her Opechee Trading Post, "... as anglers might be needing some tackle."*

I was born Barbara Beaton on July 29, 1909 in South Ryegate, Vermont. My father owned and operated a granite quarry and my mother was the postmistress there. I boarded with relatives in Barre during high school, graduating from Barre High School in 1926. I earned a BS in Library Science from Simmons College in 1930, leaving on commencement day to assume a library position at Mt. Holyoke College. I married Laconia native and angler Merton Cotton, in 1933 and moved to Opechee Street in Laconia.

Things were different in 1933 – a week's salary might be $7 or $8 and waterfront lots on Governors Island were selling for $1 a front foot.

On the assumption I would leave after a short time, I became the head librarian of the Laconia Public Library in 1944; but time flies when you're having fun and I didn't retire until 1978.

My husband, Mert, resigned as assistant treasurer of the Laconia Savings Bank and we opened the Opechee Trading Post on Lake Opechee in December 1944.

Barbara and her husband, Mert, talk with Marty Harwood about the best fly which he missed since he was not up at 3:30 AM opening day when the store opened!

Top: *A young Barbara Cotton and son, John*
Middle: *Barbara selling flies in her Orvis Shop*

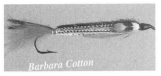

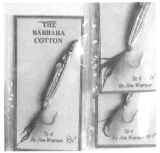

Top: *Barbara Cotton streamer fly.* Middle: *A streamer fly named after Barbara Cotton, by another Master Angler, Jim Warner*

His father Edwin Cotton and our son, John, assisted, but as years sped by, I gradually became the most dedicated partner and the sole proprietor when my husband died in 1985. For 60 years the store has been a favorite gathering place for fishermen – a place for spinning both truths and tales. As years went by, fly fishing equipment and fly-tying materials became the specialty of my store.

At the young age of 94, I am now the oldest Orvis dealer in the United States. I pride myself in being a facilitator. My son says that's because I talk the "best game in town." "Few can sell a one ounce-weight rod to a 250 pound hulk," he said about a sale I once made. Although the yellow hornberg is my favorite fly for brook trout, I'm mightily pleased with the "Barbara Cotton" — a salmon streamer originated by Ken Welch of Bow, New Hampshire in my honor.

Master Angler Jim Warner also made his own version called the "Barbara Cotton Special."

After the end of World War II and into the 1950s, the opening of salmon season was a big affair, more so than in recent years. On April 1, the Trading Post was open at 3:30 AM, and I was dishing out bait and hot coffee to those who could barely wait for dawn. Behind the store, there was open water from the current, so only 2 or 3 boats were commonly in the narrow channel in the ice. However, sometimes hundreds of fishermen would line the banks from the store down stream to the railroad bridge and beyond.

Big salmon taken on fly off Barbara's dock circa 1978 by Jack Kirk. Fishermen would gather at Barbara's place to fish, show off their catches, to buy flies, and for her free coffee.

Boats full of freezing anglers on April 1st, opening day, in front of Barbara's Opechee Trading Post.

Others would head for other open water spots like the Winnipesaukee River inlets to both Opechee and Winnisquam and the traditional favorites on the Big Lake – the bridges at Governors and Long Island, the Weirs channel, Melvin Village, Wolfeboro and the Merrymeeting River at Alton Bay. Now on April 1, there seem to be much larger ice-free areas than in past years, a likely result of global warming.

Each year surface trolling for salmon and lake trout followed the receding edges of ice. Store talk would focus on the hottest single and tandem streamers during this most productive period. Of course, one could always get skunked when trying to show off the fishery, like in 1953 when Mert and our son, John, took Tommy Evinrude trolling for a day and never got a strike. In the Lakes Region in the 1940s and 1950s, bass fishing was more subdued than today. With the introduction and reproductive success of largemouth bass, the popularity of bass fishing has skyrocketed ... as has the horsepower of the boats that chase them. Greatly diminished is the peaceful, nighttime paddling while casting surface plugs and poppers toward over-hanging limbs on darkened shores, no doubt the result of shorefront development with impassioned desire for perfectly trimmed shorelines.

One low-key fishery, past and present, is native brookie and rainbow fishing in small tributaries to the Big Lake. Naturally, fishing for natives "ain't what it used to be" but a few fishermen successfully sneak around for the best tasting little ones. And true to tradition, I will **not** reveal my best spots.

Barbara Cotton out fishing with nice brookie.

My annual fall activity was trapping shiners and roach to sell as live bait for both ice fishing and the next spring and summer season. I used mostly glass and copper wire traps. For many years, my bait was temporarily stored and transported in two 50-gallon drums mounted horizontally in my old 1937 Chevy panel truck. Later, in the 1960s and 1970s, smaller containers were placed in my 1958 Dodge Sierra station wagon. Trapping was discontinued in the late seventies. Bait would be kept over winter in large "bait boxes" with screens on the bottom placed along my 50-foot dock behind my store. I did most of my trapping in Lake Winnisquam and tributaries to the Winnipesaukee River. However, Minge Cove (before much development) was a favorite location on the Big Lake.

Barbara Cotton—the oldest Orvis Store propietor in the America, minding her store. She says, "It will soon be open again!"

Once while ice fishing with my husband, my tip-up flag went up and I set the hook on a big fish. Mert was at a neighboring bob house swapping stories. I carefully worked the monster in and finally his big head appeared in the opening in the ice. Afraid I'd break the leader, I held the line tight with one hand and reached the other down into his gills, hoisting out the biggest laker of my life! Unknown to me a game warden was standing behind me. Not seeing him, I excitedly grabbed the big trout to my chest and ran in the direction of the bob house to show off my prize to Mert. The shocked game warden thought I was running away him, and suspecting I didn't have a license, chased after me. After showing off my prize to Mert and his friends, I came out to find the game warden outside waiting to give me a citation. He asked me why I thought I could get away ice fishing without a license. I told him that I did not think that at all…and that I <u>had</u> my license, which I showed him, much to his chagrin! I asked him why he thought a nice angler lady like me would be fishing without her license. He walked away embarrassed at jumping the gun on a poor old lady!

I love the Lake and the people who fish it; they are a special breed of New Hampshire folks. Many of the other Master Anglers, like Bill Martel, Chuck French, Carl Gebhardt, and that fine gentleman fly-tier Jim Warner, are old friends of mine. I am honored that Hal Lyon has invited me to be listed in his book as a Master Angler with them. But I'm not really a Master Angler. I'm an angler who has always befriended and supported other Master Anglers! God bless them all!

MASTER ANGLER WILLIAM MARTEL, JR.
(74 Years Angling in Lake Winni)

I first met Bill Martel in the 1940s when I was a wide-eyed young boy, gazing enviously at the fishing tackle and lures, back when Bill was working in his father's shop. The old ramshackled buildings always looked like they were about to float away down the Winnipesaukee River.

Top: Bill Martel—with all the character of an old angler
Middle Left: Young Bill Martel with a large salmon.
Right: Martel's store. For years everyone feared it would fall into the river.

As a boy I remember going into his shed to the right of the store where one could peer down into the depths under the dock watching huge bass, perch, and other fish cruising around. I remember thinking how great it would be to work in such a place! I had no inkling of how hard Bill and his father worked to catch the bait, mind the store, and guide fishing parties at the same time. But to a boy who saved his allowance for lures, it was my idea of heaven!

Top: Bill Martel Sr. up close

Middle: Bill Martel Sr. with a hefty Laker, circa 1935.

Lower: Martel guiding in his father's old Johnson laker boat just after he came home from WWII.

I was born in Laconia, New Hampshire, September 30, 1924. My father, William Martel Sr., and his mother, had owned a live bait, boat livery, and guide service on Lake Winnisquam.

He married in 1923. I was born a year later. We had an 8'x40' dock where I first started fishing when I was 6 with a cane pole. Also dad took me trolling for salmon (Chinook in those days). I caught my first one at age 7. It weighed about 7 pounds, and I needed some help in landing it. It was taken on a Phantom Minnow on his salmon rod.

At age 13, after graduating from grammar school, I had to help my father with the business to replace my grandmother, who broke her hip and was bedridden. At age 17 upon receiving my master pilot's license for motor boats and my New Hampshire guide's license, I began taking out fishing parties with my dad.

At 18, WWII came and I went into the Army where I served in Europe for 33 months. I will never forget coming back home just in time for Christmas in 1945.

In 1946, I was back doing what I loved best, catching live bait and guiding fishing parties. My guide service ended in 1969 with the death of my father. I took over ownership of his bait and boat rental service, which became a seven-day a week job for many years. I sold the business in 1985 but still work part-time with the new owners now at age 79.

Bill Martel laughing in the store surrounded by fishing lures and gadgets

Martel's has been serving the fishing public for over 85 years.

Who taught you to fish, your favorite game fish, months for fishing and trolling speed?

On left is Bill Martel, Sr., with a party he successfully guided for lakers and salmon in 1949

- My father was a good teacher who taught me all I know. He had me hold his favorite rod, sitting in the back seat of his Johnson Laker boat in the days when Chinook salmon were in Lake Winnisquam. I had to have some help then in landing these big fish. He taught me how to fish, hunter safety, fur trapping, but most of all, patience!
- My favorite fish is the smallmouth black bass because they never seem to give up. I've caught several which took 15 to 20 minutes to bring to the boat with light tackle.
- My favorite fishing months are May and July, early morning and late afternoon.
- My best trolling speed is 2 MPH for lake trout and 5 MPH for salmon

Largest Salmon, Laker, Rainbow, bass and other big fish you have caught:

Salmon: 27 inches, 8 pounds in 1961 on a Mooselook Warbler trolling 8 -10' deep
Laker: 31", 10.5 pounds, in 1937 on sewed on shiner at 20 feet deep
Rainbow: 25.5", 7.5 pounds in 1946 on a night crawler 10 feet deep
White fish: 4 pounds
Cusk: Many over 5 pounds
Bass: I caught two 6-pounders

Stories of these monsters:

Bill Martel's mentor, his father with his throw smelt net, with which he supplied his store with smelt.

One weekend I was night fishing through the ice in one of my father's smelt shanties, with a 2'x4' hole cut in the ice through the shanty floor. I hooked into a monster cusk, which I finally worked to the surface of the hole. By the light of my kerosene lamp, I could see the size of this monster and realized I needed help. I hollered to a fishing buddy to come with his gaff. He came running with a bright flashlight. Upon shining the light in the hole, the fish became startled and headed for the bottom, breaking my line! We estimated his size by the size of the hole in the shanty. It was about 42" and 18-20 pounds. The one that got away!

A bemused Bill Martel watching a cat who likes smelt as much as the trout!

I've passed on my experience and skills to my grandchildren - 3 boys and a girl. I take them out fishing in my 14' aluminum boat on Lake Winni whenever I can.

Top Ice fishing tips:

1. Fish from ice-in through most of January using tip-ups with live smelt or shiners.

2. I use 36-pound squid line on my tip-ups with 9 feet of 8-pound test leader and a # 6 hook. Use a small split shot 18" up from the hook on the leader, fishing a few feet under the ice. This usually produces well. But you'll also catch salmon just under the ice, which you must carefully and rapidly return by cutting the leader near the hook.

3. Jig a short rod or bob stick with 8-pound monofiliment line on the rod. On the stick, I use 36-pound squid line.

4. I also use cut bait (sucker) on the hook with a 1.5-oz sinker or lead head jig with a piece of sucker on the hook fishing in 35'-50' of water on the bottom.

5. In Late February or March, ice fish in shallower water near or on sandbars where lake trout come in to clean themselves of parasites.

In years past, we used to eat all the fish we caught. Now I fish for pleasure so I release all the fish I catch. Over stocking of salmon in the 1950's diminished the smelt population. Then the salmon and trout foraged on the shad and that is why I think we have so few now.

A Fishing story:

Five large trout in front of Bill Martels -- a sign of success! Circa 1940s

Prior to 1946, trolling with powerboats ended on June 30th. But in 1946, a 15-day extension was given with a limit of 4 fish (lake trout or salmon) per boat.

During that 15-day extension, from July 1st through July 15th was my most successful angling time, ever. My father, in his 28' Johnson Laker, and I, in a 22' boat, each took out two parties of fishermen per day landing a total of 147 lake trout in 15 days, with an average weight of 7.5 pounds! All were caught with sewed-on fall fish (roaches) or small suckers using steel rods with Malin copper lines at a depth of about 20'!

MASTER ANGLER JIM WARNER
(54 years of Lake Winni angling)

> "If the all-ruling Power please
> We live to see another May,
> We'll recompense an Age of these
> Foul days in one fine fishing day:
> We then shall have a day or two,
> Perhaps a week, wherein to try,
> What the best Master's hand can do
> With the most deadly killing flie.
> — Charles Cotton —

Master Angler Jim Warner at age 6, getting started in his angling career

Jim Warner's name is well known on Lake Winni - especially among fly fishermen. Jim is the creator of many successful streamer patterns sold all around the Lake's Region. He is also well known among people from Wolfeboro, as the former long time owner of the main sporting and bait store on the docks in downtown Wolfeboro. Jim is a gentleman and a Master among master fly tiers, having won much national recognition for his art. He is also an ardent fisherman, as his stories reveal. I have never witnessed first hand such fly-tying skill. When the ice goes out this year, I will be trolling Jim Warner's flies — either his Lake Winni Smelt, his "Barbara Cotton Special," "Lil Warner Smelt," or his "Nine-Three" if the weather is dark and overcast.

Jim Warner -- a Master Angler and Master Fly-tier

My dear wife would probably say,"You can't write a short anything." She has always been right (she says). My fishing experience on Lake Winnipesaukee first started in 1949, when I married a Laconia gal. While she worked as a nurse at Laconia General Hospital, I fished. Actually, I fished everywhere I could in the hours that preceded the hours I worked at Scott & Williams Factory. I tied flies then, too, and occasionally I would go out with my friend Bob Moulton in Alton Bay. He ran a small tackle & gas station, and he kept me busy tying trolling flies for him. We would troll for salmon. Otherwise, without a boat, I usually fished the Winnipesaukee River above Tilton, and the Swift, the Bearcamp, and other good trout streams.

During the Korean conflict, I was stationed in France ... and my wife tagged along. I had a wonderful opportunity to fish "about" Europe, and visited many of the good angling countries, such as Norway and Sweden. After the service stint, I opened the tiny Sportsmen's Center with Bob Moulton. We were located at the bridge in downtown Wolfeboro.

Jim Warner's old bait & tackle store, the Sportsman's Center at the bridge, followed by the Lakes Region Sports Shop, at the dock on Wolfeboro Bay.

I bought Bob out after a year and he went on his way to other area businesses. I stayed and ran the Center until 1963 when I opened the Lakes Region Sports Shop at the docks. In 1976 I sold it and "semi-retired" for more angling time. All through these years, I fished the big lake when I could. When I had the small Sportsman's Center, I had my boat tied up in the river at the side of the shop and would go out almost every morning at 4:30AM. I would troll the outer Wolfeboro Bay between Sewall and Clark Points or head out into the Broads to fish the "triangle" between Little Mark Island and Black Point. It was on these excursions that I met with other fishermen, such as, Glenn Morrill. For several years, I was a licensed guide on Lake Winnipesaukee. After I changed store locations, it was not as easy to get out to go fishing, unless there was someone to take over the shop. But, I did get out on some of the early mornings and a few of the later evenings. The new shop was even busier, because I was still catching most of the bait sold during the day, doing the bookkeeping, and managing the store. During all these years, at both stores, I tied all the flies sold there and was able to create some of the better fly patterns used around the Lakes Region.

Left: A mess of Jim Warner's beaded Winni Smelt -- the fly he created and made famous for Lake Winni salmon.
Right: Jim Warner doing the work he loves, tying flies

After selling the Lakes Region Sports business, I was unlucky enough to get into real estate in the Wolfeboro area and stayed with it until 1998, when I officially retired and moved from my Winter Harbor home to a modest spot in Melvin Village. All through these years, I tied and created fly patterns. In the last 5 years I have tied only for my old establishment in Wolfeboro. In the last few years of my "retirement" I have been doing "frames" of my "Originals" which seems to take most of my time now. In a month I'll be 76. Most of my more notable accomplishments have been at the fly tying bench.

My fly-tying has been listed in several books: Dick Stewart's *Trolling Flies for Trout & Salmon*; Dick Surette's *Trout and Salmon Fly Index*; Don Wilson's *Smelt Fly Dressings*; Mike Martinek's *Streamer Fly Patterns for Trolling & Casting 1 & 2*; many periodicals such as *On The Water*, *UFT*, and many newspaper articles. I have tied flies for scores of retail outlets including Abercrombie & Fitch and William Mills in New York City, for 3 jobber accounts, and hundreds of individuals. In 1964 I tied 6 large fly books full of area streamers for New Hampshire Governor King, for gifts to visiting dignitaries. (Curt Gowdy & Ted Williams were among them.) I have taught fly tying to grade schools, high schools, summer camps, classes associated with retail stores, and under the New Hampshire Arts

Council program as a Master Craftsman. (Written up in *New Hampshire Wildlife Journal* – May/June, 1995). I've done exhibition tying at various places including under the UFT in Boston, State of New Hampshire Arts Council, and Bob Moulton's show at the Farmington F&G Club in 1951.

But I really feel that one of my best accomplishments has been a marriage to a lovely woman for 54 years (and she has put up with so much fly tying mess!) I've had a wonderful life, so far. My dear wife has promised to bury me with my fly tying vise, when that time comes.

Years angling in Lake Winni:

1950- (with break in 4 service connected years) for total of 54 years

Who taught me to fish?

My mother, who took me trolling for largemouth bass in Lake Santa Fe in Melrose, Florida. We used a jointed Pikie Minnow, and I landed a very large bass. I have a photo holding it when I was 6. As far as teaching me here on Lake Winni, I was self-taught. My mother gave me a gift when I was 12, a trip to Lake Sunapee, where I stayed in an old lakeside hotel by myself and rowed around the lake trolling for 2 days. What a gift! I was always reading the top two fishing magazines, *Field & Stream* and *Outdoor Life*. In 1949 I married a Laconia gal. In the spring of 1950, my wife & I rented a boat on Lake Winni and I remember that we caught a nice lake trout in a snowstorm off the Gilford shore. In 1950 I met a friend who owned a sport shop in Alton Bay, Bob Moulton. He & I fished a great deal, trolling mostly for salmon and trout, when we could get away. We also trolled for bass along the shoreline.

Fishing Mentor/hero?

I have had many good friends over the years who were far better than I for the title of Master Angler! But if I had to pick one out of all, it would be Glen Morrill of Alton Bay. Black Point used to be one of my favorite Lake Winni fishing spots and on numerous occasions I would encounter Glenn out with a fishing customer in his small boat usually doing quite well. Usually when I trolled alongside we would exchange information. He would shout, "How deep are your trolling?" He would then give me a hint; "Let some more line out..." or "Take in some line." And as soon as I did as he suggested, I would begin catching both trout and salmon. At that time, Glen was THE guide on Lake Winni, and his motto was, "No fish — no pay." I doubt if he ever came away empty handed. At that time, Glenn's favorite lure was a fly with red & blue and a yellow wing. In those days, even though in the middle of the summer, we trolled solid copper lines with long leaders and flies.

What did I learn from Glenn?

Perhaps most important was depth and trolling speed. And another of his tips then, is just as good now. I noticed that Glenn never trolled in a straight line. He always fished in figure "8's" and random curves. I found out then that this caused the fly or lure to slow down and drop, and then to speed up and rise. Color of flies was another hint, for he would use the darker less conspicuous flies like a "Nine-Three" for top water in the very early morning or late evening. And if the flies were being trolled on top, the longer the leader, the better the luck.

My favorite Winni fish

Well, it is not hard to pick the landlocked salmon for this category. The lake trout, pound for pound, is a strong game fish. But in the spring, when most are caught on top, they tend to throb and just use their weight. On the other hand, a salmon will fight much harder. Sometimes the acrobatics can be fantastic! Of course rainbow trout are very much like salmon in the fight. Landlocks can also be caught for longer periods too, on into the summer months, than can lakers who go down deeper. The salmon tend to stay in the top 10-15 feet on into the summer months, whereas the lakers seek the cooler temperatures of deeper water. On several occasions even in summer, I have been out on Lake Winni at a very early hour to find salmon on top, sometimes just surfacing. On one such memorable morning, I cast a fly beyond the swirl, only to hook a huge salmon, which broke off.

Which do you prefer - lead core, fly rod, or downrigger fishing for salmon and trout?

This is a big subject. I have always advocated the use of the fly rod; but then, I'm not a purist either. Other methods have their place and I have used them all. When I did most of my trolling on Lake Winni, between the 1950s and mid 1980s, the springtime was, of course, the most fished time of the year. Back then, few anglers would follow the fish into the deep. And by September, still few fished, for it was time to think fall and the coming hunting season. Leadcore, was a spring-into-early-Summer line. To have enough leadcore to get part of the way to the bottom, a pretty large reel had to be used to hold 200 yards of leadcore. I doubt that 200 yards of leadcore can get down more than a hundred feet unless one trolls at a crawl. And leadcore is difficult to work to give it action, because one tends to wear a bad spot in the outside nylon braid. In the very early years when I trolled, copper line was the most popular and cheap. But it got you down. And if you hit the bottom and broke off, you might only lose the fly or lure. Steel or Monel line was also used and its smaller diameter allowed you to get more on a smaller reel. Sometime around the sixties, a twisted steel line came into the Lake Winni scene and there were men who trolled these steel lines with flies who were very successful.

My method of trolling in the spring, especially, was with 3 rods (2 anglers). Two rods would be on top water, whether they be with fly or other lure, and the third rod would be deeper — a heavier rod with leadcore. The leadcore would be let out no more than 5 colors, which would put the fly down about 5-15 feet, depending on trolling speed. If the fish were not hitting on the top lines, then I would switch the arrangement with 1 top and two down.

When downriggers first came to the market, in the 1970s, the need for most of the leadcore/steel lines was over. The downrigger enabled fishermen to catch good fish with much lighter lines and tackle. I had a pair of the early downriggers. They were too clumsy and far from the technology of the present. I never used them that much, but they looked good on the back of my boat — sort of a status symbol. The downrigger, properly used, can be a deadly method to catch fish, especially in the hotter summer months.

For the most part, when spring was over, it was high time for me to buckle down to the business of running a sports shop for 18 hours a day!

Favorite fishing months:

Of course, spring is my favorite time with fly-fishing. But winter has always held a spot in my heart ... when my arthritis wasn't so bad that I could brave the cold. When I lived in Laconia, and long before I opened the sports shop, I used to like to bob or jig for perch through the ice. My brother-in-law and I would trudge out onto the Broads, use a hand chisel and cut through a couple feet of ice. We'd fill a bucket with nice yellow perch. We used the small pin smelt for bait on hand lines. Even later in the years, I can remember having a series of cusk lines in front of my Winter Harbor home and, with my daughter, pulling up some very nice cusk for chowder.

Best time of the day for angling:

For me, definitely the early morning for trout and salmon. But for bass, I prefer the evening hours.

JIM WARNER'S CHART OF FISHING DEPTHS AND LURES BY MONTHS FOR VARIOUS FISH

MONTH	SALMON	LAKERS	RAINBOWS	BASS
MAY	Top to 5-10'	Top to 5-10'	Top to 5-10'	0-5'
JUNE	Top to 5-20'	10-25'	Top to 5-20'	0-10'
JULY	5-30'	20-50'	5-20'	15-25'
AUGUST	10-35'	20-50'	10-35'	15-25'
				0-10' night
SEPTEMBER	10-20'	20-50'	10-20'	15-25' 0-10' night
OCTOBER	closed	closed	closed	5-10' 0-5' night
ICE FISHING	closed	depth varies	depth varies	Bottom

Best speed for trolling:

Early in the spring, I believe that the speed should be slower than later when the water warms up. I remember a customer at my store, The Sportsman Center, who came in and bought some very small No. 1 brass Mepps spinners. When I questioned him, out of curiosity, he told me he was catching salmon like gangbusters. I found out that he had a small rowboat and was just letting the spinners out on a long line while slowly rowing across Wolfeboro Bay. I tried to copy his technique, but could not get the proper slow speed. It could be that the variable speed one achieves when rowing gave him his advantage. Flies, in general, should be trolled faster. Lures - depending on their proper action, which one should always check in the water by the boat - should be trolled slower. For years the

ChevChase lure was the rage. And I found that the Mooselook, with proper bending and a pearl spinner blade in the back, worked almost as well. My best advice as to trolling speed is to put the lure into the water beside the boat, and observe which action is best with which speed.

Comments on lures in general:

Jim Warner tied flies to look like the old classic balsa wood Flat Fish lure

- **For spring trolling for cold water species** (trout and salmon): streamer flies. Lures such as Mooselooks, Chev Chase, spinners with bait such as a worm or minnow, live smelt on single small hook, Rapala type lures, pimple lures, etc (just about anything on the market which imitates a swimming bait fish.) I even created a fly to imitate the old popular balsa wood Flat Fish lure.
- **Summer fishing** might include all the above but only trolled at different depths. Though **fall fishing** can be "iffy", use the same flies and lures.
- **Different tactics for the warm water species** such as bass and perch.

Some of these lures mentioned above are OK, such as the Rapala type lure, but live bait is usually more effective for daytime fishing. One of the favorites for bass is the hellgrammite, the larval stage of the Dobson Fly. Bass go crazy for helgies if fished properly. Some helgies can be found along the shore of Lake Winni, but crawfish are the natural food for bass, as they can be found most anywhere on the bottom of the Lake. (Although not the norm, I have found crawfish in the innards of salmon.). Minnows are also a good part of the bass diet and many kinds of shiners or minnows can be found along the Lake's shoreline. Where minnows can be fished at all depths, helgys and craws are usually fished on the bottom. Night crawlers are sold in great quantities around the Lake and they have resulted in the catching of many good bass by young and old.

Bass fishing on top water in late spring, daytime into the evening hours is fantastic! Top water gurgling, bubbling noisy plugs are my favorite. Casting into shore is best, but trolling is also good, but, at night, one is not sure of navigation around boats and various buoys.

- **Ice Fishing:** Bait for ice fishing is 90% the live type. Live smelt, if they can be found, are the best. Jigging with pieces of smelt can provide the angler with some nice perch, a laker, or a cusk. Live swimming smelt on the tip up can be deadly for all species. There are some very deep holes, which some fishermen covet over the years to bob out jack smelt. When the bait smelt are not available, then there is the emerald shiner that was introduced into Lake Winni in the 1950's. They are far more hardy and live longer than the fragile smelt. The red fin shiner, a native of Lake Winni, is nearly extinct. However, these are used for tip ups too. There are other types of shiners imported from New Hampshire waters and sold for bait around the Lake. As far as ice-fishing lures go, the pimple type is used most of the time. Ice flies have been tried as well, but not often.

My largest fish taken on Lake Winni:

Landlocked Salmon: May 1957, 7 pound 2 oz. On a small Marabou fly. Off the dock at Wolfeboro in 15 feet of water
Lake Trout: Many, but none enormous enough to list
Rainbow Trout: September 1958, 6 pounds, 5 oz "Wolfeboro Bay Special Fly", off Clark Point out side of Wolfeboro Bay in 5-10 feet of water.
Smallmouth Bass: July 1966, 6 pounds, on a Crazy Crawler at 7 PM Behind Melody Island in Alton on the surface
Yellow Perch: 1949 2+ pounds through the ice off Rattle Snake Island on cut bait
Cusk: 1970 or 1971, 11 pounds, in Winter Harbor on small yellow perch
Pickerel: Almost 5 pounds, off my dock in Winter Harbor on a daredevil in shallow water

I share below two stories about the above and "The one that got away."

- **A true salmon fishing story:** Years ago, in the late 1950s into the early 1960s, the dockside at the Smith River, as it enters Lake Winni at Wolfeboro Bay, was a Mecca of fishermen with bait or flies. The better fishing would depend upon the amount of water being released out of Crescent Lake upstream. To swim into the river mouth, salmon needed a current. As owner and proprietor of the Sportsman Center, I ran an "off the dock" fishing contest in May of 1957. There were many entries of salmon to 4 pounds or better. On any given day, I would take my lunch break and take a turn with my fly rod at the salmon in the river. There was one particular salmon that had caught every angler's eye, and it moved back and forth in the clear current, refusing all morsels that came its way. Damned if I didn't hook and land that fish! He weighed in at 7 pounds 2 ounces, and a picture of him is here in these pages.

The 7 pound salmon Jim Warner caught himself from his store dock ... which did not win the prize!

There was a bit of hard feeling amongst the fishermen that day, but they all calmed down when I "disqualified" myself and went back to work. Just one week later a fisherman from Milton Mills landed a salmon of 8 pounds 14 ounces, which clinched the prize.

• Smallmouth Bass angling

In Lake Winni it has always been fantastic. When running a store, fishing time is limited to early mornings or late evenings. A friend and I used to leave my dock at 8 in the evening with a canoe strapped on the car and down the lake we would go to the Whorttleberry Island area, where there were lots of rocky shoals and spots where the bass would come into the shallows to feed late in the evening. This was a great area. Another excellent area for bass was a pothole behind Melody Island, where bass would come in from the deeper waters to feed. (I guess I am old enough to be willing to violate Hal's statement that we Master Anglers will not share our secret spots!) I was fishing there with a buddy and we were catching a few smaller 2-3 pounders. It was getting really dark and I said that I would make just one more last cast. An explosion engulfed my black Crazy Crawler plug and I was fast to a real monster! Two guys in a canoe is bad enough, but this fish decided to go under the canoe and with it my spinning rod bent in an almost complete circle under the boat. Then the monster jumped. What a magnificent fish! But its next jump was over the front of the canoe that wrapped the line twice around the canoe! How we ever landed that fish had to be a miracle, but it was very well hooked! The next morning it was on display at my store on ice in downtown Wolfeboro…which caused quite a stir among the local anglers. How I wish I had that adventure on video!

• "The fish that got away…"

…Did so with fly and leader. It was a magnificent salmon — perhaps 8-9 pounds. I was trolling between Ship Island and Black Point in the "triangle," an area known for good deep lake trolling. I had a full 200 yards of copper wire line out with a yellow marabou fly attached to my long leader. I was trolling the "8's" and circles as Glen Morrill had taught me, when a fish hit hard. Before I could reel in the slack, I saw the fish break water and leap clear into the air. He came down on my light leader and it broke! I just kept reeling in the slack…but I had the sight and the memory of a truly beautiful fish — the biggest I have ever hooked.

• Passing on my skills:

A framed display of the Warner Smelt in various sizes

This is a sticky question for me. In one sense, I must answer with a qualified "no," except through these pages. But in my career running a successful fishing store, I believe that I had a unique opportunity to share and pass on much of my experience, not only to my customers and friends, but also to the younger generation of anglers. I tried to freely pass on all I had learned. The field I am most noted for in the Lakes Region is that of tying streamer flies. After almost 53 years of tying and creating new patterns, I have also taught fly tying to young people in many of the boy's camps, high schools, and other places.

I believe that I am the original creator of many well known Lake Winni flies including the "Lake Winni Smelt." Perhaps this is how I will be remembered more than I will as a "Master Angler." One of my proudest achievements was teaching a young man in 1995 to tie flies under the auspices of the New Hampshire Council of the Arts. Yes, fly tying is a creative art.

My top 5 tips for each fish:

Salmon:

Jim Warner created this Bicentennial Smelt at the urging of outdoor writer, Roger Conant.

1. Adjust your trolling speed to the action of the lure trolled.
2. Try to increase and decrease your speed to put different action on the fly or lure.
3. Do not troll in a straight line.
4. Fish early or late in the day, and fish the shoreline where the water is roughest from the wind, as baitfish tend to congregate in these spots.
5. Dark flies such as "9-3", the "Magog Smelt" or the Bicentennial Smelt are best in the early morning hours as well as evening.

Lake Trout:

1. Trolling live bait is the best for lakers.
2. A slower speed is necessary for lakers to get the trolled lure or bait below or under the other salmonoid species that are above the lakers.
3. An important rule for lakers, or any big fish, is to use a large net and when landing one, always lead the fish to the net headfirst.
4. Big lakers and salmon can sometimes be found "on top" at first light in the morning. Cast a light line and lure beyond their swirls and sometimes they will strike on instinct.
5. When trolling deep in the summer months, try to bring in your fish as slowly as possible, if it is your intention to release it. Coming up from the deep-water causes a case of the bends for the fish, and it is mostly impossible to revive and save them.

Rainbow Trout:
I never went out fishing just for rainbows. They were introduced into Lake Winni only in later years. On one occasion in 1958, before they were stocked, I caught one off Clark Point. This species was not a native of Lake Winni. I can only think that this one I caught was "there" because of a stocking mistake, or this might have been one of the "Bows" that got away when the Melanesian Pond dam broke years before in Wolfeboro. But any tips I might list for rainbows might follow those I have listed for salmon as they are quite similar in habitat and feeding, except that the rainbows consume more terrestrials (insects) than salmon and they often come nearer to the surface.

Black Bass:
1. Bass are easiest to catch when on their spawning beds in the shallows in the spring. This is also the time to catch and release!
2. The best time for bass in the summer is after dark. This is when most boating ceases and you are virtually alone to fish. Bass come into the shallows looking for a late dinner and are easily fooled by noisy top-water plugs.
3. When fishing with live crawfish or hellgrammites, use a fairly large egg sinker so that when the bass picks up the bait and runs with it, there should be little or no resistance on the line. The bass might feel it and spit out the bait.
4. After a bass has run out a measure of line, then stops running, then takes off again, it is then on the second run that you should set the hook. He has usually swallowed the bait by then and he is yours...if you play him carefully and do not let him break the line. If you keep him for eating it is fine, but if you want to release a gut caught fish, you must clip the line inside his mouth. The hook will later rust out of his gut.
5. Some of the best bass fishing on the Lake can be found in October. Try casting toward the shore where the bass have moved back to cooler water.

Ice Fishing:
1. Stay off the ice until it is safe! I can remember a scary time out on Wolfeboro Bay with the cracking and sinking just under my weight. Of course, I HAD to be there because I had a smelt house there for my store...and was carrying a pail of fresh-netted smelt back to shore.

2. When tip-up fishing on very cold and windy days, scuff some snow into the hole. This will insulate the opening and it will be easy to clean out to check the lines.
3. Never use an ice chisel without a line tied to it.
4. Tie your bob house down with sticks in the frozen ice, or the next warm windy day you might find your house (and you in it!) sailing down the lake.
5. Put big skis on your bob house as runners, so that it can be moved to shore after the heavy March snowstorms.

Catch & Release

At this time of my life I do mostly catch & release. To clarify, there comes a time in your life when you just feel sorry for the other being, whether it be animal, fish or fowl. I shot my last deer 10 years ago. I remember feeling so sorry about it, that I gave up deer hunting that day. After I put my last hunting dog down, I gave up bird hunting. Unless a fish obviously will not live after catching it, I throw it back. This has not always been the case. In younger days, I felt it necessary to feed the family. We enjoyed lots of salmon filets, fried brook trout, deer steaks, duck stew, cusk chowder, etc. Now, I jokingly state that my wife refuses to clean the fish, so I throw them back. But catch & release has always been a good part of my fishing life, too. We never kept everything. I can remember fishing the Winnipesaukee River in 1950 and rarely keeping a nice fly rod caught salmon. There were many fish caught in Lake Winni in my trolling days that were released. I love to fish! Having one to eat was OK too, but not necessary.

Over the years I have fished in many countries, mostly, though, in North and Central America. Except for "camp food" fish were rarely kept. So practice catch & release? Yes!

What happened to the Lake Winni Yellow Perch?

Well, I have a theory. It is my opinion that they have fallen prey to the thousands of Mergansers that flock to Lake Winni in the fall, on their migration south. In the fall of the year, I used to see large schools of newly hatched perch from my dock in Winter Harbor. It was not uncommon to also see schools of red fin shiners, horned pout, and lots of bass fry from my dock. But in the 1980's through the 1990's, every late fall before ice forms, hundreds of these ducks would land in the Harbor and spread out, moving along the shore, diving and feeding for hundreds of yards. This had to contribute to the decline of forage fish like the yellow perch. Smelt, on the other hand, are found in deeper water where the ducks cannot get at them.

What about the Whitefish or "Shad?"

A year or so ago, I asked Pete Lyon, an ex-game warden and fishing friend, about the shad. He said that Lake Winni's shad population was never that good, although early last century the shad were a wonderful fish to catch and eat. But they were never that abundant. He felt that Lake Winni is on the southern most fringe of the shad habitat. In lakes such as Squam and Sebago, White fish or shad can be found in more abundance. Years ago I asked a Fish & Game biologist this same question. His theory was that shad spawn in the late fall or early winter and under the ice. If the Lake has not frozen when this spawning occurs, then the eggs are washed to shore. I tend to agree with Pete's theory…but who knows for sure?

A salmon sniffing dog: By the way, Pete Lyon is the famous game warden who trained a black lab to seek illegal salmon that poaching ice fishermen had hidden in the snow. He trained his dog, "Poacher" to ignore trout, perch, and all fish except salmon. The story is told that on one occasion he stopped in at a bob house on Lake Winni where three men were keeping warm while jigging.

Pete asked, "How you doing, boys?"

"It is slow," one replied.

While talking with them, one of the men looked out the window and said, "Your dog is going wild out there digging in the snow banks!"

Pete replied, "Yes, he likes to dig in the snow."

A minute later the dog was scratching at the door and Pete let him in carrying a nice frozen salmon in his mouth which he dropped at Pete's feet.

One of the anglers stammered, "Where did he find that salmon!"

Pete let him out again and he repeated this strange act …5 more times!

Finally, realizing that the jig was up, one of the men, said, "That's the most amazing thing I have ever seen! We surrender! Whatever we owe in fines, it is has been worth it just watching your amazing dog!"

Would I stock Lake Winni with other species?

NO Way! There can be no good reason to bring a new species to Lake Winni to compete with an already scarce food supply. If more species were introduced, they would have to find forage fish. Can you imagine what coho salmon might do to the smelt population? And brown trout rarely are caught until after dark, and it is unlawful to fish after the sun goes down for the salmonoid species in Lake Winni.

One more fish story

Jim Warner, who once tied 25,000 flies in one year, puts together an order of flies for the customers

The one true happening, which comes to my memory, occurred on a hot day. It was a traditional family gathering at a camp on the Lake in the late 1950s. It was a hot 4th of July. The beer was plentiful and the spirits were high. My brother-in-law suggested that we go fishing. Well, I'm never without some sort of fishing tackle. This day, I had a heavy 9-foot trolling rod, loaded with 10-pound test wire trolling line and a tackle box full of lures. Out we went onto the smooth, windless lake. I had few thoughts about catching anything, but we trolled for an hour with fishless conversation. Finally I suggested that we troll along the shore back to camp. I mentioned to Leo that I would put on a large Rebel Minnow and let out most of my line. And I said, "When I hit bottom and lose the lure, we'll go back to camp." I didn't hit bottom, though it could not have been deeper than 15 feet. Suddenly I had a fish on…and it was a monster! After a brief throbbing struggle, I was able to bring it along side the boat. It was the biggest laker we had ever seen! And it was thoroughly hooked on the rear hook of the Rebel. It kept swimming around the boat with me just holding on…and Leo grabbing the only net - a small 12-inch diameter one. We should have never tried to net it but rather just go to shore and beach it. But we tried…and it just rolled off, with the hook suddenly pulling out. Both of us just watched open jawed, as it swam slowly away. Later that week I asked a fish biologist how much it must have weighed, telling him the dimensions, as its back was fully 8 inches across and he told me that this was probably one of those 20+ pounders. What a day! What a memory of my biggest "… fish that got away!"

My Favorite recipes

Master Angler and fly tier, Jim Warner, works on tying his famous streamer creation, the "Lake Winni Smelt."

Well, we have cooked and eaten about every game species in Lake Winni. And the tiny smelt is, in my opinion, the most delicious. There have been many good "messes" of fried smelt, with heads intact and without, at our table over the years. The best way to prepare them is to pop them into a hot, greased frying pan, and when golden brown, enjoy!

Yellow perch, although larger, I cook and fry the same way.

Cusk is best for a chowder, but cusk fillets are also truly delicious!

Pickerel are very bony, but also make a great chowder.

Hornpout, once skinned, are a very tasty fried fish.

I prefer Lake Trout to be baked in milk.

Salmon, I fillet and grill over an outdoor fire with lemon and butter.

Bass, according to size, can be baked or fillets can be grilled or fried.

What about the Mercury warnings and scares?

Though I do not know much about this, I am sure that it has been a problem for a very long time...we just did not monitor it or know about it.

MASTER ANGLER AL STEWART
(33 years of Lake Winni Angling)

People often ask me why I enjoy fishing, and I cannot explain it to them because there is no reason in the way they want meanings described. They are asking a man why he enjoys breathing when he really has no choice but to wonder at its truth." — A.J. McClane —

Al Stewart telling fish stories . . .

I first learned about Al Stewart from a man who fishes out of Center Harbor. He claimed that this hardy man and his wife, who live in a cozy little solar heated cottage built on the rocks of Little Two-Mile Island only a few hundred yards from one of the Lake's hottest salmon and laker holes. I heard the story, later confirmed by Al, that one spring Al and a party of angling friends came to fish and stay at his cottage. They carried little to eat, being over confident that they would catch their supper. The story goes that they did, indeed, catch a mess of nice salmon. Al, who has no waste disposal on his small island, decided to efficiently clean the fish aboard his small boat; he skillfully did this, placing the guts and skins in a yellow plastic bucket, and the nice fresh filets in a tin one. Al kept trolling, while he performed his fish cleaning chores, until he had a nice strike and boarded and released a good 22" salmon. Being very excited by the thrilling battle the fish put up, Al was eager to head in with dinner. He quickly dumped over board the contents of the tin bucket and headed in with the yellow bucket of fish heads and guts! Since that time, his friends joke that if one wants to catch already filleted fish, troll just off Little Two-Mile Island!

In 2003, when I visited Al on 2 Mile Island, I was sad to see that he was connected to an oxygen pump. But I soon learned that he had 4 small 2-hour portable pumps that he could take out in the boat while fishing. He told me that one had failed to work while fishing and he had to rush back in and connect to his bigger machine on the island...where, he has only solar power except for a portable generator. That's angling dedication! Sadly Alan wrote to me in early 2004:

"We will probably not be going back to Little 2-Mile Island this coming summer because of oxygen logistics and other infirmities which keep us close to home.... Too bad and so sad after more than a 56 year association with Sandy Island Camp, Little 2-Mile Island, and beautiful Lake Winni...."

Left: Al Stewart telling another fish story, with the author laughing.
Right: Al Stewart's Little Two-Mile Island -- near good Laker waters

I've been fishing in lake Winni 33 years in 2004. I had a late start, beginning at age 45. Lewis Derby, my young protégé who was a salmon fisherman, taught me to fish here. But my earlier mentor was Chuckie Gordon from Dalton, Massachusetts, who taught me how to fish for brown trout both trolling and still fishing. I learned from him how to thread a live smelt or shiner on a line with it still alive. He also taught me how to play a big fish so it would not break my line.

My favorite Winni game fish is the landlocked salmon. It is the best eating and fighting fish in the lake — lots of action and a very smart fish.

Al Stewart, "Destined for greatness, but pacing himself...."

I prefer leadcore more than the higher tech downriggers as I am forever getting hung up!

My favorite fishing months are April and September, early in the morning. Fishing is dead after 11 AM.

I troll at 2 MPH.

Chart of fishing depths and best lures

	Salmon (depth & lure)	**Lakers** (depth & lure)	**Rainbows** (depth & lure)
May:	6-8' Maynard Marvel fly	same	same
June:	10-25' Maynard Marvel	same	10' Maynard Marvel
July:	same	same	same
August::	same	same	same
Sept.:	25-30' Maynard Marvel	Maynard Marvel	same

Top: Close up of the Maynard Marvel, Master Angler Angler Al Stewart's favorite lure...and that of many other anglers.
Middle: Al Stewart's grandson with nice catch of salmon
Bottom: Al Stewart with nice salmon

Largest salmon, laker, rainbow and bass you have caught in Lake Winni

Salmon: 5 pounds in 1986 on a Maynard Marvel at 15' deep

Laker: 10.5 pounds in 1994 on a live shiner at 30'

Rainbow: 3.5 pounds in 1999 on a Maynard Marvel depth at 10'

My story about the monster trout

I used my old sewed on shiner technique for this fish. I had to play the 10.5 pound monster trout for 45 minutes before he tired out and came to the net. I had only 6 lb test line on my 30' leader which made it a delicate and interesting fight!

I have passed on my skills to my son and grandson by taking them fishing very often at an early age. My son is an excellent fisherman now.

My top 5 tips for salmon

1. Use very light leaders (6-pound test) and 30 feet long.
2. Don't use snaps or swivels beyond the end of the leadcore line as the fish can spot them.
3. Keep trolling speed as close as possible to 2 MPH.
4. If you have a decent fish on, reel in all other lines and keep them inside the boat. Then slowly play and land your fish.
5. Patience - play your fish until he is tired and then net him.

9 pound 14 oz, 30" Laker taken by Al Stewart on one of his hand sewn smelt trolled deep and slow.

I try not to catch lakers and if I do I release them, with the exception of my one trophy laker which was caught on a live shiner and very small treble hook.

Rainbow trout are, for me, just a matter of pure luck. I do not purposefully fish for them, but every now and then a bonus rainbow hits my line.

Catch & release

I practice it some of the time. Smaller marginal fish and all lakers are released. And some get eaten. When you live on a small island with no electricity, fresh fish are a delicacy not to be wasted!

If I were the Commissioner of Fish & Game, I would not mess with nature, by stocking other species of fish, but let well enough alone. The salmon catch has been steadily improving in size and quantity so the Fish & Game people must be doing a good job of keeping the right balance between salmon and smelt. I would not favor the introduction of any new species.

A fishing story

Al Stewart and his friends with an early morning mixed catch

3 of us were fishing. We had 6 rods all with Davis spinners and live bait - quite a few rods with lots of complex tackle! Bingo! We got 6 hits all at the same time! We must have trolled though a school of fish. We each caught them, somehow without getting hung up in one anothers' lines! By the time the chaos was over, we had 6 fish flopping around in the bottom of the boat — all with treble hooks in their mouths. What a joyful mess!

• Why do I fish?

Al Stewart's cozy solar powered cottage on Little Two-Mile Island, waving goodbye

During the Great Depression, money and food were very hard to come by. At the age of 8, I began fishing and digging clams to put food on the table for my mother and 3 sisters. We ate just about anything I could catch or dig. This became ingrained within me. Thirty years later, I bought a new 14' runabout. In order to partly justify spending the large amount for the boat, I started fresh water fishing for perch, trout, and horned pout. We also used the boat for our recreation and camping trips to Lake George and Winnipesaukee. We bought Little Two-Mile Island on Lake Winni in June 1969. The following year I was hired as the camp carpenter at Sandy Island and my wife was hired to run the craft shop. We worked at Sandy Island for 35 years and our 4 children also worked there for several years. We commuted daily by boat from Little Two-Mile Island to Sandy, about 7.5 miles each way. What a great life!

My young friend, Lew Derby, taught me how to fish for salmon and trout in Lake Winni. We troll at 1 3/4 to 2 MPH or 600 RPMs. Most of the time we use leadcore with a 30' 6 lb test leader and a Maynard's Marvel streamer fly. We have had great success over the years with this fly. I would like to use live bait, as I believe it is better than the imitations, but it is too much of a hassle to go ashore, get in the car, and drive to town to get it.

Over the past 30 years, Lew and I have shared many more triumphs than disappointments. My son, Robert, who lives in Gilford, New Hampshire, is also an excellent angler, and we have shared many happy fishing trips together. Bob, Lew, and I have fished in snow, sleet, rain and ice as well as many days of rough water as well as calm sunshine. Bob and Lew use downriggers, but I do not. Every time I have tried these high tech downriggers, I have gotten into a mess - so "Humbug" I say to downriggers!

I have always lived in a house full of women with the exception of the years when my son was growing up, but then he and I lived in a house full of women! I still live in a house full of women, so fishing is a good way to get "out with the boys" once in awhile for some male bonding.

My Best day of fishing

Was on July 30, 1994. I started at 5 AM trolling with two rods, each with a Penn Reel with 100 yards of 40-pound test leadcore line and 25 yards of monofilament backing. My leader was 30' of 6-pound test monofilament. I had strung on a live shiner in my secret method, which I guess I will share reluctantly in this book. I use a very tiny treble hook hooked through the shiner's back so he can swim freely.

When my big fish struck that morning, at first I thought I was hung on bottom. I took the motor out of gear, then looked at the depth finder. It read 70 feet! Quickly I put the motor back into gear and began reeling in the other rod, which had no fish. Meanwhile the rod with the fish was clicking off line - the sweetest sound in the world! After bringing in the empty rod, I shut off the motor and concentrated on landing the big fish. I knew that he must be very big by the way he ripped line from my reel. I set the drag for what I guessed to be about 3-4 pounds of pull and proceeded to work the fish. After awhile, he would come part way in and then rip off another 10 yards of line … and so it went for about 30 minutes or so. My arm was tired. He finally began to tire as well to the point when I could gradually reel him in. As he approached the boat, I couldn't believe his size! My net was old and I was certain that he would break it. But at the end of our 40 minute fight, he was so pooped out that he could not even flip or flop! Once I got him in the boat, I weighed him. 10.5 pounds and 31" long! What a thrill to catch this biggest fish of my angling career!

Since I was alone and had no one to brag to, I couldn't resist going over to the only other boat I could see in the area and showing off my prize. I then went home to Little Two-Mile Island and had my wife take a bunch of pictures of me with my fish. I cleaned and filleted him, and into the freezer he went to feed some hungry mouths! On the ocean I have caught several striped bass that were much bigger than this fish. But that was done with steel wire and lots of muscle, which required no finesse whatsoever. But getting a 10 1/2-pound laker on a 6-pound test line is a proud accomplishment!

Al Stewart with his big 10.5 pound Laker caught with a slow trolled smelt

Here's how I rig up a shiner, minnow, or smelt for trolling: I make a 4" long threader out of piano wire with a very tiny hook on one end and a handle loop on the other. I insert the piano wire into the fish's mouth and push it through his digestive tract and out his vent.

I hook a 2-foot leader onto the piano wire hook by a loop in one end, and pull it back through and out his mouth. I then attach a very small treble hook to the end of the line coming from the shiner's vent and insert one hook of the treble hook through the fish's back just behind his dorsal fin. Where the leader loop comes out the fish's mouth, I attach it to my 30' 6-pound leader on my line. Rigged this way, the shiner swims normally when I troll him behind my boat at 1 3/4 to 2 MPH.

Favorite recipes for cooking Lake Winni fish

My wife cooks both salmon and lakers the same way. We put a whole fish filet in foil, sprinkle it with lemon and/or white wine, salt, and pieces of butter, (bigger for bigger fish) (1 quarter pound of butter to 2 pounds of fish). Close foil and cook over grill for 10-15 minutes until done.

Am I concerned about mercury levels in Lake Winni fish to the degree that I restrict my fish intake? No.

MASTER ANGLER MARIO DECAROLIS
("Angler") (51 years of Lake Winni angling)

"Most anglers spend their lives in making rules for trout,
and trout spend theirs in breaking them."
— George Aston —

Mario smiling in George's Restaurant after stealing a blind man's sausage (Donald Duck's)

For many years, I heard a man with the call sign "Angler" on the CB radio. He seemed to always be catching salmon when I wasn't! One day in 1990, I was trolling in front of my cottage on the east side of Bear Island for salmon. I was with a Russian scientist friend, Andrei Naumov, a solid state physicist who loved to fish, whom I had sponsored and brought to Dartmouth College. The Angler called for "Aardvark," and when I answered the CB radio, he asked me if my boat was blue and white. When I responded affirmatively, he said that he was following me. I saw a funny old aluminum boat with a big American flag on the bow several hundred yards behind me and waved to him. Impulsively, I suggested that he join us for lunch. I told him to follow me to my East Bear Island dock, which he did. We three enjoyed a great lunch of Lasagna, washed down with ample glasses of red wine and stimulating fellowship. We toasted the sport of angling in Russian, Italian, and English that day, and have been best fishing buddies ever since.

Mario is one of the most generous and humorous anglers I have ever met, ready to teach or give tips to good people any time. I feel compelled to tell a story or two about him. I once took him turkey hunting. I told him to go out that evening before the opening of the spring gobbler season, since I was busy, and listen for gobblers going to roost to help us get to them the next morning. He took his nearly blind 88 year old friend, Ed Meyerhoffer, with him. He told Ed to wait by the car and hiked out into the woods to listen for turkeys, but Mario fell asleep somewhere in the forest. While snoring, he expelled his teeth without realizing it. When he awoke, it was dark and he hurried back to the truck where poor Ed had been waiting, holding on to the truck for hours dutifully listening for turkeys as Mario had instructed, since he couldn't see them.

I arrived just before Mario returned and found Ed anxiously concerned, as Mario had been gone for such a long time. When Mario got back to the truck, he realized he had lost his teeth and was panicked. "Battle Axe" (his wife, Ann's radio call sign), "...will have my hide! That's $2000 worth of teeth," he said.

The next day, while joking about finding a turkey with a set of teeth in its mouth, a small miracle occurred. Mario, not knowing exactly where he had fallen asleep the night before, disappeared into the woods to take a leak. Miraculously, he emerged 10 minutes later with a big toothy smile. He had, against all probability, found them on the ground!

I cannot resist another Angler story. During the fall Salmon Derby a few years ago, Mario and I were fishing together. Now, Mario does not like to net fish, as he hates to get the hooks tangled in the net. I caught a nice 4 3/4-pound laker which Mario refused to net.

Ed Meyerhoffer, Mario's good fishing buddy who is blind but still helps Mario drag his bob house out onto the ice in winter. He has some great stories about pushing the bob house out on the ice while Mario is pulling it, and shouting, "Push harder, Eddie! We've gotta stay ahead of the cracking ice!"

Since then, I always bring my own net along when I fish with him just in case I catch a trophy fish. I lifted the laker by the jaw into the boat and we weighed it: 4 3/4 pounds. Mario, who doesn't care for lakers, said, much to my protest, "Release it! It isn't big enough to win the derby." I argued for putting it onto a stringer, but Mario insisted on releasing it, and I was a guest on his boat. An hour later, I caught its twin; but back in the water it went... against my better judgment again. That afternoon, Mario had to leave 3 hours before the derby was over for some appointment. As he drove past Silver Sands Marina, he decided to stop and see what fish were hanging as potential winners of the boat and motor prize. The biggest laker on the boards was 4 1/2 pounds! I also stopped in, an hour later. When I saw that my laker that Mario had released would have won the boat and motor, it is an understatement to say that I was one very frustrated angler! There was one hour left before the Derby was over and I raced back to my boat and started trolling furiously in an attempt to catch another winner, to no avail. We now joke about my laker, which would have won the Derby if Mario *had not released it. And he knows that he owes me! In spite of this, Mario is, in my opinion, the best salmon angler on Lake Winni. And he always has good Italian food and drink aboard for those who are fortunate enough to spend a day angling with him. He has been angling in Lake Winni for 52 years since he was 18 years old. He is also an excellent ice fisherman, fly fisherman, and good all around sport! Here he is in his bob house which he and his friend, Ed, drag onto the ice as soon as it is at least 4" thick.*

Mario in his ice bob house with his grandson's 1st grade teacher in photo, who also happens to be a Patriots Cheer Leader

Master Angler Mario DeCarolis

I've been fishing Lake Winni for 52 years. I started fishing when I was 18 years old. I did not have an instructor. I just had to try it because of the many fishing tales. I used our proven methods from Massachusetts on rivers and ponds. where we were spin and fly fishermen.

There are quite a few people who were mentors for me. At age 12 my oldest brother Rocky — we were 2 of 8 boys and 2 girls (10 in our Italian family!) I was the 4th son. We had 7 boys first before the 1st girl was born. Rocky was 6 years older and taught me hunting & fishing. The first shot I fired was with a 16 gauge double barrel at a black bird on the ground; needless to say, nothing went to waste. What was left of the black bird, ended up in the tomato sauce. With 10 kids the more protein the better! Rocky had a tremendous influence on me in work, hunting and fishing.

The next mentor was Rocky's best friend, Frank Trotto, whom he met in the navy during WWII. He was from Medford, Massachusetts. They maintained their friendship all of their lives and both were hunters and fishermen. He was a graduate of NE University as a civil engineer. Frank made his own homemade brass wobblers and handed them out readily. If there were 5 fishermen fishing and 20 fish were caught, Frank would catch 50% of them on his homemade lure, even though all of us were using the same lure! This happened repeatedly on Walled Pond in Massachusetts. Frank is now in St. Petersburg Florida and he wades in Tampa Bay still spinning fishing for anything he can catch at age 76. Sometimes he wades all night into early morning. His favorite answer to the question of why he catches so many more than others is, "It's all in the presentation, boys." He wades far off shore in Tampa Bay at night and has many a shark circle him in the shallow water. I am surprised one hasn't got him yet!

Left: Mario fishing in his boat
Right: Keep it secret!

A good friend and neighbor who was 20 years my senior also had an influence on my hunting and fishing. Ray was a trapper and he traveled all over Maine with my brothers and me. Ray got his deer every year. On occasions we would stay in Canaan, New Hampshire, on Canaan Lake at Roberts Camp for 2-4 day hunts. On one Saturday morning, Ray was hit with 4 out of 5 bullets fired from a 30-06 rifle shot by an irresponsible hunter from Connecticut. The first shot grazed his stomach, the next 2 grazed his thigh, and the 4th was the worst of all, hitting Ray in the kneecap, rolling around his kneecap and exiting where it had entered! The shooter was "shooting at sounds," and, believe it or not, he was a NRA Safety instructor! He later had a nervous breakdown. Thank God he was a lousy shot.

After these three mentors, I took over on my own to learn my way with my brothers, Joe (who I believe is a better all-round fisherman, who ties his own flies which we all use) and Phil. I taught them some things on Lake Winni. For the next 25 years I was on my own. Then I met my neighbor, Paul Philippe. For nearly 2 years, we never spoke, other than a wave in passing boats. Then one morning Paul traded his 20-foot bass boat for a 23-foot open console Well Craft boat. Paul (known to many of us as "Bean Counter" on the CB, as he was an accountant) asked me if I would join him on his shakedown fishing cruise. I parked my old 1968 I/O at his dock across Fish Cove from me, and we started fishing at the Post Office at the north end of Bear Island heading south on the east side toward Ozone Island. We each had a leadcore and a fly line out. About a half-hour later, Paul's leadcore line reel started screaming. He told me to take his rod. I looked at him as if to say, "You gotta be kidding?" I replied, "Paul, this is your first fish on your new boat! You catch it yourself!" He hollered for me to "Take it!" I replied, "Paul, he can run all your line out and I WILL NOT take it!" Remember that this was the first half-hour of our first meeting and here we were having our first argument already! He finally grabbed his rod just before the line ran out and fought and released a nice 3 pound salmon.

About 10 years ago Paul caught a 16.5-pound lake trout. I believe that this was the record laker at that time, though bigger ones were caught before. He kept this monster and had it mounted by a taxidermist from Tilton. It is the finest mounting I have ever seen. The same taxidermist mounted a 7.9-pound salmon I caught in Lake Winni a few years later and did a perfect job at a reasonable price. When Paul passed away in October 2002 of cancer, we held a fitting memorial ceremony to him at the same spot off Timber where he caught his big laker.

Paul and I fished many days together. Though we argued often, we always parted in laughter. I believe we helped each other learn many of the finer points of trolling and ice fishing. Paul's garage was a show place, loaded with rods & reels of all sizes, varieties, and prices. He had hundreds of small drawers filled with antique lures, flies, jigs and curiosity pieces. The door was always open, and he told his friends to help themselves anytime.

His final Lake Winni boat was a 28 foot Wellcraft Coastal with twin V8 inboards and a 25 HP Evinrude trolling kicker. He had mounted 4 Cannon electric downriggers with two 4 foot and two 6 foot booms. In the summer months if 3 were in the boat fishing, they could use 6 lines out, with 4 down riggers, and 2 leadcore lines. If a leadcore line hung up on bottom, Paul would not change course or speed. You either got the line off or broke it. I would always go back and try to release it in my boat, being the frugal Italian I am ...and then usually end up hanging up another line, or getting lines caught in the prop. I learned from Paul to change my ways. To this day, I do not turn and go back to try to save the line, unless it is the only one out. For some reason, Paul's 6 lines rarely tangled with one another. I know that Hal had planned for Paul to be one of the Master Anglers in this book, but he left us for happier fishing grounds before that could happen except in memorium. Paul, we anglers salute you! You were, indeed, a Master Angler!

What's my favorite Lake Winni game fish and how do you fish for them?

Open water trolling for salmon. Pound for pound the landlocked salmon is the best fighter. I love its aerial acrobatics!

My favorite fishing is with a fly rod with sinking fly line for spring angling. After June, I prefer first, leadcore, then downriggers. I use a spinning rod on my downriggers. They are more comfortable to catch salmon with than lead core. There is no greater fly-fishing than in spring and this is absolutely my favorite, to have a salmon strike my fly line while working the rod in my hand is a great thrill. My favorite time is from April to the end of May. August is the next best month. September is not usually good.

The best times are early morning from 9 AM to 12 noon, (I am not a happy early riser in spite of Hal trying to get me up for early angling!) Also it is good the last 2 hours before dark. I troll at 1-1.5 MPH, slower than some salmon fishermen.

Chart of fishing depths and best lures

	Salmon	**Lakers**	**Rainbows**
May:	3' deep on Streamer flies	15' deep - Streamer flies	3' deep - Streamer flies

June: 15-25' deep on flies, Suttons and Top Guns (when water is above 65°, 20-40' deep)

July: Same as June

August: My best month for size and #s of salmon caught. 25-40' down on Suttons. I rarely ever fish below 40.' Lakers are not my favorite. I never take one home!

September: I will bring out my fly-rods mid September just to end the season. I rarely catch salmon in September, though the largest salmon I ever caught in Lake Winni was September 10.

Largest salmon, laker, rainbow and bass
I have caught in Lake Winni

Salmon: 7.96 pounds on September 10 using a gold & silver Sutton at 20'. I have it mounted.

Laker: 7.5 pounds while ice fishing, jigging with a Swedish Pimple at 45'

Rainbow: 5 pounds on a live smelt through the ice at 10'

Other large fish: White perch with night crawler on a jig: 2-3 pounds, through ice with 3-4' light rod. Lots of fun and an excellent eating fish!

Stories about these monsters

Paul Philippe and I were fishing around Buoy 80 trolling one fly and one leadcore each with 5 colors out on September 10. I said to Paul, "It looks like I am hung up." Paul said, "NO way! That's a fish!" But my rod was not moving. I said, "The only thing I have is New Hampshire real-estate." Then all hell broke loose. The salmon came out of the Lake about 3 feet in a jump. Then the fun began on my 6-pound test line, which made me treat him tenderly. He was out of the water as much as he was in. This was my largest — a nearly 8 pound salmon.

Mario's 7.96-pound salmon

I have passed on my skills to just about everyone I know. If you ever want to keep anything a secret, do not tell Mario, as everyone knows. What fun is it to have something nice, if you don't share it? That's my philosophy. If you ever get into my boat, you will see and experience all my secrets! I have also passed this on to my children and grandchildren as well as good friends. Just ask, Hal (Aardvark) if you don't believe me!

My top five tips for salmon, lakers, and rainbows

1. Troll at the right speed: 1-1.5 MPH with either a fly or lure.
2. If fishing a lure, make sure it is not spinning, but wobbling. To adjust this, change your speed with your lure in water watching it to see if it has proper action.
3. Troll slower with a smaller fly.
4. Salmon and rainbows like a little red on the lure.
5. Use brass colors after June. (I am never without at least one brass and silver Sutton on one rod. "Top Guns" have also recently proven very effective.

My top five ice fishing tips

1. Make sure you have plenty of libations.
2. Make sure you have plenty of propane for your heater.
3. Make sure you leave your bob house unlocked in case someone wants to use it.
4. Make sure you have thick enough ice to fish (minimum of 4") when bringing out your bob house.
5. Make sure you have extra food in case unexpected hungry company shows up.

- **Catch and Release:** I practice catch and release most of the time, unless "Battle Axe", (my wife's CB Handle) and I want fish for dinner. If I keep one, it will always be a freshly caught salmon under 18" I keep no fish in freezer except for someone very special who might be visiting soon.

- **What do I think happened to the Lake Winni yellow perch?** They used to be a nuisance when trolling. I am glad to see them gone away, though I do not know why.
- **What do I think has happened to the Lake Winni whitefish ("shad")?**

I have never caught one on Lake Winni. For many years I saw the term "white fish" and never realized it was what I call shad. About 7 years ago, I was fishing with my good buddy and neighbor, Ed Meyerhoffer. I have been fishing our Fish Cove with him longer than with anyone else. He bought his lot in the 1940s for $750, set up a tent in March, and would go down Old Hubbard Rd. on the path to fish Fish Cove with a sled and toboggan. No roads were maintained and the paths were rough. Ed & his late wife, Ruth, spent their honeymoon in that tent just after WWII when Ed got out of the Army after serving in Europe and then the Pacific. Ed & I spent a lot of fishing time together. When we were fishing out of Browns 7 years ago, I asked Ed what year he had stopped catching shad. He said it had to be over 20 years ago. While we trolled along talking about shad, Ed had a strike from a good fish. He played it for 10 minutes and brought it to the net. Once in the boat, it looked initially like a salmon, but Ed went nuts! It was a 5-pound shad, the biggest of his lifetime! In the 1950s and 1960s when Ed & his brother wanted to catch shad, they always fished in their favorite shad hole off Brown's marina. And we were together when he caught his largest in 20 years in the same spot ... and this was his last.

If I were NH Commissioner of Fish & Game, what initiatives would I take to improve Lake Winnie angling?

None. I am not a marine biologist. I do not like to see salmon caught through the ice. And I believe 40-50% of the salmon caught die after being caught because of internal injuries. But neither would I do away with ice fishing as I love it. I am also against introducing other species. There are enough species to satisfy all types of anglers now. Do not fool with Mother Nature!

Angling in the Smile of the Great Spirit

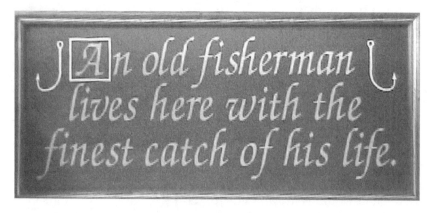

Sign about Mario's wife, Ann, the finest catch of his life!

My favorite recipes

My wife, Anne, squeezes lemon over salmon filets, lets them sit for 10 minutes, and then puts on Italian seasoned bread crumbs and salt & pepper. She drizzles on melted butter, sprinkles with thyme, and bakes in an oven at 350° F for 25-30 minutes. This is my favorite! And my wife, Anne is the, "Best catch of my life," as this sign in my home proudly proclaims. My personal fish recipe is simpler. I wrap it in aluminum foil and put on a grill for 20 minutes.

Am I concerned about mercury levels in Lake Winni fish to the degree that I restrict my fish intake?

Yes, my wife and I (children and grandchildren as well) have only 2 meals/month average. I prefer salmon over rainbow and white perch. I do not eat lakers, like the author of this book!

Mario and his trusty dog, Tag, speeding away in his angler boat

MASTER ANGLER TED ST. ONGE:
58 Years angling in Lake Winni

Left: Ted St. Onge with a big salmon.
Right: Ted St. Onge trolling with Osippee Mountains in the background. You can see the Dave Davis spinners attached to the downrigger ball on this side of the boat. He uses them as an attractor and has his release device 18" above them on the cable with his sewn shiner spinning slowly just behind the Davis spinners and he always catches salmon and trout with this rig.

I first encountered Ted while trolling in August with Mario DeCarolis just north of Diamond Island in 2002. He was in a small "low tech" open boat with a small hand crank downrigger attached to the rear. At first we thought he was still-fishing or stranded, as he appeared to be sitting still, but we could see that his small kicker was firing and that he was moving very slowly with his lines almost straight down. In contrast to Mario and I, he kept netting large fish. We were curious and approached him, asking what he was using and how deep. He said he was fishing at 44 degrees. "Don't you have a thermometer?" he teased.

Ted trolling very slowly for salmon or lakers.

Ted always fishes for salmon at 44 degrees and takes the temperature frequently. And Ted catches fish! I videoed him for a few minutes, watching his unconventional technique and success and thought to myself, "This man is a Master Angler," but I lost contact.

Three years later, I was watching a Wildlife Journal show on New Hampshire Public TV called, "Salmon Legacy - Part I" when I saw Ted trolling on the TV demonstrating his techniques. I jumped for a pen when his name was flashed and scribbled it down. Some months later, while speaking with Fish & Game biologist Don Miller, I mentioned the TV show and asked if he knew the angler in the show, "St. Onge." He confirmed that he was a friend of Ted's and that Ted was, indeed, a Master Angler. I got his phone number and, at last was able to connect with this unique angler. More so than all the other Master Anglers, Ted relies on temperature readings to direct his trolling depth. He fishes MUCH slower than any of the other Master Anglers at a 1/2-MPH crawl. Ted is almost jigging while moving slightly to cover more water. He sometimes uses his own home-crafted lures but mostly he uses a fairly large shiner sown onto his hook so as to give the bait a spin. I know no other Master Angler who can make this statement, but Ted St. Onge makes the claim that he has never fished on Lake Winni for salmon or trout without catching at least one! That's an amazing record for one who has been fishing the lake for 58 years! And if he were any other angler I know, I wouldn't believe him. But I do.

My Dad and Mom liked to fish for warm water fish such as horned pout and eel. They never had to go very far to get them. My brothers and I were started on fishing on the banks of the Merrimack River and the nearby ponds around Manchester. Every Friday night after work our parents would take us fishing. I was 7 years old and that was how it all started. As I got to be 13 or 14 years old, my Uncle Oscar Nault would bring in a large lake trout that he had caught on Lake Winnisquam. I used to marvel at these big wild looking fish. I knew that I had to catch some of these fish. I passed on the things that I have learned to my friends and family. My son loves fishing as much as I do and I know that some day I'll still see the beauty of Lake Winnipesaukee and those beautiful salmon through his eyes and I told him so.

I've been fishing Lake Winni for 58 years, beginning at age 18. My friend, Larry Roy, a well-known sport fisherman in New Hampshire, taught me to fish here.

But my dad, Bill St.Onge and my Uncle Oscar Nault were my mentors. They taught me as a boy to read all I could about the professional anglers in the outdoor magazines and to be persistent in the methods that they used.

What's my favorite Lake Winni game fish?

The landlocked salmon, because of the spectacular jumps and endurance they demonstrate when I use light tackle.

Fly rod, downriggers, or lead core?

After ice out I like to see the fly rods snap back when the fish are on top. I prefer lead core beginning in June; but downriggers are better when the lake forms a thermocline.

My favorite fishing months

June, July, August, and September. And unlike some of the others, I find 10:00 AM to 12:30 PM, to be the most productive angling times when the fish are down and not so light sensitive. Just after ice out when the fish stay up high near the top, dawn and dusk are best.

My best trolling speed

I'm a loner on this one, but I have most success trolling at 1/2 mile per hour, which will lower the average speed of the 15 Master Anglers in the "Chart of Secrets" found in Chapter 14, but in my opinion, slower is better.

By using a thermometer, I know exactly where the fish are holding and at 1/2 mile per hour, I can troll at that depth. One color of 18-pound-test lead core will take my lure down 10 ft. 3 colors - 30 ft. down, 4 1/2 colors - 45 ft. down. I prefer to use downriggers when the salmon are down at least 15 ft. and more. I use sewed on bait, Mooselook Warblers, Suttons, Hinkleys, Needlefish, and streamer flies.

Chart of fishing depths and best lures

May: On top to 10 ft. down for all
June: 20 ft. - 25 ft. down for all
I fish strictly using thermometers and that determines my depth
July: 25 ft. - 35 ft. down.
difficult to say just how deep a fish will be.
Usually salmon are in 54 to 56 degree water.
August: 35 ft. - 45 ft. down   Lake trout are in 48 to 52 degree water.
Rainbows are 58 to 60 degree water.
September: 35 ft. - 45 ft. down for all

My Largest salmon, laker, rainbow in Lake Winni

Salmon: 10 pounds in July 2003. Lure: sewed on bait. Depth: 38 feet. But my largest was 11 pounds, 4 oz. 32" long in 1975 which I caught in Squam Lake

Laker: 14 pounds in August 1999. Lure: sewed on bait. Depth: 100 feet. (Diamond Island)

Rainbow: 3 1/2 pounds in May 2003. Lure: sewed on bait. Depth: 3 feet. (Bear Island)

My stories about the monsters I have caught

A photo of Ted St. Onge with a 31" 10 pound salmon in front of his boat

One day when I was fishing the broads on Lake Winnipesaukee. It was a very hot day in August. It was the kind of day that gets so hot that you keep soaking your hat in the lake to cool down. I lowered my thermometer into the lake. At the depth of 90ft the temperature was 54 degrees - the temperature I always seek. I then let down ten colors of lead core line. I was using florescent orange Mooselook Warblers. The day was going pretty slow on the lake and I was having no luck. Two fishermen came close to my boat and asked what I was fishing for. I told them "Salmon". They were trying to be helpful and said that I was trolling too slowly and that I would be capable of catching lake trout only. But I had tried this time proven method for a long time and knew that it worked. I was thinking about changing the lure colors when all of a sudden my outboard motor stalled. I couldn't get it started. I was afraid that I would hook bottom with the ten colors of line that I had out. I turned up the throttle and pulled the starting cord. It caught and gave me quite a thrust forward. I thought, "Too late, I'm hooked on the bottom!" I then noticed the rod bucking back and forth almost touching the water! The bottom turned out to be a 31" 10-pound salmon. After a 30-minute battle, I finally got the fish in the net. You should have seen the look on the faces of the two fishermen when they saw this fish. This day that started out slow, once again become a great day of fishing for me.

One morning I decided I would fish Lake Winnipesaukee from Brown's Boat Basin. It was a beautiful day with a blue sky and a light wind. This is what we call "a 4 inch salmon chop". I launched my boat then headed out past the U.S. Post Office on Bear Island, near the ledges on the side of 3 Mile Island. I had no sooner put out one rod when the action began. I caught quite a few salmon in the next two hours. These salmon weighed up to 3 pounds and most were about 19" to 21" in length. At 11 o'clock I had a wicked hit on my rod. The way the reel sceamed I knew that I had a good one. After about twenty minutes of this fish putting up quite a fight, I reeled it in. I had landed the 7 pound salmon in the photo that you see on the left.

Ted's wife, Pauline St. Onge holding two salmon

My wife and I went fishing by Little Bear Island one day. It was the first week of June and the salmon were starting to go down from the surface where they are just after ice-out. We took a water temperature reading with a thermometer I attach to my hand crank down rigger. We had a reading of 54 degrees at a depth of 20 feet. We started to fish at that depth and began to take salmon almost immediately. All the salmon were to 2lbs to 3lbs. We released all the fish. It was a beautiful day with a blue sky and white puffy clouds. We were enjoying the beauty of the lake and it's surroundings. Then suddenly Pauline's rod whipped back and forth. This time the rod bent to the breaking point. The reel was screaming! After a 20-minute fight she landed a huge salmon. We had not even finished re-baiting that rod when her other rod, on the other side of the boat, got a huge hit with the reel screaming. After another fight she landed another huge salmon. Needless to say, Pauline did not throw these two back.

Passing on my angling skills to others

I have shared my experience and skills with my wife, my son and a lot of close friends.

My top five tips for Salmon

1. Just after ice out, fish early in the morning and late before dark. Salmon are light sensitive and as the sun rises, they tend to go down.
2. Use sewed on smelt or minnows and troll 1/2 mile per hour. Find the depth the salmon are. This method never fails.
3. Always use thermometers to find the thermocline. Just a few degrees off can make a difference between a slow or fast day of fishing.
4. Fish close to the boat. 6 1/2 ft. from the ball of the downrigger and tie an attractor to the ball of the downrigger.
5. Use a Dave Davis spinner, 48 inches long on the ball of the rigger an attractor and run your bait 2 feet back of the spinner and 18 inches above the last blade on the spinner so it will not catch on the spinners.

My top five tips for lakers

1. Use larger baits than you would for Salmon
2. Use a thermometer to find 48 - 52 degrees
3. Run the bait close to the bottom near the shore line or near a reef
4. Suckers about 6 - 8 inches long work fine. Try to bump the bottom occasionally.
5. Troll slowly (1/2 MPH)

My tips for Rainbows

I find that Rainbows take with the same method that I use for salmon except that I run my bait at a temperature reading of 58 degrees for rainbows instead of the 54 degrees I use for salmon.

My top tips for Bass

I am basically a salmon fisherman. I do catch a lot of bass, but only by accident. The same goes for rainbows. Last season I caught nice rainbows and salmon on Newfound Lake but, all and all, the best fishing last year was on Winnipesaukee.

Catch & release?

Most of the time I release my fish. But I'm always looking for trophy fish and will usually keep a very large fish.

What do I think has happened to the Lake Winni yellow perch?

I have seen yellow perch disappear in the lake also. I don't know why.

What do I think has happened to the Lake Winni whitefish?

I still catch a few. My son, Scott and I had just caught a nice salmon while actually watching him on the fish-finder come up to the lure behind the downrigger. Scott said to me, "As soon as we mark another fish in the sonar, I'll try to jig the rod up again and see what happens. "It wasn't very long after we had caught the Salmon that another big fish appeared on the sonar. After waiting a few minutes of watching the fish shape following the bait but not taking, Scott picked up the rod and popped the lure free from the release. This time after pumping the rod just a few times, the rod bent down as if stuck on the bottom. After a fifteen-minute fight, he brought the fish to the net and we couldn't believe the size of this fish — a whitefish! We believe this whitefish was a record fish but we didn't have it officially weighed. On our scale, the fish weighed 5 1/2 pounds and was 24" long. After showing the picture of this fish to Mr. Wheeler at the New Hampshire Fish and Game Department, he said that we should have had it weighed because it probably was a new whitefish record as the current record is 5 pounds 1 ounce!

If I were NH Commissioner of Fish & Game, what initiatives would I take to improve Lake Winni angling?

The fishing I experienced last season was some of the best I have seen in 30 years so I don't think it needs much improvement. I would like to see more state launching boat pads, however. Paugus Bay charges 20 dollars to launch a boat! For us fixed income or retired folks, that's way too high!

My favorite fishing stories

Ted St. Onge with New Hampshire Fish & Game Wildlife Biologist - Don Miller. My friend Don Miller told me about the surprise he had gotten when he did a net study. The smelt population had exploded. This created really improved conditions for salmon fishing. I decided to try my luck. I had one of the best fishing days of that season. This is a photo of two salmon that Don and I took together that day. I thanked Don for all the information that we anglers get from the biologists net studies each season.

My wife and I were fishing Squam Lake in 1975 and one morning we fished near Church Island. We had not had a hit for about 3 hours. We were using live minnows and that is usually very good bait. Finally a little breeze came up and it started to break up the surface. Shortly after, we got a little chop. The rod on my side of the boat went crazy. It turned out to be the largest salmon I have ever caught in New Hampshire. It took me almost 40 minutes to net it. It weighed 11 pounds, 4 ounces and was 32 inches long.

A lot of salmon fishermen including me like to fish the Big Lake, but often overlook Paugus Bay. Some of the friends that I hunt with in New York came to New Hampshire to do some salmon fishing with me. They are never disappointed with the great fishing on Paugus Bay. That's why they come back year after year. This year, they arrived on June 15th and the Salmon were 28 ft. down. We caught salmon up to 5 pounds but most were between 2 1/2 and 3 1/2 pounds.

I was fishing Alton Bay a few years back. It was a gray day with no breeze. The lake was like a mirror and I wondered if it would start to rain. It goes to show you that you never know. It turned out to be one of my best days of the season. I set the 2 fly rods with long leaders of 100 feet because the smelt were still going up the brooks and also up on the gravel banks on the side of the lake to spawn. The long leaders help to get the salmon that the boat scares off, close to the shore where the smelt are running. After the boat goes by, the salmon come back to catch the spawning smelt. About 100 feet behind the boat, the smelt that you are trolling come up to the surface. I caught and released many salmon that day. About the rain? It never rained a drop the entire day. I had a great day of fishing on the lake.

Ted St. Onge with a big salmon

Am I concerned about mercury levels in Lake Winni fish to the degree that I restrict my fish intake?

Yes

What is angling really about?

With me, fishing is an addiction. I can't get enough of it. It's constantly on my mind. It's a thrill that I can't explain and I just want to keep doing it.

CHAPTER 12

OLD BUT NOT THE OLDEST MASTER ANGLERS

Hal Lyon, Chuck French, Carl Gephardt, Rick Davis, and Steve Perry

Life is not about fishing. Fishing is about life.

MASTER ANGLER HAROLD C. LYON, JR. (Hal)

(65 years angling in Lake Winni)

Fishing as the sun begins to rise

Harold C. Lyon has an unusual background: graduate of West Point, Rangerparatrooper officer, and posts in government: Director of Education for the Gifted, Associate Commissioner of Education for Libraries and Educational technology and project officer for "Sesame Street." In the academic world: assistant to the president of Ohio University; the faculties of University of Massachusetts, Georgetown University, Antioch College, Dartmouth Medical School, Notre Dame College, and University of Munich, Germany. A Fellow of the Koop Institute at Dartmouth, he is the recipient of the Gold Medal in the 1990 International Film & TV Festival of New York, a CINDY Award, and the Blue Ribbon in the 1991 American Film & Video Festival. He's the author of three other books and has been angling in Lake Winnipesaukee for 65 years.

I've been fishing Lake Winni for 65 years, beginning when I was 4, off our dock on Meredith Neck. My Uncle Gordon, who was one of the best anglers on the Lake in the 1930s-40s taught me the finer points of fishing. My mother and I lived with her sister and Uncle Gordon and their two children, my cousins, Bill and Janet, neither of whom liked to fish. I was fortunate to be my uncle's fishing student and he my mentor. This was during WWII when my father was away in Europe. My uncle taught me to fish for bass (mainly with hellgrammites and crawfish), salmon and trout, trolling with flies in spring and with heavy gear like Monel wire lines and Dave Davis spinners followed by a sewed-on shiner. I often wonder how these fishing customs and rituals begin. Is there any empirical background behind these practices?

Angling traditions remind me of this true story about the gauge of the railroad tracks, which comes from one of the rail road museums of the West in Fillmore California:

> The US standard railroad gauge (distance between the rails) is 4 feet, 8.5 inches. That's an exceedingly odd number. Why was that gauge used?
> Because that's the way they built them in England, and English expatriates built the US Railroads.
> Why did the English build them like that?
> Because the first rail lines were built by the same people who built the pre-railroad tramways, and that's the gauge they used.
> Why did "they" use that gauge then?
> Because the people who built the tramways used the same jigs and tools that they used for building wagons, which used that wheel spacing.
> Okay! Why did the wagons have that particular odd wheel spacing?
> Well, if they tried to use any other spacing, the wagon wheels would break on some of the old, long distance roads in England, because that's the spacing of the wheel ruts.
> So who built those old rutted roads?
> Imperial Rome built the first long distance roads in Europe (and England) for their legions. The roads have been used ever since.
> And the ruts in the roads?
> Roman war chariots formed the initial ruts, which everyone else had to match for fear of destroying their wagon wheels. Since the chariots were made for Imperial Rome, they were all alike in the matter of wheel spacing.

The United States standard railroad gauge of 4 feet, 8.5 inches is derived from the original specifications for an Imperial Roman war chariot. And bureaucracies live forever.

So the next time you are handed a specification and wonder what horse's ass came up with it, you may be exactly right, because the Imperial Roman war chariots were made just wide enough to accommodate the back ends of two war horses.

Now the twist to the story...

When you see a space shuttle sitting on its launch pad, there are two big booster rockets attached to the sides of the main fuel tank. These are solid rocket boosters, or SRBs. The SRBs are made by Thiokol at their factory at Utah. The engineers who designed the SRBs would have preferred to make them a bit fatter, but the SRBs had to be shipped by train from the factory to the launch site. The railroad line from the factory happens to run through a tunnel in the mountains. The SRBs had to fit through that tunnel. The tunnel is slightly wider than the railroad track, and the railroad track, as you now know, is about as wide as two horses' behinds. So, a major Space Shuttle design feature of what is arguably the world's most advanced transportation system was determined over two thousand years ago by the width of a horse's ass.

I'm certain some of our fishing tips and customs have a similar convoluted history!

Who is my fishing hero/mentor?

My Uncle Gordon and my brother, Bob, who is an outdoor writer and fly fishing guide for Steelhead on the Deschutes River in Oregon, (though he now lives on Lopez Island off the coast of Washington State, were my mentors). I also had a great uncle, Fred Turner who was a great fisherman I did not see often, but when he was with me when I was a boy, he was always teaching me new fishing lessons. He taught me to cast while holding a card between my elbow and body without dropping it out. He even taught me that my own earwax and the oil by the side of my nostrils were the best rod ferrule lubricants!

What were the principal things I learned from him?

Patience, creativity, sportsmanship, patience, respect for the fish, patience, and fly-casting.

What is my favorite Lake Winni game fish?

It use to be smallmouth black bass and I still believe them to be, pound for pound, the best fighting fish in the lake. But now I prefer the land-locked salmon which are also great fighters known for their acrobatics and finicky feeding habits. Sometimes you catch them faster than you can get your line out and other times they will not hit at all. But the bass is the most ferocious fighter.

Which do I prefer, leadcore, fly rod, or downrigger fishing for salmon and trout?

I prefer fly-fishing on the surface in springtime when the water is cold and the salmon feed on top. There's no better thrill than a big salmon hitting my fly line and fighting him with a 6-pound leader. I catch more on leadcore line than downriggers and my theory explaining that is that the lead ball on a downrigger provides no action for the lure following it while a leadcore line — particularly on a long flexible rod which I use — bounces up and down in waves providing a jigging motion to the lure which triggers more strikes than a stationary lure behind the lead ball of a downrigger. I believe I have the honor of having brought to Lake Winni in 1971 the oldest downrigger on the lake, an old hand-crank Luhr Jensen which I used successfully until 2002, when I got a new boat with Big Jon downriggers.

Here's a shot of my current "angling machine" with the new electric Big Jon's.

My Angler Fishing boat with 150 HP Suzuki 1990, kicker, and new electric downriggers -- a fishing machine!

My favorite fishing months
May, June, July, and August!

Best time of day?
Early morning before the sunlight pushes the plankton down, with the smelt following them and the salmon following the smelt to deeper waters. And I also love to fish in the evening just before dark.

My best trolling speed?
Between 1.5-2 MPH...but I like to vary my speed

The author with a nice salmon

My largest salmon, laker, rainbow, bass, and other fish
Salmon: 5 pounds in spring 2003 on a Pumpkin Head streamer on top.
Laker: 6.5 pounds in 1976 on a Pearl Wobbler 50' deep.
Rainbow: 5 pounds in summer of 2002 on a silver and red Needlefish at 40' deep.
Smallmouth bass: 6 pounds caught September 10, 1986 on a hellgrammite
I caught 2 large cusk through the ice on the same morning, one 9 pounds and one 6 pounds. Each had swallowed a smaller cusk on my line so that there was no hook in each, only the smaller 10-12" cusks wedged in the bigger ones' stomachs!

Chart of fishing depths and best lures

MONTH	SALMON	LAKERS	RAINBOWS	BASS
May:	on top with flies with sinking line	on top with flies	on top with flies	Too early for bass
June:	15-20' flies, Top Guns DB Smelt	40-50' Suttons (#61)	10'-20' flies, Top Guns DB Smelt	Fly fish the beds with poppers and Bass Bugs
July:	25-40' Top Guns DB Smelt Suttons Hippytad	45-65' Suttons (#61) Live Shiner	10'-30' Top Guns DB Smelt	off structure 15'-20' with Hellgrammite, crawfish or live frog
August:	40-50' Top Guns DB Smelt Suttons Hippytad	50-65' Suttons (#61) Live Shiner	20-40' Top Guns DB Smelt	same as July
September:	Same as August Plus flies with Sinking line	Same as August	Same as August Plus flies with Sinking line	same as August
Ice fishing:	cut line when you catch salmon	15-60' Live Smelt jig w/bait	5-10' small Smelt or night crawler	

My stories about these monsters?

See earlier chapters of this book where I have told my stories!

Have I passed on to others my angling skills?

The author with sons Eric and Gregg in 1970 with great string of bass. We don't catch as many big ones now that there are over 85 bass tournaments per summer on Lake Winni.

Yes, to my sons, Eric, Gregg, Roy, Dan, and my daughter Laural. I taught my brother, Bob to fish when he was very young and he has since become a much more successful angler than I am as well as an outdoor writer, and guide. And I have passed my skills on to my grandchildren, Taylor, Jordan, Miranda, Amanda, Crystal, Tiiersten, Brittany, Hans, Heidi, and my next door neighbor and friend, Vince's son, Michael. And, God willing, I will also pass it on to my other two grandsons, James and Jaymie who are infants as I write this. I hope that through the publishing of this book, I will be able to pass on some of it on to thousands of others.

My top 5 tips for salmon

The author heads out to his boat on Bear Island at sunrise for some salmon trolling -- the most peaceful time of the day.

1. Fish very early in the morning or late just before dark.
2. Vary speed and course so as to make "S curves."
3. Use light long leaders: 4 to 6-pound test.
4. Give action to your lure by jigging.
5. If you do not get hits, try a radically different lure.

Angling in the Smile of the Great Spirit

Left: My granddaughter, Crystal's first smallmouth bass!

Top Right: Meredith News Clip, 1969, Lyon family with big catch of bass. Every year the paper would contact us for pictures of one of our catches which, they told us, were good for tourism. We did our bit to help!

Bottom Right: Mike Giuliano, son of my friend Vince, with a white perch.

My top 5 tips for Lakers

1. Troll as slowly as you can but fast enough to make your lure have some action (1-MPH).
2. Troll off deep drop-offs.
3. If you do not get hits trolling one way change your direction to the other way as big lakers sit facing one way and will not chase your lure like a salmon.
4. Use big lures or large bait for big lakers.
5. Stop where you see large fish on your fish finder suspended above deep water and jig for lakers there.

My top tip for rainbows

When fishing for salmon, I see rainbows as bonus fish and use the same tackle and lures as I do for salmon. I consider rainbows as occasional rewards for patience.

The author with a rainbow trout caught on a dry fly

My top five tips for bass

1. Fish in late evening off structure and if you have no luck do not stay long in one place but move on and try another spot (buoy hopping).
2. Let hellgrammites or crawfish sink slowly without a weight stripping the bait back in slowly after it reaches the bottom (less than 3-5 minutes/cast) as a bass often hits the bait as you bring it back in slowly.
3. Let the bass run until they swallow the bait. They will take off on second run and that is the time to set the hook.
4. If you have no luck, either pull in your anchor and throw it out several times as this attracts bass and then they will hit. Or dive in the water with fins and snorkel and swim around the structure and then get back in the boat and fish, You will often attract them and they will hit.
5. Use a large Eagle Claw hook (#2 or 1) as bass have large mouths.

My top 5 ice fishing tips

1. Bring hot thermos with beverage.
2. Dress warmly.
3. Drill many holes to check ice thickness. And if you do not catch something, move on and try another hole.
4. Fish off of drop-offs.
5. Fish with others for fellowship in the cold.

Catch & release?

Much of the time I release the fish that I catch, but my entire family loves bass, trout, and salmon, and we look forward to cooking and eating some each summer.

Sons, Eric & Gregg with father with very large bass!1969.

What do I think has happened to the Lake Winni yellow perch?

I believe that they have been displaced by the white perch, which have proliferated and competed for the available forage fish along with the salmon. Maybe also they now stay in the more fertile bays where the water is not as clean as it is out in the open areas where we troll.

What do I think has happened to the Lake Winni whitefish?

I have not caught one in 10 years now, though I used to catch one or two each year while trolling for salmon. I believe it is the same story as with the yellow perch: too much competition for forage fish. We are also at the southern tip of the whitefish range.

If I were Commissioner of Fish & Game, what initiatives would I take to improve Lake Winni angling?

I would introduce no new fish. I do not believe in messing with Mother Nature and there is already too much competition for the forage fish which the salmon and trout need.

My favorite fishing stories

See my fish stories under the chapters on smallmouth bass, salmon, and lake trout.

One summer, I was having a dry spell and couldn't catch a salmon for 2 weeks. I was bemoaning this, and a fisherman on the Lake told me I must have been offending the fishing Gods. He asked me if I ever had bananas on board my boat. I told him that I ate a banana almost every fishing morning. "That's your trouble!" he exclaimed, confidently. "Salmon are allergic to the smell of bananas! I always inspect the lunches brought on board by fishermen and if any has a banana, I insist he leave it on the dock and wash his or her hands thoroughly before boarding. You need to scrub your boat and stop bringing bananas on board. Same thing goes for bass slime. I never board a bass on my boat. I cut the line and let it stay in the water...even if I lose the lure. You've been bringing bass on board your boat? That's certain salmon repellant!"

I thought he had to be pulling my leg. I told him that I had heard always to wash hands when you got petroleum products, like gas and oil, on your hands as they repelled salmon. And I was careful about that, but his response was that he knew a charter captain who always dipped his lures in the oily bilge and he caught more fish than his competitors. When I told my friend, Vince, about this, he went directly to the Internet and did a search on "Bass and Bananas." There is a whole cult-lore about fishing and bananas - especially among salt-water fishing captains who superstitiously never allow bananas on board their vessels. It apparently came from back when the slave ships also brought bananas from southern climates and the smell of them was noxious to those on board. But then we also found a Web site where a man swore on bananas as the key to good fishing. He always brought them on board and rubbed his lures on the bananas before trolling and caught many more fish on banana scented lures than without! (This guy even made a lure out of a rubber banana!) So what are we anglers to believe? There is a theory supporting almost every technique. Where is Bean Counter and his empirical data-gathering when we need it? He is probably laughing from heaven watching us as we struggle.

My favorite recipes for cooking various Lake Winni fish

Salmon:

I love salmon smoked on my smoker. I season it with lemon and salt (Kosher large grain salt) and smoke them on my fast water smoker for about 30-45 minutes. When cleaning fish for smoking, I learned from my Alaskan Tlingit Indian brethren to always split them wide open cutting down one side of the spine from head to tail so the fish will open, allowing the smoky flavor to permeate well.

I also like salmon filleted and broiled with lemon. I sprinkle sliced almonds on them for the last 5 minutes of broiling. Salmon are also excellent fried in olive oil. I bread the fillets with corn flake crumbs first.

Lakers:

First of all, I am in a minority among many anglers in my liking of the oily lake trout. (I also love the oily blue fish broiled with lemon butter and cheese!) A baked stuffed laker is a gourmet dish to satisfy even my German gourmet friends who, when they visit, love this great dish. I always keep all cold water fish (trout and salmon) whole with the dignity and beauty of their heads left on, out of respect for these noble fish.

- Spray the laker inside and out with olive oil spray, salt and pepper it, and stuff it with Pepperidge Farm stuffing.
- Sprinkle the fish with corn-flake crumbs and adorn it with thin lemon slices greened up with basil leaves.
- Bake a 4 pound laker at 375 degrees for about 40 minutes, taking it out for the last 10 minutes.
- Grate cheddar cheese all over it and sprinkle it with sliced almonds. The cheese melts over the fish and those who get to eat that side, have the best of feasts! I always put a small tomato or raw carrot in the trout's mouth (like a roast suckling pig) and serve it on a garnished platter — a fish dish for a king!

Lake trout fillets are also excellent fried.

Smallmouth black bass:

Smallmouth bass are my family's favorite. We often have fried bass and grits for our summer after-fishing-late breakfast in summer time. The tradition of eating fish and grits comes from my wife's southern heritage mingled with my mother's. I never skin a bass or salmon, but scale it and fillet it.

- Dip the fillets in a mix of one egg and a cup of milk

- Toss the fresh fillets in a mix of half flour and half corn flake crumbs.
- Fry them in hot olive oil until golden brown and serve them hot with lemon wedges and grits.

Left: A plate fit for a king! Baked stuffed Lake Trout and land locked salmon from lake Winni! I prepare such a dish for my best guests and also once a year for our annual Christmas party. Here's how: Rub the fish (with head on as such a noble fish does not deserve to be decapitated!) with olive oil and lemon juice. Salt it inside and out. Sprinkle it with Corn Flake crumbs. Stuff with Pepperidge Farm stuffing, following the directions on the package. Bake a 4 pound fish on a greased baking dish for about 35 minutes at 375 degrees. Remove from oven and sprinkle trout (not salmon as it's delicate flavor will be eclipsed by the cheese) with grated cheese and slivered almonds. Bake for another 5 minutes until almonds are brown. Remove from oven and serve with wild rice and a green veggie, washed down by a nice dry white wine!

Right: a baked stuffed lake trout, dinner fit for a king, as served to my German guests, who still talk about it.

Cusk:

In winter, cusk is a great eating fish (caught only in winter on fixed cusk lines). The white meat, filleted and fried like Tempura in olive oil after breading, is excellent. But traditionally, cusk is for great chowders.

- Take the meat after skinning (and backbone with the meat on it) and boil in 2 cups of water for 5 minutes. Let it cool.
- Remove meat from water and backbone (so as not to dissolve it).
- Add diced potatoes and an onion or two to the fish stock and boil until potatoes are firm but not falling apart.
- Add the already cooked fish for the last 10 minutes.
- Serve in steaming bowls with fresh ground pepper and lemon slices, and several shakes of Tabasco.

Add sourdough bread for great winter chowder! Delicious!

White Perch
White perch are one of the best eating fish in Lake Winni. I always skin them and filet them. I dip them in an egg mixed with milk, roll them in a mix of half corn flake crumbs and flour, and fry them lightly in olive oil. They are a white firm fleshed fish and delicious!

Horned Pout:
Horned pout are the sweetest fish in the Lake. My father was a master at cleaning them. He'd make a deep cut behind the dangerous dorsal spine slanting his knife toward the head. He would then step on the partially severed head, and with a smooth pull, strip the skin off the pout body in one move. I have never been able to duplicate his art, so I use pliers to grab the scale-less skin and peel it off. The firm red meat is delicious breaded and fried. We use to catch them on worms at night when they come out to feed.

Yellow Perch:
These used to be one of the sweetest fish in the lake, back when we could catch them by the bucket-full. But in the past 10 years, I have caught fewer and fewer yellow perch, though the are present in bays and around some dock structure. I cut off their heads, skin them, bread them and fry them in olive oil.

Whitefish (locally known as "shad")
Again, one of those fish we now seldom catch. However, they were one of the best eating fish in the lake. I filleted them, breaded them, and fried them in olive oil. A very sweet firm white fish. I wish they were still here!

Pickerel:
Pickerel are another very sweet fish. However, the challenge is the numerous "Y"shaped bones. There is a way to cook and dissolve the bones. After filleting them, you score the sides of the fish every half-inch or more in a checkered pattern. This enables the hot oil to penetrate the skin, which if done properly, will dissolve the "Y" bones.

Fish Cheeks — a delicacy!
I learned about this delicacy from my Alaskan Tlingit brethern who work in the salmon processing plants. As they clean salmon for quick freezing and shipping back to New York City for Lox, they scoop out the scallop-like cheeks from each side of the large fish heads, and drop them into a bag by their feet. In a large king salmon, the cheek is the size of a silver dollar, and it is a piece of sweet firm meat! They take them home

and fix the best meat from the entire fish for their family. I eat the cheeks of most fish I cook, after they are cooked.

Am I concerned about mercury levels in Lake Winni fish to the degree that I restrict my fish intake?

We are concerned to the point that we restrict our daughters and granddaughters from eating lake fish more than once a week. Also, the scientists tell us that the bigger fish on top of the food chain, contain the most mercury, so we tend to avoid eating the biggest trophy bass and trout. The scientists also advise that salmon are not as apt to collect mercury as bass and trout. Certain large ocean predator fish like tuna, sea bass, swordfish, and halibut contain high levels of mercury, and people consuming large quantities of them are often at risk, according to reports of Dr. Jane Hightower, a physician, who tested 720 patients who regularly consumed a few meals of these fish per week. The results were alarming: nine out of ten had high blood-mercury levels.[36]

But as I see it, the mercury was even more present a hundred years ago, when so many factories were burning coal and before we had emission standards, and we seem ok! Or do we? I doubt it has gotten worse, but I expect it is somewhat better than in the "old days." The scare is one more reason to practice "catch and release, especially with big fish."

MASTER ANGLER CHARLES B. FRENCH
(37 Years angling in Lake Winni)

"The true fisherman approaches the first day of fishing with all the sense of wonder and awe of a child approaching Christmas. There is the same ecstatic counting of the days, the same eager and palpitant preparations, the same loving drafting of lists ...."
— Robert Traver —

Master Angler Chuck French tying flies by the fireplace

I first met Chuck French in my church, the First Methodist Church of Gilford, New Hampshire, where he had a reputation of being one of the best fly fishermen in the church. We have grown to know and respect each other. One morning at church I heard him tell, with intense reverence that there was "... a rainbow trout in the Town of Gilford under the main bridge into Town which would go at least 3 pounds!" This is the kind of information which gets the attention of every decent angler. I later heard about his son catching 6 to 7-pound largemouth bass around the docks at a local marina, where I dock my boat. Word around the church was that, even when he was a school administrator, he would be out on the trout ponds, streams, and Lake Winni catching an hour or so of fly-fishing before school would open. He is one of those meticulous anglers who ties flies and prepares all winter for April 1st Opening Day.

I was born on May 18, 1938 in New Boston, New Hampshire and graduated from New Boston High School in 1956. I completed a B.S. degree in Forest Management at the University of New Hampshire in 1961, where I served as president of TKE fraternity. I married Barbara Kane of New Boston on May 6, 1960. I served in the Army as an artillery officer at Fort Sill, Oklahoma, and then at Fort Hood, Texas from 1961-1963 in the 2nd Armored Division. Following active duty, I served in the 368th Engineer Battalion, an Army Reserve unit in Laconia for 5 years.

I completed a practice teaching program at the University of New

Hampshire in 1963 and began a teaching career in September 1963, at Memorial Junior High School in Laconia, New Hampshire. I served as President of the Laconia Education Association and was a Vice Principal in Laconia from 1967-1974. I completed a Masters degree in school administration at Plymouth State College and have served in a variety of educational positions including science department head, guidance counselor, and team teaching leader. I have also served as president of the Lakes Region Day Care Center, president of the Lakes Region Scholarship Foundation, Chairman of the Administrative Council, First United Methodist Church, in Gilford/Laconia, and President of Trout Unlimited, Winnipesaukee Chapter. I'm a former registered Fishing Guide in the State of New Hampshire.

Barbara and I have 5 children; Carolyn, Pamela, Dianne, Linda and Andrew. We are now the proud grandparents of fifteen wonderful grandchildren, all of whom have learned to like the sport of fishing.

I retired from teaching in 1997 after 34 years of teaching and administration, but remain active as a tutor for individual students. I'm a long time dealer in antique and collectible books and fine prints. My current interests and pastimes, in addition to fly fishing, include: fly tying, nature & family photography, watercolor/oil painting, astronomy, baseball, hawk watching, raising chickens, gardening, and passing on a love for learning to our grandchildren.

Tying on a new fly....

I've been fishing Lake Winni for 38 years, beginning when I was 27. My father-in-law, Howard Kane of New Boston, is the person who introduced me to landlocked salmon fishing on Lake Winnipesaukee back in 1965. At that time, he had many years of salmon fishing under his belt, especially on Winnipesaukee, and also on Lake Moosehead in Maine. He used, almost exclusively, tandem flies such as the "Gray Ghost," "the Pine River," and the "Nine-Three." Every so often he would even put out a lure, and usually it was the "Pearl Wobbler," or a version of the "Mooselook Warbler". I always looked forward to being out on the water with "Howie" as we attempted to track down landlocks in his pampered 19-foot Thompson lapstrake.

Chuck French's favorite lures: Antique Pearl Wobbler, Red & White Streamers, and blue Flash King

In addition to my father-in-law, I have a second person that must be considered my fishing mentor. My very good friend and professional colleague, Martin Harwood of Lakeport, New Hampshire, is the one who has been most influential in cultivating my fondness for the sport of fly-fishing. This influence began in 1963 and continues even today as a result of the sharing of dozens and dozens of fishing trips taken all over the states of New Hampshire and Maine.

Both "Howie" and "Marty" have taught me countless things about fishing, but I have gained much more than just angling techniques from each of them. These two men, each in their own way, have been a very positive influence in my life, and they have done this mainly through teaching by example. By observing their actions, I have learned how to prepare for, and carry out, successful fishing excursions; but more importantly I have learned to have a deep respect and reverence for the lake, the fish species, and all the other natural surroundings when out on the water.

What is my favorite Lake Winni game fish?

The landlocked salmon is definitely my favorite Winnipesaukee game fish species. A hooked landlock's fighting characteristics are, of course, legendary; and it is known for its strong runs and its tail-walking abilities. I must admit, however, that a nice 3-pound rainbow can give a good account of itself too. I would describe the landlock as a handsome species. Its overall shape, silvery scales, and unique markings make for a creature that is something to behold.

Which do I prefer, leadcore, fly rod, or downrigger fishing for salmon and trout?

My strong preference for a salmon tackle system designed for trolling is a 9 foot fly rod, a Pflueger Medalist Reel (#1498), a #7 or #8 sinking fly line, and a 12 foot/6-pound test leader. I use a seventeen-foot I/O fiberglass fishing boat but I don't own any downriggers. I ordinarily put out three trolling lines when accompanied by at least one other fishing companion. Each fly rod is secured in a Downeaster rod holder. I have only used lead core line on a few occasions, and that was several years ago. The deadening effect of lead core line on the fish's jumping ability is the main reason I don't use it anymore. By fishing a sinking fly line the fly or lure ordinarily travels through the water at approximately one to two feet deep, depending on the trolling speed.

Chuck French with a salmon and rainbow trout, both caught on streamer flies.

Since I am usually fishing within the top 2 feet of water my favorite months for fishing the waters of Lake Winnipesaukee are April and May. My reasons include:
1. The salmon are feeding on top, where the smelt population is running.
2. The anticipation level is way up there after a long winter's wait.
3. I like the cold, rough lake weather in the spring.
4. There are fewer recreational boaters to watch out for.

The very early morning hours are my definite preference for salmon fishing. I'm an early riser and I love that time of day. Often the salmon are chasing smelt right on the surface well before the sunrise. Late afternoon is my second choice. However, I have had some great success fishing right in the middle of the day too.

I like to vary the trolling speed periodically until I find the one that seems the best for the conditions of that particular day. Salmon don't seem to have any difficulty hitting a fairly fast moving fly.

Chart of fishing depths and best lures

Note: During May, June, September, and October much of my fishing time is spent on small fly-fishing ponds in NH & Maine with the Eastern Brook Trout as the quarry.

MONTH	SALMON	LAKERS	RAINBOWS	BASS
April:	1-2 feet	(same as for salmon)	(same as for salmon)	
Red & White tandem				
Gray Ghost tandem				
Pearl Wobbler				
Live smelt				
May:	1-2 feet	(same as for salmon)	Hornberg	
	(same as above)	(same as above)	Muddler Minno	
			Red & White	
			Golder Demon	
June:	3-6 feet	(Don't fish lakers after May)	(Busy fishing trout ponds)	Popping bugs
	Red & White tandem			Muddler Minnow
	Winnipesaukee smelt			Furry Mice
				Flash King
July:	I'm pond fishing July and August			(same as above)
August:	(same as above)		(same as above)	(same as above)
September:	2-4 feet			
	Gray Ghost Tandem			
	Winnipesaukee Smelt			
	Mooselook Warbler			

Ice fishing: Varying depths from under ice to bottom smelt/shiner Jigs such as the Swedish Pimple

Largest Salmon, Laker, Rainbow, bass and other fish I have caught

Salmon: 6 pounds. in May 1972 on a Gray Ghost 2 feet deep
Laker: 7 1/2 pounds in February. 1970 on a live smelt at: 30-40 ft.
Rainbow: 3 1/2 pounds in April 2000 on a Flash King at 4 feet
Cusk: I've caught 3 and 4 pound cusk.

Chuck French's son, Andy, with a nice spring salmon. Chuck's main role is to be a good mentor and to pass angling down to his sons, daughters, and grandchildren. Andy is the artist who created the cover for this book.

Stories about these monsters

The 6-pound salmon that I caught back in 1972 was memorable because of the horrendous weather conditions we had to contend with. A fishing friend and I foolishly decided to venture out on to Lake Winnipesaukee in my little 12-foot aluminum boat one very cold and blustery day in May. The fish struck while we were trolling off the south side of Timber Island. I played the fish for nearly twenty minutes and, as a result, we drifted out from the leeward side of the island and into very rough water. We were lucky to land a salmon of that size in such unfriendly conditions; but more importantly, we were lucky to make it safely back to shore and be able to show off our prize fish to the folks at home.

Passing on to others my angling skills?

One of the biggest sources of enjoyment for me as a fisherman is derived from helping others learn the skills involved with fishing, especially the skills of fly fishing and also fly tying. Because of this my wife, Barbara, plus our four daughters and one son have all found success as anglers. Now I'm able to introduce several of our fifteen grandchildren to the world of fishing. I've also helped two of our son-in-laws become very adept fly fishermen. Fishing trips have been a way of life in our family for more than forty years now.

There is an abundance of family photographs on our refrigerator and in our photo albums showing off the big one that "didn't" get away.

Chuck French's son, Andy and friend, Ed, early in the morning learning from Dad

My top 6 tips for salmon

1. Keep all fishing equipment organized and in tip-top shape.
2. Go to bed early, get up early, and get out on the water early.
3. If the salmon are surfacing early in the day, try fly casting to them with a #6 Maynard's Marvel.
4. When trolling a sinking fly line be sure to put the entire fly line in the water for better action of the fly as it move's through the water.
5. Try float fishing with a live pin smelt that is allowed to swim freely as far away from the boat as possible.
6. Always cut your motor as soon as possible following the strike so that you can fight a fish that has retained maximum stored up energy.

Chuck French's grandson, Payson Searle, holds his first salmon

My top 6 tips for lakers

(Note: The only time I go after lakers is through the ice.)

1. Maintain and organize your equipment.
2. Get out on the water real early in the morning.
3. Try using a portable bob house for greater mobility.
4. Maintain a "packing list" of the equipment you need for ice fishing.
5. Fish at a variety of depths until you determine the optimum level.
6. Be sure to try jigging with varying sizes of the Swedish Pimple.

Chuck French's son, Andy, and Chuck's two grandsons, Will and Tom MacPhee.

My top six tips for rainbows

1. Maintain and organize your equipment.
2. Fish early in the day, and late in the evening.
3. Try the "Red & White" tandem and different versions of the Flash King lure.
4. Rainbows can become very active on the surface

during a good chop.
5. Try stopping, drifting, and fly casting with a #10 original Hornberg pattern.
6. When the "Hex" hatch is on be sure you have a good selection of large mayfly patterns on hand.

My top five tips for bass

1. Try top-water lures in the "Grave Yard."
2. Don't pass up shaded dock areas during the mid-day hours.
3. Fly-cast a #8 Muddler Minnow and also a furry mouse made with cropped deer body hair.
4. Focus on fishing areas of the lake that have "structure", but use weedless lures.
5. Concentrate on casting in between lily pad areas.

My top five ice fishing tips

1. Jigging a Swedish Pimple at varying depths can be very productive.
2. Use live smelt with a very small non-lead weight.
3. Keep your equipment well maintained and organized.
4. An 8" power auger is all I've needed for fishing in Lake Winnipesaukee. (There are optimists who believe they need a 10" auger!)
5. Set traps at varying depths until you locate the optimum fishing depth.

Catch & release?

I'd like to think that most fishermen keep only a small percentage of the fish they catch. I ordinarily keep 3 or 4 salmon at the beginning of the season so we can have one big family dinner of baked Winnipesaukee salmon. After that most all the salmon are released to fight another day. A fish is much more valuable as it fights on the other end of a line than it is lying dead in a frying pan.

What do I think has happened to the Lake Winni Yellow Perch?

It appears to me that the average size of yellow perch has dropped off significantly over the past 15 or 20 years, but the quantity seems to be holding its own. I often rely upon having an abundance of perch available while introducing my grandchildren to the very basics of fishing. We have found plenty of "takers" at any of the marinas we've visited. Usually when a species declines in either numbers or in average size the cause is related to a reduced food supply. One reason for a species' food supply to drop involves a more intense competition for that food by one or more other species. For instance, we know that Winnipesaukee's bass population is doing very well right now. This certainly could partially explain why other species such as the perch would be affected. There are, of course, a myriad of other possible causes also that could include disease, parasites, water pollution, and/or reduction of suitable habitat.

What do I think has happened to the Lake Winni White Fish?

I can only speculate that some "combination" of the factors mentioned above is involved in the demise of the White Fish in Lake Winnipesaukee.

If I were NH Commissioner of Fish & Game, what initiatives would I take

Here are a "few" of the initiatives I would take:
a. After conducting research on the current smelt population in Lake Winnipesaukee, a program should be implemented to upgrade the population.
b. Figure out how to effectively control the growth of Milfoil in the lake.
c. Push for reasonable limits for the types and numbers of gasoline engines on the lake.
d. Establish a section or two of the lake for "no kill" fly fishing for salmon, and perhaps even for bass too. That would stir things up a bit.
e. Push for limiting the use of "personal water crafts" in the more ecologically sensitive coves of the lake.

My favorite fishing stories

"Under the Cover of Darkness"

Back in the 1960s it was an opening day tradition for my good friend and mentor, Marty Harwood, and I to put our little 12 foot aluminum boat in at the Opechee Trading Post and fish the Winnipesaukee River just above the Messer Street Bridge in Laconia. By starting as early as 4 AM we could fit in a good two hours of great fly fishing before the start of school, which for both of us was just a couple of blocks away from our launch point. In those days the salmon population in the river through the center of Laconia was very impressive. There was no shortage of fishermen either. The abundance of salmon in the river drew fishermen in from all over the northeast. The natives, especially the younger ones, were also out in sizeable numbers on April 1st. They would be lined up on the bridges in town well before daylight - a virtual maze of lines, bobbers, smelt, and lures dangling over the bridge railings.

The anglers on the bridge near Barbara Cotton's Opechee Trading Post who's lines Church French and Marty Harwood wiped out on one April 1st opening day of salmon season with their anchorless boat!

As Principal and Vice Principal at Memorial Junior High School, Marty and I were seen as avid fishermen by many of our students who also ventured out at 4 AM on opening day. There was not a hint of daylight as we eased our boat into the frigid water near the dock owned by Mert and Barbara Cotton; and who had already given us a jump start with a hot cup of coffee. As usual the anticipation of some fly fishing action with one or two Winnipesaukee "landlocks" was running in high gear. Our plan was to move out and upstream from the dock area and anchor in what we had come to regard as a "hot spot" for fly-casting. After we got there and the word had been given to drop anchor we each waited for the familiar tug of it as it found a holding spot on the bottom. It quickly dawned on us, though, that we were free floating in the rather strong current directly toward the bridge and that maze of fishing lines that were hanging from the bridge. Each of us had "assumed" that the other guy had actually thought to tie the anchor to the boat. We were now rapidly drifting helplessly broadside, in the darkness, right into all those lines!

It all happened very quickly and before we knew it we found ourselves well below the bridge and luckily able to avoid a very dangerous situation considering the temperature, depth, and swiftness of the water. Needless to say, we had caused a considerable uproar on the bridge as many of the lines were taken out by our boat as we traveled under the bridge. We heard more than a few negative references to our basic intelligence and common sense abilities. We floated well down river - away from sight of the angry anglers on the bridge before we decided to row to shore and end our fishing expedition for the morning. I will always be able to re-create in my mind the image of Marty trying to untangle a large red and white bobber that had attached itself to one of the guides of his fly rod. Later in school that day we each overheard several versions of the story about the two "knuckle-heads" that caused havoc on the Messer Street Bridge. Marty and I were thankful for the cover of darkness that served to conceal our identity that cold April morning.

"An Unexpected Salmon Bonanza"

Grand Dad French passes down his fly tying skills to his grandsons, Tom & Will MacPhee.

It was late April on Lake Winnipesaukee and the ice had been out for approximately a week. My ten-year old daughter #3, Dianne, and I had already clocked in more than six hours of plying the waters in the Saunders Bay area. After minimal success we decided to troll back in to Glendale via the Broads side of Locke's Island. The weather was perfect for early season boating - bright, sunny, calm, and warming up rapidly. It certainly was not what most salmon fishermen would call prime fishing time or conditions. We were trolling 3 sinking fly lines, each sporting a different tandem fly pattern; a beaded Gray Ghost, a Pine River, and a Red & White. As we slowly cruised past the pair of blacktop buoys, 2 of the Pflueger medalists "sang out" simultaneously; a "double!" We managed to lose one of the eager salmon due to a little confusion with handling of 3 rods. But Dianne was as proud as could be after successfully landing a beautiful 3-pound landlocked. It wasn't long before we were traveling back through the same "hot spot." It was then my turn to bring in another fish of comparable size. This was the second hit on the old beaten up Red & White that we were using. But this was only the beginning of our unexpected bonanza. Between the hours of 11 AM and 1 PM Dianne and I were each able to bring in three salmon, each one in the three-pound, 22-inch size range. The old beaten up Red & White tandem fly was the fish's choice in 6 of 7 hits. When we finally decided to call it quits for the day that "super" fly was almost totally destroyed. The silver tinsel was a tangled mess and there were less than a dozen sprigs of red and white buck tail remaining intact. We returned 4 of the salmon to the water and were able to provide a big feed for our family with the remaining 2. This is an experience that Dianne and I have regularly been able to reflect upon with great joy even though it took place almost 30 years ago. It certainly made me alter some of my theories about ideal conditions for salmon fishing. I still have that Red & White and have "ruined" good many additional ones over the years in the waters of Winnipesaukee.

"The Guide Learns A Valuable Lesson"

Master Angler Chuck French -- close up

He was one of my first clients during the years I was a New Hampshire fishing guide. It was late in the month of May when I contracted with an older gentleman from Massachusetts to spend a day on Lake Winnipesaukee stalking the sometimes-elusive landlocked salmon. During the events of the day, this person would show me that he was the epitome of the patient and forgiving man. We had trolled in the Melvin Bay section of the lake for more than four hours with only one short hit. My client had had some experience with salmon fishing several years beforehand so he was very understanding about the chances of having a non-productive day of fishing. However, he exhibited unswerving optimism about our prospects for the remainder of the day. It was early afternoon when we connected with what appeared to be a three to four-pound landlocked. My client proved to be quite adept at playing the fish as it tail-walked on the surface on several occasions in its attempt to go free. I was successful in bringing in the first of the two remaining vacant lines. And when more than half of the second line was in, the "prize" fish that was being played by my client made a strong run directly over the line I was retrieving. The fish then reversed direction and crossed the line again. When the vacant line reached the gunwale, it was obvious that it might interfere with the landing of the fish. I wanted to be sure that it would not happen so I hurriedly reached for my clippers in order to free up the "live" line. The fish was now near the boat and at the surface; a beautiful sight, indeed. The fish was still very active and was capable of several more short runs. I was more than willing to sacrifice a leader and a Gray Ghost to ensure my client's chances for success. As I clipped the leader in front of me I breathed a sigh of relief, until....... it became terribly obvious that I had cut the wrong leader! That sinking feeling I experienced as we watched the silvery form disappear below the surface will be forever etched in my memory bank. I don't know how many times I apologized for my stupidity to this fine gentleman but it was quickly obvious he was above it all and was able to demonstrate immeasurable patience and understanding with his young guide. I think he probably felt as badly for me as I did for him. Luckily in the remaining daylight hours we were able to give him two more opportunities to land a Winnipesaukee salmon. He was successful both times and we parted at the end of the day, each with very positive feelings. I'll never forget the lessons this man taught me that day "under the Smile of the Great Spirit."

MASTER ANGLER CARL GEPHARDT
(22 Years angling in Lake Winni)

"There are times when no amount of persuasion, skill or use of some so-called infallible lure will make a fish strike. I believe that everyone who fishes will admit that, at least to himself if not to the public."
— Ray Bergman —

Carl Gebhardt, Master Angler of Lake Winni

Carl is one of those outdoorsmen who could not hide it if he wanted to. He exudes outdoorsmanship! He retired from his post as a forester in the White Mountain National Forest several years ago to have more time to fish with his family. He has fly fished all over the United States with his sons, and wherever he is, when the talk turns to big fish, game, sportsmanship, Carl is in the midst of it all. Carl is an avid fly fisherman and does not go deep for salmon or trout. So his main Lake Winni fishing is in May and June when the fish are up top. He has been an exemplary Scout leader for many years and loves to pass on his love for the outdoors to youth, especially his own children.

Carl Gephardt awaiting a strike on his fly

Fishing, and especially fly-fishing, has been a beckoning force during my entire life. I was raised in rural New Jersey and began my fishing career with a bent straight pin, cotton thread line and tree branch in a brook near home. My fishing interest was inspired by 3 uncles with long passionate discussions of fly fishing, fly patterns, fishing riffles, long pools and eddies, heavy insect hatches, and memories of long bicycle rides to the river, patched waders and 3-piece bamboo rods.

Fishing led me to a degree in Forest Management earned at Michigan Tech where the spring steelhead and brook trout fishing was phenomenal although often more than a match for my old bamboo rods. A short tour with the Army interrupted my fishing career, only for it to continue after being hired by the US Forest Service. The next nine years in Missouri with the Forest Service were spent raising 2 sons, Ken and Jim and fishing the rivers and ponds for smallmouth bass and bluegill. They became some of our most memorable years. Another career move brought us back to Michigan as project leader for the National Wild and Scenic River Studies of the AuSable, Manistee, Pere Marquette, and Pine Rivers, and the trout fishing was superb. Although this was a "desk job," it also required many long days and cold nights on the rivers, some of which was not always directly related to the project.

A frozen Carl Gebhardt with two frozen salmon

A final transfer in 1980 to the White Mountain National Forest introduced us to the many fine lakes, ponds and rivers of New Hampshire, and it was here that our boys taught me the true joys, and frustrations of fishing. Meanwhile fishing has drawn us to backpacking trips in Colorado and Montana. As luck would have it, our oldest son, a Fish Biologist with the Forest Service, reintroduced us to steelhead fishing in Upper Michigan and recently relocated adjacent to the St Joe River and cut throat trout fishing in Idaho.

I've been angling in Lake Winni for 22 years, starting when I was 38.

An uncle, John Gebhardt of Schenectady, New York taught me to fish. He spent a lifetime trolling for lake trout and rainbows on Lake George. He was constantly creating and modifying new techniques, equipment and fly patterns. I spent many long days in a boat with him, but probably learned and listened more intently in later years.

There were 3 uncles, Gottfred and John Gebhardt, who nearly raised me, and another great uncle, Joseph Kichline, who, unknowingly, inspired three plus generations of our family to become anglers. Each had a life long passion for trout fishing that was more focused on techniques, fly patterns the water and experiences than taking fish. However, there were always fish to eat and we certainly enjoyed them.

I learned from them, patience and a profound appreciation for fly-fishing, rivers, lakes, and forests.

What is my favorite Lake Winni game fish?

Probably the landlocked salmon because they take a fly well and can be taken on fly tackle in rivers or from a boat. They are also an especially attractive fish and great eating.

Which do I prefer, lead core, fly rod, or downrigger fishing for salmon and trout?

First Day Catch

Ken (left) and Jim Gebhardt of Gilford brought what should be the last snowstorm, pulled in three land-locked salmon at 6:30 but the early morning catch was no April this morning near the Lakeport Dam. The Fool's jest. first day of the fishing season for salmon

Carl Gephardt's sons, Ken and Jim with opening day catch of salmon from local newspaper.

Although I prefer wading and fly-casting on incoming rivers during the first few weeks of the season, we do very well trolling with a fly rod off the back and a spinning rod on a downrigger to the end of May.

My favorite fishing months?

April and May on Lake Winni and June – July on the ponds. And I love early morning best.

Stories about the monsters I have caught?

There were 3 extraordinary years during the late 1980s during which we - mostly my son, Jim - caught and released many large salmon and several very nice rainbows on the Winni and Merrymeeting Rivers. It was a strange and wonderful experience. Those fish ranged from 23-28 inches and were taken while wading on a Pinfish bucktail and small unnamed wetfly.

Passing on to others your angling skills?

I have passed my love for angling on to my sons, by example, support, and lots of practice.

My top five tips for salmon

1. Morning fishing from 7-9 AM.
2. Lightly dressed flies on single long shank hooks seem to attract the most strikes. However, we lose fewer fish on tandem hooks. Fly size and pattern may be more important than color, materials and precision tying.
3. Long leaders or monofilament lines.
4. Switch flies or lures often if they don't produce.
5. Don't overlook that "short surface line" off the back of the boat.

Catch & release

Yes, most of the time I practive catch and release, although I really enjoy eating fresh fish. There are fish that have taken a fly and fought so well that I hate to kill them. I might prefer to bring home several small injured fish, and I'm more likely to bring home a "stocked trout" than salmon from the lake.

If I were NH Commissioner of Fish & Game, what initiatives would I take?

Eliminate politics from Fish and Game management and follow the professional advice of our hired professional biologists. Consider the long-term impact of derby fishing. Although derbies may be an economic stimulus and bring people to the sport, they may need further study and perhaps greater restrictions. The decline of quality fishing is startling - particularly in the rivers. Above all let's initiate and support efforts to protect and improve water quality and habitat, but let the "experts" tell us what and how that can be accomplished.

Fishing stories:

Our sons are better storytellers than I am, but of course most of the stories somehow reflect humorously on dad and, of course, none of them are true. I have been caught in the boat, unfortunately on film, with my eyes closed only momentarily while the boys caught and released dozens of fish. And somehow only dad can lodge a fly high in a tree and become hopelessly entangled in fly line during a heavy hatch on Sky Pond. I WAS SET-UP! That new fishing vest they gave me with "dozens of pockets" is appreciated but has become a source of their amusement as I frantically fumble through each pocket looking for some indispensable item at the height of the hatch. Only we can fly fish 3-in-a-canoe during that heavy hatch with fish rising everywhere and only dad can manage to entangle himself in fly line or hook a flying bat.

Carl Gephardt with big rainbow trout caught on a fly

Only dad would be up late on a hot humid night fighting mosquitoes while finishing that "bushel" of 3-inch bluegills our young sons had to bring home to the table.

I outfished Jim once on a cold wet very snowy opening day when he was called to the riverbank and I moved into his riffle. I cherish the photo proof of that event.

Time and wisdom have broadened our view and grandchildren have become a welcome opportunity to pass all of this onward, but this is what fishing is really all about. Memories and stories of the big fish we lost outlive those that we brought to net. And, although I readily dispense highly valuable advice to the boys, I probably listen and consider more of what they have to say now than ever before.

My favorite recipes

Those salmon fillets wrapped in foil with a little cooking wine, sliced onion, lemon, and thyme are great either on the grill or in the oven they are just hard to beat.

MASTER ANGLER RICHARD L. (RICK) DAVIS
(56 years of Lake Winni angling)

"Scholars have long known that fishing eventually turns men into philosophers. Unfortunately, it is almost impossible to buy decent tackle on a philosopher's salary.
— Patrick F. Mcmanus —

Rick Davis, founder of the annual Spring Salmon Derby

I first met Rick Davis in 1979 when he owned the Paugus Bay Sporting Goods store and followed his successes as he started the Salmon Derby. He was a man who lived for salmon! He has dedicated his life to creating a healthy salmon population in Lake Winni. He is the founder and the workhorse President and Executive Director of the annual spring Winni Salmon Derby, founded in 1981. He has been angling in Lake Winni for 56 years, since he was just 5 years old. In 1999, his garage burned down, destroying his boat and all his fishing tackle. He was, as any angler will understand, deeply grieved by this loss. But his indomitable fight on behalf of the landlocked salmon fishery continues.

I was born in Moultonborough in 1941 and resided there for 60 years until moving in 2002 to Center Harbor, New Hampshire. I served the Army in the United States and Germany. I worked as a meat cutter for several years before bursitis forced me to change occupations. My wife and I owned a retail sporting goods store, Paugus Bay Sporting Goods Co., in Laconia for 20 years, selling the business in 1989. Since then I have owned another business, Wilderness Pursuits International acting as a sport travel agent selling hunting and fishing adventures primarily in Canada. We work with the best outfitters and sell trips for them for groups up to 20 people. The trips include such adventures as hunting for moose, caribou, bear, deer, mountain lion, elk, etc., and fishing for arctic char, lake trout, Atlantic, Pacific and landlocked salmon, walleye, northern pike and more. I started the Winni Derby 23 years ago and have been its President and then Executive Director for that time. I fished a few times with my Father before he died when I was 6 years old. After that I gathered knowledge on my own or from older experienced fishermen.

Rick Davis with a 2000 Prize Winni Salmon Derby winner

What is my favorite Lake Winni game fish?

The land-locked salmon — an unpredictable fighter.

Which do I prefer, lead core, fly rod, or downrigger fishing for salmon and trout?

Downrigger fishing with light tackle.

My favorite fishing months?

All of the fishing season, but spring and the month of September would be my favorites in the evening.

Best trolling speed

2.0 – 2.2 mph

Chart of fishing depths and best lures

MONTH	SALMON	LAKERS	RAINBOWS
May:	5 colors of 18-20# leadcore, Sutton Spoons, Flash King Mooselook Warblers (sm. lures).	10 colors leadcore copper Mooselook	same as salmon same as salmon
June:	7 colors leadcore Same lures as above	10 Colors leadcore copper Mooselook	same as for salmon
July:	Change to downriggers 30-40' same lures	40-50' copper Mooselook	same as for salmon
August:	Downriggers 40-50' same lures	40-60' copper Mooselook	same as for salmon
September:	Downriggers 30-40' same lures	40-50' copper Mooselook	same as for salmon

Ice fishing

For Lake Trout, use smelt and either jigs or tip-ups.

Fish shallow 12-18 inches off bottom or 3-4 feet below the ice. Find the drop-offs.

Largest salmon, laker, and other fish I have caught in Lake Winni?

Salmon: 6.0 pounds Depth: 20'
Laker: 9.0 pounds Depth: 65'
Other large fish: white perch: 3+ pounds; cusk: 8 pounds; whitefish: 3 pounds.

Passing on to others my angling skills

Rick Davis relaxing

I have passed on my knowledge through my retail outlet, The Paugus Bay Sporting Goods store which I used to own. I've also taught in the "Let's Go Fishing Program" sponsored by the State Fish & Game, and I like to think the Salmon Derby with its mentored Junior Division competitors and winners the Derby is my form of passing it on to the next generation of anglers.

My top 5 tips for salmon

1. Work your flies; don't just drag them.
2. Run one fly in the prop wash or no more than 10' behind the boat.
3. Long leaders in the spring and shorten them up as you go deeper.
4. Watch your lures to make sure you are getting the right action.
5. Patience, and then get ready for a show if you get into them!

My top 5 tips for lakers

1. Lake trout feed when they are off the bottom 15-20'.
2. Run a short leader off the downrigger ball, 10-12' back
3. Use small copper Mooselook Warblers for lures
4. Black lures work well, too.
5. Go slow. If using live smelt or suckers you can just drift and do very well.

Tips for rainbows

I'm opposed to stocking rainbows in the lake, so I don't fish for them. They're eating the resources the salmon need to grow. There is a fight for the plankton., smelt, and other forage fish. The salmon need this forage.

My top 5 ice fishing tips

1. Keep bait alive and check it often
2. Fish for lakers in 30' depth of water or less.
3. When fishing for white perch, drill a lot of holes and keep moving

from hole to hole jigging. You can tell right away if you're in the school or not; but when you are, it will be hot!

4. DO NOT fish just below the ice as you'll hook salmon. They are easily injured if taken out onto the ice and returned to the water.

5. Take lots of good food and relax!

Catch & release

I practice it most of the time. I'll kill 1 or 2 fish a year for my neighbor to eat.

What do I think has happened to the Lake Winni yellow perch?

Years ago, when there were very few smelt the game fish ate small yellow perch and depleted them.

What do I think has happened to the Lake Winni white fish?

I believe the department that controls the water level drops the level after the shad spawn, leaving their eggs to spoil.

If I were NH Commissioner of Fish & Game, what initiatives would I take?

No fish will survive without food, and forage food should be maintained or increased. Adding more fish or different species will not do a thing without the food to feed them.

I would also ban the high-speed boats, i.e., Cigarette boats, Bertrams, and the like.

Recipes for cooking Lake Winni fish?

I don't eat much fish, but do like white perch battered and fried. Cusk is good the same way or in chowder.

Am I concerned about mercury levels in Lake Winni fish to the degree that I restrict my fish intake?

Mercury has always been here. It's only since the equipment to measure it came along that the stories about not eating fish have started to appear. I don't feel there's enough to matter. I'd be more concerned with the gasoline on the water than mercury levels.

I lost my boat in a fire 3 years ago and haven't replaced it. I've since moved off the lake also. The fight for space on Winni is so bad during tourist season that it takes a lot of the fun out of fishing for me.

The Lake Winni Spring Salmon Derby

Pictures of the Winni Derby winners over the years from 1986-2000 are in Chapter 10, along with a history of the Derby I wrote.

Rick Davis awarding the Grand Prize to the 2000 Winni Salmon Derby Ladies' Division

To illustrate the variability created by varying smelt populations, we had one year when only 10 fish were entered into the Derby! After the Derby worked diligently to enhance the smelt population things improved and today we have fish that are at an all time high for length/weight ratio. The average fish in 2003 in the nets was 4 pounds and they are getting larger.

MASTER ANGLER STEVE PERRY
(45 Years angling in Lake Winni)

"Fishing: the art of casting, trolling, jigging, or spinning while freezing, sweating, swatting, or swearing."
Henry Beard and Roy McKie

I first met Steve Perry 6 years ago, attracted to his writings and studies on Game Fish in New Hampshire and Lake Winni. He is one of the most scientific of outdoorsmen, having had the good fortune to make his career be about what he most loves - angling. He is a born and bred local angler, having grown up fishing Lake Winni. He adds a genuine scientific contribution to this book, and he may be the only one of us Master Anglers, (other than me, of course) who one can fully believe!

Steve Perry stripping eggs from female salmon in fall

I began spending weekends and summers on Lake Winnipesaukee in the late-1950's at the age of 4. My folks had a cottage on the Saunders Bay side of Varney Point, a mere 200 feet or so from the Gilford Town Beach. This is the place where I spent almost every waking hour fishing off the dock for bucket loads of yellow perch, unless it was raining, and then I would head for our boat house in search of horned pout. It was always a big thrill to catch the occasional smallmouth bass and pickerel since it required a net to land such a prize. Back before the expansion of Gilford Marina, it was also possible to catch a limit of brook trout from the end of the dock during the month of May, as these fish were able to make their way into the lake, and along the sandy shore after being stocked into Gilford Brook. But the best excitement of all was catching the crowned jewel, a landlocked salmon. Each April, I would hop into our leaky wooden row boat and head for a floating piece of ice in a small patch of open water, where I would row fast enough to force the front end of the boat up onto the small "iceberg" and then begin casting a gold Kastmaster with the hopes of hooking into one these spectacular fish.

My early passions for fishing eventually led to an interest in the sciences while going to school. By the time I was a junior in high school, I knew I wanted to pursue a career in the field of natural resources and participated in a "Future Scientist of Tomorrow Program" that was hosted by Virginia Polytechnical Institute and State University. During a week-long stay on campus I was exposed to a number of different fields of study including Forestry, Parks & Recreation, Wildlife Management and low and behold...Fisheries Science! This exposure resulted in applying to a variety of colleges and universities offering fisheries science as a major study during my senior year in high school. I was fortunate to be accepted to Michigan State University where I completed a Bachelor's of Science degree while majoring in Fisheries and Wildlife Management. Upon completion of college, I returned to New Hampshire intent on trying to secure a job with the New Hampshire Fish and Game Department. I still remember the war hoop that came forth when I found out I was hired as a Fish Culturist at the Department's New Hampton Fish Hatchery. For the past 25 years I've held a number of different positions within the Department with the sole purpose of trying to give back to the state's fisheries resources all that it's given me during a life filled with the joys derived from fishing. During my years with the Department I've held a number of positions including Fisheries Biologist (1980-1989), Regional Supervisor (1989-1997), and Inland Fisheries Division Chief (1997-present). I can tell you that I feel "The Smile of the Great Spirit" each and every day, as it first presented me with the opportunity to embrace fishing as a passion and to turn that passion into a career that is based on trying to continue this lake's angling legacies for the generations yet to come so that when they visit these waters, they too can share in its soothing powers.

I have been fishing for 45 years in Lake Winni beginning when I was 4.

My paternal grandparents, Henry and Ena Perry, taught me how to fish. It started with digging worms in the garden; placing enough in a coffee can to outlast the constant nibbles of the yellow perch and sunfish while my eyes were transfixed on the red and white bobber, as I waited patiently or maybe not so patiently, until it was the right time to set the hook. My grandparents also had a boat, and the whole family would clamor aboard and head out on the lake in search of smallmouth bass. We would anchor in all the likely spots, and bait our hooks with crayfish or hellgrammites. Then we would wait for the action to begin.

Master Angler Steve Perry with nice salmon and rainbow trout

I still remember vividly the time my mother hooked into a monster bass only to be disappointed when it came off the hook a short time later. I know it was a big one because it wasn't 5 minutes later when my older brother, who was 6 years old at the time, said he had something heavy tugging at his line. Fifteen minutes or so later a 5-pound smallmouth bass was hoisted into the boat, and during the picture taking ceremony that occurred later, we both had a tough time keeping the fish's tail off the ground. Each spring my grandparents used to gather us all up for a day spent fishing the area's trout streams. We all looked forward to the feed of trout we had at the end of the day, but the highlight was the picnic lunch my grandparents packed for these excursions, particularly the raisin squares, which were my grandmother's specialty.

My fishing heroes are my parents and grandparents. They gave me the opportunities to fish and their patience, encouragement, and support turned fishing into a passion.

The principal thing I learned was that fishing is the best way to spend time with your family because it's fun, relaxing and it puts you on, in, or at the edge of the water.

What is my favorite Lake Winni game fish?

My favorite game fish is the landlocked salmon because of its slamming strikes at the end of the line and it's spectacular jumping abilities. I think pound for pound smallmouth bass are the best fighters. When they turn their slab side to the boat and start to bulldog, you know you're in for a battle.

Two nice Land Locked Salmon from Steve Perry

Which do you prefer, lead core, fly rod, or downrigger fishing?

All 3 methods can be productive given different conditions. There's nothing like the strike of a landlocked salmon hitting a fly while you're trolling and working your fly rod during early spring. Fishing with downriggers is great when the fish go deep because you can play the fish on light tackle. However, fishing with lead core can be very productive when your trolling pattern and variations in speed impart an array of erratic motions to your lure or fly. If I had to choose which method has produced the most fish for me I'd have to say downrigger fishing followed very closely by working flies with a fly rod.

Favorite fishing months?

April-May-September

Best time of day?

When the colors of dawn first appear on the eastern horizon.

Best trolling speed?

1.8 mph

Chart of fishing depths and best lures for Salmon and Trout

May:	0-15'	Grey Ghost
June:	0-30'	Size 2 Needlefish White w/Pearl
July:	30-45'	Size 2 Needlefish White w/Pearl
August:	30-45'	Size 2 Needlefish White w/Pearl
September:	0-45'	Size 1 Needlefish White w/Pearl

Largest Salmon, Laker, Rainbow, bass and other fish you have caught?

Salmon: 25", 5.5 pounds in 1978. Lure: Red Ghost fly on the surface
Laker: 25.5", 6.25 pounds in 1980 on a live smelt at 45' deep
Other large fish: Lake whitefish (Shad): 20," 4 pounds in 1978 on a live smelt at 60' deep

Stories about these monsters?

The salmon was caught early in the spring when I was trolling a small patch of open water near Governor's Island Bridge. I was trolling a tandem Red Ghost with beads on a flat line and had just enough monofilament out that when I lifted the tip of my rod to the 12 o'clock position, the fly would break the water's surface. After the fish hit I was having a pretty good battle with it though at that point it was a stand-off. The guy I was fishing with, who is a long-time friend, didn't want to stop trolling because he'd seen several other salmon roll right around the boat. My friend kept urging me to hurry up and get the fish in the boat, and after a time I did, despite the fact that the boat was moving the whole time.

Steve and friend with nice catch of Lakers, salmon and rainbow trout

4-pound Lake whitefish caught by Master Angler Steve Perry in Lake Winni in 1978 while ice fishing on Paugus Bay off Christmas Island

My largest lake trout was caught while I was ice fishing during the Meredith Rotary Club's 1980 Fishing Derby. I had a bob house over an underwater hump that was located in about 50 feet of water between the south end of Rattlesnake and Ship Island. The fish was caught on a tip-up baited with a live smelt. The lake trout was on the prize board until it got bumped off late Sunday, finishing 11th, while prize money was only being awarded for the top 10. This particular location was very productive that winter and on many occasions when a flag went up 2 or 3 others would pop up simultaneously, as the lake trout moved over the hump in waves, apparently chasing schools of smelt.

The lake white fish was caught on January 1, 1978 while I was ice fishing on Paugus Bay out in front of Christmas Island. The tip-up was set out where the old channel is located, being around 90 feet deep in that particular spot. The ice conditions that day were tenuous at best, as you could see the ice move up and down as you walked, although it was clear black ice. I remember the ice conditions because we were having luck catching lake trout that morning and you could see them being brought to the surface when they were still 30 feet below the ice because the ice was so clear. When my flag went up, I thought it was another lake trout until I saw it when it got to about 30 feet and it was light colored rather than dark. Thinking it was a salmon I started getting prepared to cut the line. But when the fish was closer to the hole I saw it was a shad, so onto the ice it came. If I had known then that it was an unusually large lake whitefish I would have had it mounted rather than eating it that night for supper.

Passing on to others your angling skills

I have a son and daughter who spent many days fishing with me as they were growing up. They both continue to fish on occasion even though they are in their early 20s. There are times my daughter will outfish her boyfriend, who lives and breathes fishing.

Master Angler Steve Perry with large male salmon in fall

My top 5 tips for salmon
1. Go early.
2. Watch for surface activity.
3. Find the schools of smelt.
4. Match the size of your lure or fly to the most prevalent smelt size.
5. Troll erratically.

My top 5 tips for lakers
1. Go early.
2. Fish deep or near deep under water structure.
3. Troll as slow as possible.
4. Use big baits if you're after big fish.
5. Jigging works well whether you're ice fishing or fishing open water.

My top 5 ice fishing tips
1. Go early.
2. If you're using tip-ups check the condition of your bait regularly.
3. If you're jigging, chum your hole with cut bait and add a piece of cut sucker to your jig hook.
4. Cut big holes so you can get that big trout through it and onto the ice.
5. Always, always, always check the ice conditions.

4 nice Lake Trout from Steve Perry and friend.

Catch & release

I practice catch and release most times. The only time I'll keep a fish is if someone I know asks for one to eat, or the fish is injured to the point that it's likelihood of survival is low. I practice catch and release primarily because the salmon and trout in Lake Winnipesaukee are a finite resource and are too valuable to be caught only once.

What do I think has happened to the Lake Winni yellow perch?

I think shoreline development has had a detrimental impact on the lake's yellow perch. The proliferation of large-scale homes and condominium complexes with concurrent removal of trees, shrubs, and other natural vegetation along the lake's shore, and installment of lawns right to the waters edge that get fertilized regularly, provides unregulated input of non-point source pollutants each time it rains. A variety of chemicals that are contained within lawn fertilizers can cause harm to fish and other aquatic organisms.

What do I think has happened to the Lake Winni whitefish?

I don't think anything dramatic has happened to the lake whitefish in the lake rather I think the methods used to catch these fish during the yesteryears have been forgotten.

If I were NH Commissioner of Fish & Game, what, if any, initiatives would I take to improve Lake Winni angling?

The primary initiative I would take is the restoration of a buffer zone along the shoreline so that water run-off is filtered prior to entering the lake. Another initiative would be developing a watershed scale plan for the lake so that issues affecting water quality could be identified and strategies adopted to mitigate adverse impacts.

My philosophy, science, and specifics of how the F&G Department controls the population of forage fish (smelt),

The smelt population has such a close bearing on the health of the salmon populations. Is the present time the best for salmon size and numbers in Lake Winni? How delicate is the balance between the various fish populations?

Steve Perry with large hooked jaw male salmon in fall

The New Hampshire Fish and Game Department manages the lake's smelt population by quantifying each year's production of young-of-the-year smelt using a scientific quality echo sounder. The annual abundance estimate of smelt then forms the basis for adjusting the landlocked salmon stocking rate in an attempt to balance the predatory pressure landlocked salmon exert toward smelt with the smelt population's ability to sustain that predatory pressure without being impacted significantly. This management strategy has stabilized salmon growth at an optimal rate.

Although salmon growth has been more consistent over the last decade, I don't believe it has resulted in establishing "the best" time for salmon size and numbers. The average size of the salmon in the lake is more closely related to the age composition of the population. The older individual salmon are in the lake, the larger the "average size" will be. Angling pressure and harvest play a major role in the salmon population's age composition. Currently, fishing pressure is at a level that results in most salmon being harvested within a minimum of 2 years of reaching legal size (15 inches). Typically, in the fall of each year, 85% of the salmon population is age 2 and 3, while only 15% of the population is age 4 to age 6. I believe this age structure is tied to the advent of downrigger fishing, which from a practical manner, lengthened the active salmon fishing season on the lake. Prior to downriggers appearing on the scene, anglers fished for salmon primarily during April and May and maybe late September. There were a few anglers that would fish for salmon when they went deep, using lead core or wire line. With downriggers, more and more anglers fished for salmon during all months of the season, since fishing with light tackle, when the salmon went deep, made it a more enjoyable experience than fishing with "heavy equipment".

Results of latest significant studies of various fish (salmon, lake trout, rainbows, and bass) in Lake Winni? What changes in game fish management did/do the results of these studies indicate and prompt?

Salmon Study Results

Steve and colleague working the fall salmon nets which by the disturbance on the water are full of salmon ripe for egg harvest and milt fertilizing

Salmon stocking rates influence salmon growth. Analysis of a long-term data set determined a statistically significant negative relationship existed between the annual weight of yearling salmon stocked and the average size of the salmon captured by trap nets the following year. What this means is when the total weight of yearling salmon stocked into Lake Winnipesaukee increased, the average size of salmon decreased the following year and conversely, when the total weight of salmon stocked decreased, the average size of salmon increased the following year. This finding resulted in the establishment of a base-stocking rate for salmon (0.07 lbs./surface acre), which is intended to meet a management objective of maintaining an average size salmon, captured by trap nets during the fall, that ranges between 18 and 20 inches.

Smelt Study Results

Rainbow smelt populations fluctuate widely and it is important to identify these fluctuations before salmon growth is affected. Quantifying the abundance of young-of-the year smelt on an annual basis, allows adjustments to be made to the base-stocking rate of yearling landlocked salmon, so that optimal growth of salmon can be maintained in conjunction with balancing predatory pressure being exerted by salmon on the lake's smelt population. The age structure of smelt spawning in tributaries to Lake Winnipesaukee is unusual since age 1 individuals dominate the run and typically smelt don't become sexually mature until age 2. This may be due to the slower growth rates, resulting in age 1 smelt becoming sexually mature at this age rather than at age 2, and high predator based mortality rates. These findings further support the need to balance predator abundance with prey abundance.

Lake Trout Study Results

The increase in lake trout minimum length (from 15 inches to 18 inches) resulted in protection of first time spawning lake trout in Lake Winnipesaukee. This is important since natural reproduction is being relied on to sustain the lake trout population.

The introduction of rainbow trout (years and numbers stocked) and the prevalent theories as to why this did not create too much competition for salmon for forage fish.

Rainbow trout were first stocked directly into Lake Winnipesaukee during 1990 and have been stocked with 10,000-15,000 yearlings per year since that initial introduction. The principal reason behind initiating the stocking of rainbow trout into the State's large lakes (>1,000 acres) was to provide winter anglers an alternative trout fishery that would take some of the angling pressure off lake trout during the ice-fishing season. Rainbow trout were selected for stocking in these waters because of their propensity to forage on whatever prey item was most prevalent or available, while also maintaining consistent rates of growth regardless of what they are feeding on. Additionally, rainbow trout will inhabit relatively shallow water during the winter months, particularly in areas where water is flowing into the lake, so winter anglers' fish for rainbow trout in different locations than when they're fishing for lake trout. Lastly, the numbers of rainbow trout stocked into the lakes are kept at relatively low levels in an effort to reduce any negative affects they may have on the lake's salmon population.

What is the biggest rainbow, salmon, and laker found in my netting operations?

Biggest rainbow trout:	25 inches	7.25 lbs.
Biggest salmon:	29.5 inches	9.5 lbs.
Biggest lake trout:	35.6 inches	14.6 lbs.

Annual census methods and objectives in Lake Winni (seining in rivers, at 2 Mile Island, annual high tech electronic scanning operations).

Spring Smelt Assessment

The objectives of this annual assessment are to determine size, age, and sex ratio characteristics of smelt spawning in tributaries. Comparison of these estimates through time provides information on the status of these spawning populations. Samples of spawning smelt are obtained from selected tributaries with sampling occurring between 2100 and 2400 hours. Smelt are collected using a long handled (2.4-m) dip net (38-cm diameter) with 9-mm wire mesh. A minimum of 100 smelt is netted from each tributary and total length (mm), weight (g) and sex are recorded for each fish processed. A sub-sample of up to 5 fish per 10mm length interval are kept in separate containers in order to obtain representative samples for age determinations.

Summer Smelt Assessment

To improve landlocked salmon management practices, the New Hampshire Fish and Game Department annually conducts acoustic surveys with the objectives to:

1. Estimate the annual abundance of pelagic forage fish (kg/ha);

2. Determine the species composition, size characteristics, and spatial distributions of pelagic forage fish;

3. Estimate the annual abundance (kg/ha) of juvenile rainbow smelt; and,

4. Adjust landlocked salmon stocking rates to provide consistent growth.

Mobile hydroacoustic surveys are conducted during late-July and August when lakes are thermally stratified and rainbow smelt were restricted to the hypolimnion. Surveys are conducted at night, when limnetic fish tend to be more evenly dispersed, making acoustic quantification easier and more accurate. Acoustic transects, spaced approximately 1.6 km apart, are perpendicular to the shore and span the pelagic area of the lake. Near-shore littoral areas (depth less than 10 meters) are excluded from each transect. Two major functions of the acoustic sampling system are echo integration and dual-beam processing. Echo integration provides an estimate of relative fish densities that are converted into estimates of fish abundance. Dual-beam data provides information on the target strength of individual fish or groups of fish. The target strength data is used to compute relative fish size information and to calculate the scaling factor necessary to convert echo integrator survey data into estimates of absolute fish abundance. A 3 x 7-m rectangular midwater trawl is used to verify fish species and size-class compositions. The net is 18 m in length and has stretched-mesh sizes of 10.2, 5.1, 1.9, and 1.3 cm. The cod end is 3-mm-mesh knotless nylon netting. Species occurrences are determined from discrete samples of fish collected from the 0-5m, 5-10m, and 10-15m depth strata. This reduces bias in apportioning estimates among the species of fish found in the limnetic zone. Tow times vary from 0.03-0.50 hrs, at speeds of 2-3 km/h. Fish captured in the mid-water trawl are identified, enumerated, measured for total length (mm) and weighed (g). Forage fish are identified as the proportion of targets that fall within a target strength range of -64 and -46 decibels (dB). The estimated forage fish biomass (kg/ha) for the lake is based on the mean number of forage fish/m2, the mean forage target mass (g) and the estimated pelagic area (ha). Each depth stratum is analyzed separately and strata biomass estimates are summed to determine the lake totals.

Landlocked Salmon Assessment

Bringing in the fall harvest of salmon ready for stripping and fertilizing

The primary objectives of this annual assessment are to evaluate the age and growth characteristics of adult landlocked salmon in New Hampshire lakes. Adult landlocked salmon are sampled with trap nets set during the fall spawning season. Representative samples of the landlocked salmon catch are sexed, measured for total length (mm), weighed, and examined for excised fins to determine their age, since each landlocked salmon cohort is marked by excising different fins prior to their release as juveniles.

Steve Perry showing children large male salmon before stripping him of milt.

Lake Trout Assessment

The objectives of lake trout assessments are to evaluate spawning lake trout in terms of mean length, weight, and relative weight and to compare these statistics to long-term data sets. Lake trout are sampled by both small mesh gill nets and trap nets in the fall of the year. All captured lake trout are measured for total length (mm), weighed, and sexed and then are released at the site of capture. Relative weight values are derived as a measure of fish condition. This index compares the actual weight of an individual fish with a standard weight for a fish of the same length.

Am I concerned about mercury levels in Lake Winni fish to the degree that I restrict my fish intake?

No.

CHAPTER 13

THE YOUNGER MASTER ANGLERS: ALAN NUTE, JASON PARENT, AND TRAVIS WILLIAMS

"In the world of fishing there are magic phrases ....
Among them are: 'Remote trout lake, 'fish up to 13 pounds,'
'the place the guides fish on their days off,'....
There's power in words like that."
— John Gierach —

MASTER ANGLER ALAN NUTE
(AJs Bait & tackle)
38 Years of Lake Winni Angling)

Alan closeup

I FIRST MET *ALAN* when he took over ownership of the landmark bait and tackle store on Main Street in Meredith — the angling community's communication hub known as AJ's Bait and Tackle (AJ standing for Alan James Nute). He was not only a highly knowledgeable angler who knew first hand about all the tackle he carried in his store, but he was also completely generous in sharing that wisdom with all who entered his store, which is not something one can take for granted. He is also a creative experimenter with various lures and baits, being the only Master Angler on our list who is a master at catching salmon on worms! Alan is also a master fly-tier, having created hundreds of his own successful patterns, which he, himself, tests, before selling them. When I first invited him to fish with me on my boat, I did not expect to witness such a creative use of varied lures and baits. But he managed to catch and land a nice salmon, 4 bass, a rainbow *and a white perch in an hour of August fishing with me by trolling a nightcrawler — something I would never have tried!*

Left: Alan Nute with a rainbow trout he caught trolling his night crawler rig. Right: Alan & the author discussing fishing techniques

Alan Nute discussing, with the author, his new favorite fly, which he ties to order right in his store

I was born in Nashua, New Hampshire, on May 5, 1962, just as the good salmon fishing begins on Lake Winni. Angling and football were the two sports I excelled in. I caught lots of fish and I was an All-State linebacker in high school. I also played while at Plymouth State College. I have been in the retail fishing tackle business since I was 16. My dream was to someday own my own tackle shop and I achieved that goal in 1997 when I bought Waldron's Bait Store and became the owner of what is now AJ's Bait & Tackle in Meredith. I want to use and try everything I sell which gives me lots of research and development time on Lake Winni, testing new lures and flies which I tie myself right in the shop.

Thanks to my wife, Beth, who watches the store for me, I am able to get out to fish and to catch most of my own hellgrammites (which I do with a snorkel and mask in the rivers, turning over rocks near shore and grabbing them in my hands), crawfish, smelt, and shiners for the store.

Alan Nute smiling. He is the only Master Angler to use night crawlers successfully for salmon! He rigs it on his line using a small wire which he threads the night crawler on, passing it onto his line.

I've been fishing Lake Winni for 38 years beginning at age 5-6. My uncle first took me Ice fishing on Bear Island and trolling in the spring. My aunt, June Fuller, owns a place on Bear Island right across from Cattle Landing and it was there that my uncle taught me to fish.

My Uncle Cyp which is short for Cyprian Kvedar, was my fishing mentor. He taught me many successful methods of fishing with live bait, jigging through the ice, and trolling with flies in the spring.

What's my favorite Lake Winni game fish?

Landlocked salmon- they are unpredictable and put up a great fight, jump a lot, and are strong fighters.

Which do I prefer, lead core, fly rod, or downrigger fishing for salmon and trout?

I use them all. They all work, in their time and place.

Favorite fishing months?

August, as I can get up early, be out on the Lake at first light, and come back with a limit of salmon or trout by working time in the early morning

Best trolling speed?

1.5 mph

Chart of fishing depths and best lures

	Salmon	Lakers	Rainbows	Bass
May: A.J.'s flies,	top to 25 feet Top Guns	40 feet on bottom Sutton spoons	on surface small flies&crawlers	shallow 0-10 feet Gold bombers
June:	20-40 feet Dodger& fly, Top Gun	40-50 feet Sutton spoon	20-25 feet flies crawlers	still shallow spinner bait
July:	40-55 feet Dodger -fly, DB Smelt	50-65 feet Pro Eye spoons	25-40 feet Top Guns	10-20 feet Gitzits/Sinkos
August:	50-70 feet Harry's Willow,DB Smelt	60-110 feet bucktail jigs	25-45feet Pheobe spoons	20-40feet Zoom lizards
September:	30-55 feet Flash King	60-110 feet Suttons & jigs	top-40 feet streamer flies	15-30 feet Silver buddy
October:	season closed	season closed	season closed	25-40 feet Silver Buddy
Ice fishing	40 feet bucktail jig or sucker meat	just under ice salmon eggs	35 feet shiners	

Largest salmon, laker, rainbow, bass, and other fish I have caught in Lake Winni

Salmon: 9.5 pounds in September on an Egg Sucking Leech fly in 5 feet of water

Laker: 10 pounds in January 3, 1980, 10:30 AM on live smelt through the ice at 30 feet

Rainbow: 5.25 pounds In April on a night crawler trolled on top

Other large fish: 8-pound cusk jigging with a swedish pimple. 3.5-pound white perch on a small jig with worm.

Passing on my angling skills on to others

The icon for AJ's Bait & Tackle run by an angler for anglers!

I have a daughter who does not fish, so instead, I pass on my skills to customers in my store, AJ's Bait & Tackle in Meredith, New Hampshire.

When I tell them to try my pumpkin-head streamer for salmon, I have been out there using it with success. People now know that and they take my recommendations. Many summer novice fishermen and women come into my store, and after I learn about their experience, I guide their decisions on a rod and reel, line, lures, technique, and even...sometimes, places to go. They keep coming back as a sign of their trust in me and what I sell them. I take pride in having happy and successful customers! I tie and fish with all the flies I sell in the store.

My top five tips for salmon

Alan Nute always uses scent -- Dr. Juice -- on his baits, flies, and lures.

1. Fish early in the morning as the plankton are still high from the darkness and the smelt will be where the plankton are and the salmon will be where the smelt are. As the sun rises, the plankton go deeper to dark cool waters near the thermocline.

2. Give your lure action either by stopping and going with your motor, by jigging, or by a mechanical device to impart that action to your lure or fly.

3. Fish the temperature. Find what depth 55 degrees is and fish that depth.

4. Change lures frequently if fish are not hitting yours. I use dark lures in early morning or when it is dark (black, blue, gray, green) and light lures (orange and yellow) on light or sunny days.

5. Use scent. I put scent on all my lures and bait, whether it is a worm, live smelt, fly or spoon. Fish are very scent sensitive and given a scentless lure or one with scent, they will go for the smell. I like Dr. Juice's salmon scent.

My top 5 tips for lakers

1. Fish the bottom.
2. Fish slowly.
3. Use scent.
4. Fish the deep drop-offs.
5. Use live bait.

My top tips for rainbows

1. Fish shallow sandy areas.
2. Fish the mouths of brooks.
3. Use night crawlers.
4. Use the same techniques and flies as for salmon.

My top tips for bass

1. Use rubber lures off structure and near shore.
2. Use hellgrammites, crawfish, and night crawlers.
3. In summer and winter fish slower and deeper.
4. In fall, jig using bucktail jigs.

My top five ice fishing tips

1. Make sure ice is 4" thick for walking and 6" for snowmobiles.
2. Use live bait and jig for lakers.
3. Fish near shore in very shallow water for rainbows.
4. Use a fish finder. This is the newest and greatest breakthrough for ice fishermen, as it can save hours of waiting for fish who are not where you are. I use a Vexilar Fish Finder which fits into a 5-gallon pail.

Catch & release?

Most of the time I practice it. But I also love to eat fresh fish!

What do I think has happened to the Lake Winni yellow perch?

The competition with other species, like white perch, salmon, and lakers, has forced them to warmer coves where the salmon and Lakers will not go. Also the use of Copper Sulfate, currently being used to kill milfoil, takes oxygen from the water, which kills the plankton, small fish, and eventually the perch and other fish. Opechee Lake has been heavily treated with Copper Sulfate and it has killed the smelt there.

What do I think has happened to the Lake Winni whitefish?

I think we still have some but no one seems to fish for them like the old timers did.

If I were NH Commissioner of Fish & Game, what initiatives would I take to improve Lake Winni angling?

Smiling Alan Nute in his AJs Meredith NH store. He's one fishing tackle store owner, who knows from which he speaks...not unlike three other Master Anglers, Bill Martel, Jim Warner, and Rick Davis, all of whom have had their own stores in the Lakes Region

I would stop the use of Copper Sulfate and spend the money trying to find a new way to get rid of milfoil. The Fish & Game biologists have basically done a good job of adjusting the salmon stocking to the number of smelt in the lake. (I recall back in the mid 1980s when they overstocked salmon, and the salmon the next year were skinny as pickerel!) That mistake moved me away from salmon fishing to bass fishing. But I believe there are too many small needle smelt now and few of the big jack smelt we use to have. I never find big smelt in the stomachs of fish anymore. Perhaps smelt should be netted and taken to hatcheries or other lakes to allow them to grow large and then re-stock them back in Lake Winni.

My favorite fishing stories

On occasions when either ice fishing or trolling all morning with no luck, a front, snowstorm, or squall will come upon the lake and fish will start hitting faster than you can manage them! My friends and I were ice fishing one cold winter morning out off Bear Island. We had not one flag on our tip ups all morning. Suddenly we found ourselves in a snowstorm - a real white out. As soon as we could see, there were a half dozen flags all up at the same time and we were hauling in trout! The lesson here is not to give up after hours of fishing, but change something - the lure, the speed, the depth ...or if you are powerful like God, the weather!

I was fishing one morning with a friend who had a new electric trolling motor. Halfway out, suddenly the motor disappeared! His mount had broken and his new motor was gone. Six months later a customer came into my store, and when I asked if he had caught anything, he said, "Yes, an electric motor!" Sure enough he had snagged my friend's motor while trolling past the same spot we had lost it!

My uncle Cyp, his son, and I fished the first Winni Ice Fishing derby in 1980. We won first and third in the laker contest! But this was one of the years when to win the big prize, you had to catch a trout with tag and then the tag number had to be drawn - with odds like the state lottery. My cousin caught a tagged trout and we rushed in to enter it. The big prize tag number was identical to his number in all digits...except for the last digit that missed by one number! We like the Derby better now that it is based on fish size more than just the luck of the draw...but then, luck is one of the most important ingredients in all angling!

My current favorite lures

People often ask me what my favorite lures are. This keeps changing with the seasons and when new lures come out, but I sell more of three lures than any others and I also would put them on one of my lines at all times. And two of them are new comers to the angling scene. What are they?

1. The Top Gun in various colors. I have sold over 3000 of these new spoons manufactured in Vermont.

2. The DB Smelt is the next new lure in various colors. "DB" stands for its inventor, Dave Broder, a New Hampshire native who makes this slim smelt-like lure. In summer and fall, the DB smelt is a killer lure.

3. The Sutton spoon, an old standby lure which comes in silver and copper or brass. I like the # 66 Suton.

4. But I also catch a lot of fish on a nightcrawler, rigged to troll behind the boat. Here's my method of rigging them:

- Run a thin wire with a tiny hooked end through the length of the crawler bring it out about an inch from the end of the crawler.
- Put a loop of your leader into the hooked end and pull it back through the bait.
- Attach a #4 hook to the end of the leader and snug up on the leader until the hook is up to the exit place in the crawler.
- Add a second hook to your leader just above where it enters the bait near its front
- Attach your leader with crawler to a swivel on your line to prevent twist

This series of photos show me rigging the bait as described:

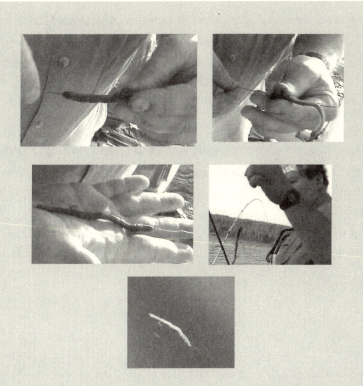

Top left: Step 1 in night crawler threading: pass the thin wire which has a tiny hook on one end through the bait and out about an inch from the other end.

Top Right: Step 2: hook your line in the small hook in the wire and pull the line through the bait and out where the wire came out, about an inch from the end.. Now fasten a hook to that end of the line and pull the line back so the hook is hidden in the bait.

Middle Left: Here's the rigged bait on your line with hook near the end.

Middle Right: Here's the completed night crawler rig, with second hook near the front, ready to be trolled behind the boat.

Bottom: Here's the rigged crawler in the water ready for a fish to take it. He uses them on down riggers as well as flat lining them behind the boat on the surface as well.

Favorite recipes for cooking various Lake Winni fish

My aunt has a recipe, which is a winner for salmon. She takes a whole fresh salmon, and stuffs the body cavity with a mix of crabmeat or other seafood, butter, and cracker crumbs. She bakes it for about 40 minutes and then pours white cheese sauce with peas over it. It is delicious!

Am I concerned about mercury levels in Lake Winni fish to the degree that I restrict my fish intake?

I'm not concerned, as we do not eat lake fish every day. Now even the farm-raised salmon are contaminated from PBCs and other chemicals from the environment and the fish food they feed them. They were probably much worse in the old days before we had any controls.

MASTER ANGLER Jason Parent
(22 Years of Lake Winni angling)

> "In a world where most men seem to spend their lives doing things they hate... fishing is at once an endless source of delight and an act of small rebellion..."
> — Robert Traver—

Jason Parent smiling while angling in the smile of the Great Spirit.

I realized a year ago while preparing this book that in 10 years, given the average age of the Master Anglers I had selected, that this book would be a book of posthumous anglers. For that reason, I began to search for several young Master Anglers who had achieved a measure of angling fame very early in their lives in order to give this book more longevity after many of us older anglers have passed. I chose two, both of whom already had excellent reputations as young guides on Lake Winni. The youngest one is Travis Williams at 29 years and the other is Jason Parent at age 32. Jason has only been fishing Lake Winni for 22 years (since he was 10), but he has been angling since he could walk.

I first heard about Jason Parent from another angler, who told me that this young Lake Winni guide was a highly successful but somewhat unconventional angler. After meeting Jason and getting to know him, I found him to be a creative fisherman, who is willing to experiment and try new things. He also fishes the Great Lakes for trout and salmon and has brought some lessons here from that experience. For example, Jason observed while fishing in the clear waters of the Great Lakes that by standing on the bow of the boat in 30 feet of water, one can see hundreds of Browns, salmon, and trout scattering off to the side as the boat trolls slowly through the water. By trolling just behind the boat, one's lures do not intersect the path of these fish which have moved 10-20 feet off to the side of the boat's path. So Jason became a believer of getting your lures out away from the boat by using side planers or outriggers of one kind or another which, he believes, results in significantly more hits. He often uses a Dipsy Diver attached to his line to get the lures out to the side. He has also invented his own "Jigging Machine" — which uses a sealed electric motor mounted in a metal box to which your line, attached to a release device, will jig with back and forth action needed to give the lure the action which entices fish to strike. I have one mounted to my boat, which is illustrated in this photo.

I'm fishing with one of Jason Parent's jigging machines mounted to the side of my boat. I have my fly line attached to the release on the arm of the machine, so that it will jig my fly, giving it more action and when a salmon hits, he will hook himself while releasing it from the release device.

Jason will custom make these for anglers for just over $200. My first year of using one of Jason's "Jigging Machines" resulted in many more strikes on my fly lines and lead core than previously, even without Bean Counter's empirical data being gathered! Of course, one can work his fly line him or herself manually, and then still get the thrill of the strike in hand! But you cannot work two at the same time...unless you have a Jigging Machine.

I now use one and swear by them! And if you want a young energetic perspective on angling and an interesting day of trolling on Lake Winni, give Jason a call to book a trip with him!

I'm a 32-year-old dedicated angler from the northern reaches of New Hampshire. I am married with two small children and I owe all my successes as a man to my beautiful wife of 8 years, Kari. We moved to Belmont, New Hampshire in 1996 and built a home in 2000. Our first son was born in August of 2000 and his name is Harrison Hunter Parent. Our second son arrived in February of 2002 and his name is Hayden Fischer Parent. I'm sure they will both be anglers!

I have been fishing since I was old enough to walk, and can never seem to get enough ice fishing, brook fishing, fly fishing, or slow trolling on one of New Hampshire's beautiful lakes, I just take it all in whenever possible. My deepest passions are embedded in New Hampshire's largest lake, which holds a bounty of wonderful fish. I have fished Lake Winnipesaukee for 22 years and learn more and more on each endeavor. Over the years I have accumulated a large resume of fishing lakes and ponds throughout New England and every year I try to add a new lake or pond to the list of accomplishments. If the lake has trout or salmon, chances are I have fished it; sometimes I do well but other times I just have to keep going back until I catch the drift.

Born in Berlin, New Hampshire, in 1973, I was quick to learn that a small city boy out in the country needed some hobbies to keep himself occupied. Thanks to my father and grandfather I did not have to look very far, as fishing and hunting were the popular choices among the Parent family men.

Left: That's me, Jason on the right, and my father and mentor on the left. I'm pretty excited holding my first trout in 1977.
Right: My grandfather holding a nice laker in 1978

I quickly learned that a worm and hook could bring a reward bounty of tasty brook trout and that a fly could tempt even the weariest of brown trout. When I turned 16 years old my first truck was a Chevy S10, and in the back were always a 12-foot aluminum boat and a 7.5 Sears Gamefisher motor. My tackle collection started at a young age, and it was not an unfamiliar sight in the North Country to see me toting my boat by hand down to the river or to a back woods pond such as Big Greenough Pond. As time went by, my appetite for bigger lakes grew and many a weekend I spent coming down to Belmont visiting my grandparents while sneaking out for early morning trolling on Winnipesaukee.

My gramp -- one of my mentors — with nice string of fish in 1967.

The fishing was not as good as it is now back then. The fish were small and skinny and the action was often slow, but the anticipation of a 7-pound salmon or a 12-pound lake trout always lurked in the back of my mind. Today, I am a fishing guide on Winnipesaukee and many of the other area lakes, and I owe all my good fortune and skills to my family and my ambition to be successful as a father, husband, and fisherman.

I've been fishing in Lake Winni for 14 years beginning when I was 16. I learned much myself through conversations with other anglers and trial and error. I am a self-taught lake fisherman and owe all my skills as an angler to determination and ambition, and of course my wife who lets me go fishing on the weekends. My fishing mentor and hero is also my fishing partner, my father. He has been there as my mentor and I, as his student, have been there for him. We fish together whenever possible and learn from each other whenever we can. He is not only my father, but he is also

You can see that my dad, here in this 1969 picture with brookies, was as excited about fishing as I was. That makes for good mentoring!

one of my best friends. I learned a lot of things not to do from my father. His methods sometimes seem out of touch, but often they prove more productive than I would have guessed. He is a master brook trout fisherman and he has shown me some of the most beautiful beaver dams and waterfalls in the North Country.

My favorite Lake Winni game fish

My favorite Winni game fish is the landlocked salmon for many reasons. Pound for pound, this fish fights its heart out every time he is in the precarious position of being hooked. Jumping and diving while displaying such antics as running the boat or playing dead make the salmon a worthy advisory during every trip.

Which do I prefer, lead core, fly rod, or downrigger fishing for salmon and trout?

A big assortment of the hotest new salmon lure on Lake Winni, the DB Smelt (DB are the initials of the creator of this new but highly successful salmon lure) which can be purchased at AJ's in Meredith.

I enjoy planer board fishing with light line in the spring for salmon, as it always seems productive. Planer boards are a floating device attached to a boom in the boat to take my lines about 10 yards out to the sides of my boat. There is a release device on the board which sets the hook when a fish hits and releases it. This set-up overcomes the problem in spring, when salmon are high up, of the boat spooking the fish directly behind or inline with the boat. The lures out to the side following the planer boards pass through the water to the boat's flanks where the fish have not been frightened by the boat.

Lead core is the most productive way I have found to catch lake trout but a good downrigger bounced off the bottom creates an aggressive hit many times as well.

My favorite fishing months

May and June, at dawn and dusk or on cloudy days.

My best trolling speed

With GPS in spring for Salmon: 2.2-2.4 MPH; summer lakers or salmon 1.7 to 1.9 This depends on lures and presentation.

Chart of fishing depths and best lures

	Salmon	Lakers	Rainbows
May:	On Top 4-10' DB Smelt/Smelt Rig	On Top 5-20' Copper Wobblers	On Top 5-15' Grey Ghost (w/beads)
June:	15-30' DB Smelt/Smelt Rig	On Bottom Wobblers/Sutton	15-30' Repala J7
July:	30-65' DB Smelt/Smelt Rig	40-70' Smelt Rig/Sutton	40-65' Dodger Smelt Rig
August:	50-75' DB Smelt/Smelt Rig	40-70' Smelt Rig/Sutton	40-65' Dodger Smelt Rig
September:	50-65' DB Smelt/Smelt Rig	40-70' Smelt Rig/Sutton	40-65' Dodger Smelt Rig

Ice fishing

I love to jig through the ice with my automatic jigging machine called "Jig-by-J." I use bucktail jigs, green and yellow or red and white and I usually set the machines over 15-35 ft of water on a drop off.

My largest salmon, laker, rainbow

Salmon: 7.25 pounds in 1996 on a Smelt Rig at 60' deep
Laker: 6.59 pounds in 2001 on CopperWobblers at 40' deep
Rainbow: 4.39 pounds in 1998 on a Smelt Rig at 35' deep

Stories about these monsters

The 7.25-pound salmon was a difficult fish to land but we were well equipped and had just returned from our yearly excursion to Lake Ontario. The fish hit on a downrigger I had just popped to check the bait. Often times when we bounce over a shelf or drop the downrigger balls off bottom the baits will get messed up. Usually, I release the rod from the downrigger and put it back in the rod holder and let it ride up nice and slow. Often you will get a strike after about 5-10 seconds. This fish hit and instantly broke water right in the prop wash. I knew right away it was a big fish and set the hook with a quick snap of the wrist. The fight was on. The fish took line to the port side of the boat and ran up along side the boat and then doubled back toward the downrigger cable. This taught me a lesson. Get those cables up out of the water when you have a monster on! Luckily I was able to use my 8 1/2-foot rod to steer the fish around the downrigger cable and away from the motor. After a short fight and a couple of quick runs the fight was over and the fish was in the net. I am strictly catch and release unless someone really wants their fish so that beauty was weighed and set free to grow and break lines in the future.

Passing on to others my angling skills

I have spent many of hours on the boat teaching my brother tricks and tactics to catch more fish and there is no doubt in my mind that he will someday soon teach me the meaning of monster fish. He recently landed a 14.5-pound steelhead on Lake Ontario and took 9th place in the Lake Ontario derby steelhead division. He is a true up and coming angler who is working toward his guide's license for 2004. I look forward to teaching my sons to fish. My wife is already an excellent outdoorswoman.

My top 5 tips for salmon

1. Lure Presentation. Make sure your speed is appropriate for your bait.
2. Water Temperature. Watch it, know it, and know what it is at different depths.
3. Use 4-6 lb test leaders lines and have good equipment.
4. Listen to other anglers on the radio, share information and keep a log of your endeavors.
5. Catch and release. (Help the population grow and get bigger.)

My top 5 tips for lakers

1. Go Slow!
2. Go Slower!!
3. Fish the Bottom.
4. Lakers like busy baits - add action to your lure (strip it or jig it).
5. Catch and release (help the population especially if ice fishing).

My top 5 tips for rainbows

1. Quick speed with streamers on jigging machines, especially in spring.
2. Use small bait. Rainbows have the smallest mouths in the trout family.
3. Slow the baits down with warm weather. Use small flies or spinners.
4. Fish around inlets or outlets to find moving water or current.
5. Ice fishing: stay shallow on sandy bottom with small baits.

My top 5 ice fishing tips

1. Jig and when you get tired, jig some more with cut bait on a bucktail jig.
2. Stay shallow with small baits for rainbows.
3. Use your knowledge of summer shelves and ledges in the winter.
4. Catch and release. Many lake trout get killed during ice fishing.
5. Use a variety of baits - shiners, smelt, suckers and/or jigs.

Catch & release

I do practice catch and release all year round except during the Derby. I wish more people would educate themselves on catch and release and put back more fish.

What do I think has happened to the Lake Winni yellow perch?

I think they have become bait to larger feeding salmon and lake trout. As fish grow in overall size, the fish they eat also grow. Young perch are a tasty morsel for a hungry salmon.

What do I think has happened to the Lake Winni White Fish?

Not sure, but I would guess an increase in other feeding fish has limited the amount of feed available and possibly the shad's feeding patterns were disrupted and they have suffered.

If I were NH Commissioner of Fish & Game, what initiatives would I take to improve Lake Winni angling?

I would increase the legal length limit and institute a slot limit to save the breeding fishing.

Favorite fishing stories:

Jason Parent waits for a strike. He's fishing two lines stacked on one downrigger line with a fly on one and a DB Smelt on the other

Several years back, I was fishing in the Winni Derby. I was about 18 at the time. My brother Dustin was 8 years old, and my then girlfriend, who is now my wife, was 16. I talked them into joining me for a day on Lake Winni. It was Saturday morning, and as usual the weather was not very good, but I had spent two days prior working on my 12-foot aluminum boat, just for that reason. I had cut two broom handles about 4 feet long and secured them in the oarlocks. I then improvised a make shift canopy for my boat out of an old piece of canvas tarp. With lots of rope and tie downs, I managed to make a pretty nice cuddy cabin for my brother and girlfriend. I knew with the bad weather that our trip to Alton Bay would be cut short if they could not stay warm. I taped off all the edges with duct tape and painted a big fish head on the front with large teeth. Then I painted a large fin on either side of the boat, and wrote a phrase on either side "It was this big!" We fished all day, or should I say they slept all day, and I fished in the cold rain with two portable cannon mini-trolls downriggers and two lead core lines. I never got a bite that day but I got more thumbs up from other anglers then ever before, and still to this day, my boat, now a 21 foot Proline, has never received so much attention.

Favorite recipes for cooking various Lake Winni fish

Take a nice lake trout. Remove the head and guts of the fish. Then purchase 3 pounds of native shrimp and 1 pound of butter. Get yourself 1 box of seafood stuffing and a turkey sewing needle and thread. Stuff your lake trout with shrimp, 3 sticks of real butter and seafood stuffing.

Jason has a large salmon which just tripped his line on one of his downriggers being trolled at 2 MPH and 40 feet deep.

Then sew the fish closed. Wrap him in about 10 layers of tin foil and bury it a bed of deep coals from fire. Leave the fish there for about 3 hours then remove carefully. Unwrap the fish and you have a meal fit for 10 kings.

Am I concerned about mercury levels in Lake Winni fish to the degree that I restrict my fish intake?

I rarely keep fish from the lake, thus I don't have any concern regarding mercury levels.

MASTER ANGLER TRAVIS WILLIAMS ("Cool Water")
(15 Years of Lake Winni Angling

The fishing is far more important than the fish.

Travis Williams on the right and the author on the left in Travis' slick boat, "Cool Water" on their way to a good salmon fishing ground.

About 5 years ago, while fishing in the Spring Salmon Derby, I was trolling in an old hole in the northern part of Lake Winni with little luck. But I spotted an open boat circling around the same hole I was fishing and every 10 minutes or so, I'd see the 5 guys in this boat whooping and hollering and netting good-sized fish. I even followed them with my downriggers set near bottom, but no fish. They must have taken 10 fish in an hour of trolling and my friend and I had not a single strike! That's enough to discourage even the most positive optimists and sink me into depression!

"Cool Water Charters" is the name of the young Master Angler Travis William's guiding service. He will take you out in his well equipped boat and teach you a lot about catching Lake Winni salmon or trout.

I finally swallowed my pride and after seeing the name "Cool Water" on the side of the boat, came up close enough to ask what their secret was. One guy with a baseball hat said, "My name's Travis and we're trolling lead-core with live smelt, bouncing it off the bottom. We're catching lakers fast as we get down there." Now, I had never trolled lead-core with live bait...so my eyes ...and hopefully my mind opened. He shouted across to me to go to his "Cool Water" Web site, which I did later that night when I got back home. A year later while in Germany for my 4-month teaching tour, courtesy of the Fulbright professorship I had, I began an email back and forth with his father, Bob, who kept me up-to-date on what the ice fishing was like.

This led to more communication on the Internet fishing board and on the Cool Water Web site: www.fishlakewinni.com, where Travis Williams was often reporting big and numerous catches...even when most anglers were not. Finally, we had the opportunity to fish together in his older boat. He since has purchased a new and nifty "Cool Water" boat, which he uses for his guiding of salmon fishing parties in spring and summer. He is the youngest of the Master Anglers in this book, not quite 30 years of age! But he is as intense, dedicated, and as successful a Lake Winni angler as can be found anywhere. I also wanted a few younger Master Anglers to give this book some longevity long after us old time anglers have gone on to the better fishing waters with the Great Spirit. You can book a charter with Travis on his website: www.fishlakewinni.com.

Father and mentor of Travis Williams, Bob Williams with nice laker

I've been angling 16 years on Lake Winni. I began at age 14. As a youngster my father would take me fishing. Like a dedicated father, he would untangle my lines and listen to my cries. As soon as I could hold a rod, my father would lug me off brook trout and pond fishing. This is just the way my father is. I have him to thank for me being the sportsman that I am today. He always took me both hunting and fishing and if the "guys" were going and they didn't want the children to go, then my father would stay behind with me.

When I moved to the Lakes region in 1988, as you might imagine, I began fishing the "Big Pond." Almost every day after school my mother would drop me off at the Center Harbor docks with a half dozen smelt, tackle box, and my rod. I would fish until dark, and on many occasions would come home with no fish, a runny nose, and somehow, a big smile on my face. I loved to fish those docks no matter what. In the rain, wind, and even snow, like a dedicated sportsman day in and day out, I would put my time in. I did manage to catch some pretty nice fish ...as well as colds and frostbite.

Though a big part of my fishing education, as you might imagine, the dock fishing grew old. My friend, Steve Ulm's family, owned Ulm's Bait and Tackle in Centre Harbor. Steve and I began trolling the Bay in his 14-

foot rowboat with one clamp-on Big Jon downrigger and two lead core rods. We did quite well and caught many fish and after a good day you could usually find us pounding our chests at one of the local bait shops!

I have many fishing mentors. There are many people who affect your life as you grow older, and, as such, many people who affect how, where, and why you do what you do, as a fisherman. However, I think the one person that deserves the honor of my respect as my hero, would have to be my dad. Bottom line, if it were not for him lugging me around when I was young, I would probably not be sitting in front of my computer right now filling out this Master Angler questionnaire because I might have been into shopping instead of fishing.

Travis Williams tied to a big salmon

I learned so much from my dad that I could write a book on it. The most important thing he taught me was good ethics and a true love for the outdoors. He instilled a love for the water and the woods in me, and I know many people reading this, right now, know exactly what I'm referring to ... and if you need a little help, close your eyes. It is May 10th and you and two close friends have nothing to do all day except fish. It's 5 in the morning; the water is flat as ice and salmon are rising around your boat like mackerel in a feeding frenzy. All you can hear is the soft chug-chug of the motor and the drag of your lead core and maybe occasional loon music. You take in a deep breath and you realize that this is what it is all about. Just thinking about it gives you that feeling in your stomach that you haven't had since you were 10 years old and Santa was coming in the morning. Now I think I have your attention. Here is where the ethics come into play. Having such a deep-seated love to do these things, I would never jeopardize this. I could not imagine not being able to enjoy the feeling of a bent rod with a furious salmon thrashing on the other end.

What's my favorite Lake Winni game fish?

Salmon. There is nothing like the fight of a salmon and the fury with which they strike your lure. They are great leapers and are made of pure muscle. Pound for pound, the salmon is the best fighter.

Which do I prefer, lead core, fly rod, or downrigger fishing for salmon and trout?

Downrigger fishing is my favorite. I like this the best because I use light tackle, and this enables the fisherman to feel every pulsating move of the fish, once the fish has struck and is free of the downrigger. You also need your angling skills to bring the fish to the boat without breaking the fish off. I catch most of my fish this way. But at different times of the year, lead core can be more effective for getting fish to hit your offerings.

My favorite fishing months

My favorite fishing months are early season, April and May, and I also enjoy a lot of success in September. This is also a beautiful month to be on the lake. I enjoy first light and have found this to be the most productive time. However, when the bite is on, it can vary throughout the day.

My favorite depths and lures for each fish

May to October:
Salmon: trolling 5 to 20'.deep. Hardware color depends on the day, but copper, gold and orange variations all are effective.
Lake Trout: drag live bait on the bottom in early season and use white, copper and orange spoons just off bottom in deep holes late in the season.
Ice fishing: My most common depth is 2-3 ft under the ice for rainbow and right on the bottom for Lakers.

My best trolling speed

Trolling speed varies. Depending on bait, time of year, and conditions. My most productive overall speed would be 2.0 to 2.5 mph.

My Largest Salmon, laker, rainbow, and bass in Lake Winni:

Travis Williams with a nice lake Trout caught on a Sutton #61 at 50' deep while trolling slowly at 1.5 MPH.

Salmon: 6.5 pounds. in April on live smelt with 3 colors of lead core with a 100'mono leader.
Laker: 7 pounds, in May on live smelt, dragging bottom with lead core line in 35 ft of water.
Rainbow: 6 pounds, in June on a copper and orange needlefish at 3 colors of lead core line.
Largemouth bass: 6.9 pounds, on live bait on the bottom.

Passing on to others my angling skills

I do this constantly in my professional guiding. Customers are always asking questions, and I enjoy passing my knowledge of fishing onto others and helping them succeed. I'm also active on the Web, passing on to others my latest tips, how deep I'm getting them, what lures. The only thing I do not broadcast is where I'm catching them. Being a professional guide on Lake Winni, I do not want to have my guests be mobbed with too many anglers!

My top 5 tips for salmon, lakers and rainbows

1. **Get out there early**. Many anglers get a late start, and I will have already landed several fish by the time some get out.

2. **Change what you do**. Do not just run what you always run and fish where you always fish. If they're not hitting, try something else; if that doesn't work, move! I always try to fish around baitfish. I will turn on my X-15 fish finder and just cruise an area before I even set up. I'm looking for smelt. If I find what I'm looking for, then I'll fish that area.

3. **Learn the seasons and the body of water that you fish.** Fish do different things in different times of year and in different bodies of water. When do the smelt spawn and where? How deep should you fish in the

fall and why? If you really want to be a good fisherman there is much that goes in to it — lots to learn. Educate yourself on the body of water, the feed of species you target, water temps, thermocline, water color, weather, currents, trolling speeds, scents, size, and structure of the lake.

Travis Williams and two friends with a nice catch of salmon from "Cool Waters."

4. **Lure speed and action.** Pay attention to your lure, making sure it is doing what it should and troll at the speeds that you should be for what you are running be it a fly, live bait, hardware, or dodgers.

5. **Ask questions and read up on fishing.** I often find myself, when telling people about different tips and techniques, sharing with them tips I have learned or read from others. I ask questions and I read, because it is fun to learn. Everyone has a variation on how they fish and what they do. What they do may not work for you. However, both reading and asking others can be productive and you can learn so much! Reading books like this one, which offers 600 years of angling wisdom from 15 Master Anglers, is a great short-cut which can save you years of learning the hard way. And now Web sites, like mine are appearing which are also excellent sources of information. Go to: www.fishlakewinni.com. On my site, I have added a Message Board were people share stories and angling tips. It's fun and most definitely educational.

My top 5 tips for bass

1. Once again, it is most important to **educate yourself to the body of water** that you are fishing. Since this book is about Lake Winni, I'll share my tips for it.

2. **Know what the bass do at different times of the year.** This is by far the best tip I can give. What works in the spring is not necessarily going to work in the late summer months.

3. **Match your line with the water.** Lake Winni is a clear lake and you should match the clarity of the water with the pound test of the line that you are going to use. When smallmouth bass fishing I use 8 to 12-pound test line. If you were fishing down south, people would look at you like you had two heads if you told them you were going to fish line that light!

Travis letting out line to get it behind the boat. We sometimes fish right in the wake 20-30 feet back in spring, as it seems to attract the salmon. At other times when the water is calm we go back 100-150 feet since the boat spooks them in the clear waters of Lake Winni -- especially in spring when the salmon are near the surface and easily scared.

4. **Keep it simple**. A good friend of mine is one of the best bass fishermen on Lake Winni. This tip is one he always tells me: "Keep it simple." For example when we fish in a tournament, I'll want to bring all kinds of different baits and he will scold me saying, "just bring what you have confidence in."

5. **Fish the structure**. Lake Winni has incredible structure. Utilize it, finding some good humps with grass and rocks. In the summer and early fall months, fish these spots. Have more than one spot to fish. If I fish a spot and there is everything I want like right depth, good grass, and rocks, but no bait, I will move to another spot until I find bait and fish there.

My top 5 ice-fishing tips

1. Again, it really depends upon what you are targeting for species. However, the basics are a good start. Always make sure you are using the right pound test line and that it is good and strong. Don't neglect your equipment. Change your line from time to time and keep it fresh. I usually rig all my lines and jig rods with 8#. green mono with a 6# fluorocarbon leader. We usually fish for white perch when ice fishing; however we will also fish for trout.

2. When fishing for **white perch** you should first fish in the correct depth of water 20 - 40 feet seems to work for us. We have found that the mouths of Coves seem to be pretty productive fishing spots, two feet off the bottom with live smelt. White perch are a school fish (They run in large groups) so if we find a "hot hole", we will pull the tip-ups out and begin to jig with either a small Swedish Pimple or just a dead smelt. Sometimes you can fill a 5-gallon pail in just a few minutes when you find one of these "hot holes!" And once again, if you set up and are not catching anything, move! They run in schools and you may make one small move and then suddenly you are into them!

3. **Lake Trout:** When ice fishing for lake trout, I prefer to jig. I use

buck-tail jigs, and red and white are my favorite colors. I use cut sucker bait to dress the hook and give the jig a little more action and smell. You can catch lake trout in almost any depth of water; however I like 40 to 50 feet and I try to fish a sandy bottom on the edge of a deeper water drop-off. When I jig, I just move the line a little, almost fanning the bottom of the lake. I also like to chum the hole with chopped up fish. On Lake Winni, you are allowed two holes so with the one that I'm not jigging, I will fish a piece of sucker right on the bottom.

4. **Rainbow Trout:** This can be a great deal of work, but also productive. I like to fish a sandy bottom in 2-6 feet of water; I will drill several holes in a line (10-15) than chum each hole with 4-5 salmon eggs. I than will rig a jig rod with a small hook and a pin smelt I also will have a tip up in, with a small smelt or power bait just under the ice. I will run around peeking in the holes counting the salmon eggs if I find any missing I plop my smelt in that hole. This can be productive and a pain in the butt.

5. **Use your head.** Since all I ice fish for is the top 3 species, my last tip is one that I like to practice when guiding. When I have customers hooked up with fish, I always tell them, "enjoy yourself." I say this because that is why we are fishing - to have fun and to enjoy ourselves. You are going to lose fish and you are going to make mistakes, so try not to get discouraged. Just have fun, keep fishing, and enjoy "The Smile of the Great Spirit!"

• Catch and Release?

For the most part, I do practice catch and release. When I'm guiding, if people want to keep fish, then we keep fish. When fun fishing, as I call it, we usually release all of them, unless we hurt a fish. I see nothing wrong with keeping fish to eat. I believe in the work of the Fish and Game biologists and I believe that they would set smaller bag limits if that were necessary.

• What do I think has happened to the yellow perch?

If I had to come up with a guess about the yellow perch, I know that the Lake has been cleaned up quite a bit from the past and the yellow perch may just not have the forage in terms of algae that they had in the past.

• My favorite fishing stories:

I have many stories but this one ties in to a couple of my previous answers. I spoke of my good fishing friend, Steve. Steve and I love to fish Squam Lake and we use to do very well there. Much like any other day, Steve and I fished the lake in his 14-foot rowboat equipped with 9.9HP kicker. We met at my house early in the morning. We then piled my rods and tackle into his truck and headed off. Sipping coffee and rubbing sleepy eyes, we drove from my house in Centre Harbor, which was just up the hill from Steve's, to Sandwich Beach on Squam Lake. When we launched the boat there, the water was flat and the summer fog was just lifting off the water. We trolled out in front of the beach, working a couple of good humps. The sun was not even peeking up over the mountains that surround this beautiful lake as we began to set up our lines. Steve had one clamp-on Big Jon downrigger and we would usually run a rod off the ball and run a stacker line above that. Off each side of the boat we would run a leadcore rod which we would hold, since there were no rod holders.

When we first started fishing together I loved to fish with my favorite lure, a Sutton spoon in copper and silver, #44. But Steve hated Sutton spoons. (Steve has a dog, which he named "Sutton." Enough said.) After a few minutes we landed our first fish, a nice three-pound Salmon. This fish was just one of several more to come. Around 6 in the morning, we started to notice a couple of other boats that were fishing in the area beginning to come closer. Finally, a man in one of the boats hollered over, "What are you guys using?" We told him how deep and with what lures we were using. These honest tips must not have helped very much as we never saw any of the boats around us land a fish.

We ended the day around 10 AM and landed 12 nice fish. Not a bad day for two kids in a 14 foot rowboat! Later that day, with a couple of the nice fish we had caught, we went to one of the local bait shops, as we loved to show off our success. We were there for awhile, when a couple of guys came in telling tall tales about these two kids in a rowboat this morning at Squam Lake. The men were saying how every time they passed them, the boys had a fish on …or even a double. The men were complaining that there seemed to be no fish since they didn't have a strike. Steve asked,"What did the two kids look like and where were you fishing?" One of the guys replied "Over by Sandwich Beach, and they were both wearing baseball hats." Steve than asked, "Like this?" and tilted his hat a bit. The guy caught on, "That was you two!" pointing at Steve and me. We confessed that it was the two of us, and we began giving the guy some tips and ideas for his next trip. The two guys just could not believe that we caught so many fish when they had not a strike. They looked at us with an amazed look in their eyes. I love this story because these gentlemen had a big fancy high-tech boat with four electric downriggers and Steve and I just had his little rowboat. It was a great feeling of triumph! It was also nice to be in a position to help the men. I hope they had better luck the next day.

Jim Wallace at the Rotary Ice Derby, explains the Rotary's million-dollar contributions to needy causes.

Close up of the Maynard Marvel, Master Angler Al Stewart's favorite lure...and that of many other anglers.

Master Angler Al Stewart

Alan Nute with a selection of his best flies

Master Angler Alan Nute

An attractor attached between the downrigger ball and cable.

The Barbara Cottom streamer fly

Master Angler Barbara Cottom

Author's son John with first laker, early 1970's

The old days of peaceful boats of real beauty, when top speed was 35 mph.

Master Angler Bill Martel in his store

Master Angler Carl Gephardt with big rainbow trout caught on a fly

Master Angler Chuck French tying flies by the fireplace

Master Angler Chuck French's grandsons, Tom and Will MacThee already tying their own flies—an art passed down to them by their mentor grandfather.

Chuck French's son, Andy and friend, Ed, early in the morning learning from Dad

Bill Wahll, aka "The Duck"

Hal Lyon's Angler Fishing boat with 150 HP Suzuki, kicker, and new electric downriggers -- a fishing machine!

Mario's fish retrieving dog, Tag, with salmon, resting after her beer.

Hal Lyon's place on East Bear Island

At the end of the day . . .

Author's grand children, Miranda, Heidi, and Hans holding a nice string of smallmouth bass in 1987

Baked, stuffed, Lake Winni trout!

A selection of Master Anger Jason Parent's DB Smelt lures

Master Angler and fly tier, Jim Warner, works on tying his famous streamer creation, the "Lake Winni Smelt."

Left: A large order of Jim Warner's hand-tied flies.

Right: The popular Gray Ghost and Bicentennial Smelt tied by Jim Warner

Left: Master Angler Mario DeCarolis
Right: His 7.99-pound salmon

A Memorial to Master Angler Paul Phillipe

Master Angler Rick Davis

a big laker caught by
Master Angler Steve Perry

Master Angler Ted. St. Onge trolling slowly

Master Angler Travis Williams approaches the dock at sunrise

Author's son Roy, with small perfect eating size bass

CHAPTER 14

The Chart of Secrets and the Top Lake Winni Salmon Lures

"When the first star sank slowly to the bottom of the lake the great fish followed and was gone from sight. I understood the water and I knew it was not time to catch a fish."
— Sven Berlin —

The "Chart of Secrets" following shows by month and for each species of cold water game fish, the average depth, favorite lure, and trolling speeds averaged for each of the 15 Master Anglers cumulative 600 years of fishing experience.

The average trolling speeds from the 15 Master Anglers are as follows:

Salmon and Rainbows 1.8 mph
Lakers 1.6 mph

Chart of secret depths and lures by month and fish

	Salmon	Lakers	Rainbows
APRIL:	Top (or 1 color) Streamer flies, Top Guns, DB Smelt	5' Suttons streamers	Top (or 1 color) streamers
MAY:	8' or 2 colors Streamers, Suttons, Top Guns, Live smelt DB Smelt	15' deep or 3 colors Copper Mooselooks streamers, Suttons	5' streamers
JUNE:	18' or 4 colors Live smelt, streamers, Top Guns, DB Smelt	32' or 7 colors Copper Mooselooks, DB Smelt, Needlefish Top Guns, Suttons	15' or 3 colors Suttons, streamers, Needlefish
JULY:	30' or 6 colors Live smelt, Suttons, Top Guns, DB Smelt	44' or 9 colors Copper Mooselooks, Suttons, Needlefish	24 feet or 5 colors Top Gun Needlefish
AUGUST:	36' or 8 colors Live smelt, Suttons, Top Guns, Needlefish DB Smelt	48' or 10 colors Copper Mooselooks, Suttons	31' or 7 colors Top Guns Needlefish
SEPTEMBER:	32' or 7 colors Live smelt, streamers, Top Guns, DB Smelt, Suttons	51' or 10 colors Copper Mooselooks, Suttons, Needlefish	28 'or 7 colors streamers Needlefish

ICE FISHING: 5-10 feet from bottom for Lake Trout in 40' of water using live smelt on tip-ups or jigging with lead head jigs. For Rainbows, in very shallow water 1-10' just under the ice with small smelt or night crawlers

THE CURRENT HOTTEST SALMON FLIES FOR LAKE WINNI

The Master Anglers' 6 most popular salmon streamer flies (all tied by Master Angler Alan Nute), from left to right: The Lake Winni Smelt (created by Master Angler Jim Warner); The Maynard Golden Marvel; the Pumpkin Head (creator: Alan Nute); the Red Marabou; the Fire Smelt (creator: Alan Nute) and; the Grey Ghost

The current best salmon flies for both spring and summer trolling on Lake Winni, according to the 15 Master Anglers are as follows:

- **Lake Winni Smelt**
- **Maynard Marvel**
- **Pumpkin Head**
- **Red Maribou**
- **Fire Smelt**
- **Grey Ghost**

THE CURRENT HOTTEST SALMON LURES

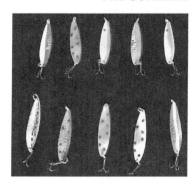

An assortment of the hot new Lake Winni salmon lures, the Top Guns, from the Moosalamoo Shoe-Horn Co. out of Rutland, VT.

Other than the flies, there is a lot of hardware available for salmon trolling. However, it is interesting that 3 lures seem to have risen to be the hottest ones on Lake Winni for salmon trolling all season long. Though some of the old timers will still stick with their old standby Mooselooks, the lures most touted and used by our Master Anglers include 2 new ones to the salmon trolling scene here, a difficult achievement given the years of the old traditional lures. These new ones among the top three are the Top Gun, the DB Smelt, and the old stand-by, Sutton. Next most popular are the Needlefish, Flash King, Mooselook (the more tarnished the copper ones become, the better they seem to produce!) and ChevChase. These lures are great for salmon but also good for rainbows and Lakers. I'd like to say a word about each of the top 3.

Top Gun

The Top Gun is a simple concave metal spoon with a small treble hook at the end, which comes in a variety of colors. Certain colors seem to be in demand during different times of the season, but mostly dark colors for dark or less light days, and brighter colors for sunny days. The Top Guns only appeared a couple years ago in AJ's Bait and Tackle owned by Master Angler Alan Nute, who used them, found them to work, and has been selling them by the thousands ever since. Already, the Top Guns have taken some of the biggest and most salmon in the spring derby. They were developed by Bill Abrahamovich.

The Winni Top Gun is the lure which won the 2000 Winni Salmon Derby. This lure and the DB Smelt have emerged as 2 of the top 3 lures for salmon on Lake Winni in the past few years.

The cable flasher which attaches in-line with the downrigger cable just above the ball to attract salmon or trout to the lure which is on a release just above the flasher, from the Moosalamoo Shoe-Horn Company.

Bill has another popular older lure, the ChevChase. He wanted to design a lure thinner than the Chev Chase for use in lake Champaign, and the Top Gun was the result. Top Guns are painted in many colors. Each has a treble hook made in France. The manufacturer, Moosalamoo, is from Burlington, Vermont and they also make dodgers and an interesting "Cable Flasher" which hooks to the downrigger ball, as an attractor. Master Anglers Travis Williams, Alan Nute, and I use a set of the old Dave Davis spinners for the same use, with our lure attached to the release just about the attractor spinners.

The Moosalamoo Company was originally started by a young machinist, Stanley Abrahamovich, who enjoyed fishing and was always trying to find a better way to catch more fish. His son, Bill now runs the business. At that time, a lot of other avid fishermen were developing a lot of other New England favorites, like the Mooselook and Sutton lures. The name "Shoe-horn" was a nickname for a flasher used with copper or leadcore line that helped to attract game fish, because of the vibration and flash it created. In 1984, after many years of developing flutter spoons, dodgers, trolling spoons, and other fish catching items, "The Moosalamoo Shoe-horn Company was formed and trademarked, "Moosalamoo," which stands for "Lake of Silver fish."

The ChevChase, another popular lure from the Moosalamoo Shoe-Horn Company.

The Original Chev Chase lure, mentioned by several of our Master Anglers, was patented in 1939 and remains one of New England's favorite trout lures. What makes the Chev Chase unique is a wire head harness that absorbs the shock of the strike and a red flipper in the tail that entices more strikes. "Top-Gun" was developed to fit the niche between the small and large Chev Chase. It is a top trolling performer, and a great downrigger lure.

They recently created a new lure called the "Mini-Gun" which has become a big producer at Lake Champlain, as the "Top-Gun" has become a new Lake Winni top producer, along with the DB Smelt and the old standby, the Sutton, according to our Master Anglers.

DB Smelt

DB Smelt

This popular lure is also a very thin spoon with treble hook on the end, which has varied colored tape actually baked onto it. DB comes from Dave Broder, the creator of this lure. Dave, an ardent angler from Berlin, New Hampshire, was fishing one day in Christine Lake when he saw a huge school of smelt splashing on the surface by a large rock. Dave scooped up a handful of them and was in awe of their iridescent sparkling colors. He went home and created his DB Smelt in 1998, modeling it after these Christine Lake Smelt. Each is still handmade, though Dave has reduced the steps from 15 to 6 to create each. The DB Smelt is colored by various tapes which are baked onto it. This lure is in much demand, having taken some of the best salmon of the season last year. One of the young guides, Jason Parent, swears by the DB Smelt.

A variety of lures made by Sutton. This Naples, New York Company had its beginnings in 1864 when Mr. Sutton, a jeweler who liked to troll for lakers and walleyes created his own spinner using his jewelry tools. He caught fish with his homemade lure and he began to make them for friends which led to his business being established. He always used real silver plate as he knew that a spectrascope shows that silver reflects the most "warm light" in low light conditions. My favorite and that of several other Master Anglers is the silver-copper #61. I like to use the thin #61 or #44 with hammered finish as it will retain action even when trolled very slowly.

Given the strong tradition of angling here in New Hampshire, It is quite an accomplishment for these two new lures to become competitive with the lures which have stood the test of time like the Mooselooks and the Suttons, which is the next on my list of the top three lures for Salmon on Lake Winni.

The Sutton Spoon

The Sutton has been around for as long as I can remember and even much longer. Mr. Sutton was a jeweler and the founder of the Sutton Company in 1864 in Naples, New York in the Finger Lakes region. Back in those days jewelers were the people with the tools and know-how to make fishing lures. He designed a Sutton Spinner with tandem treble hooks which was popular for catching walleyes and lakers on nearby Lake Canandaigua, where Mr. Sutton had a cottage. Fishing was highly competitive even back then. Mr. Sutton kept his lure a secret until word got out about it and he made a few for friends. Soon after he decided to go into business making them by hand in his jewelry business.

Hand-line fishing was the way of those times and they needed a lure that would flutter even at slow speeds. This led to the very light silver hammered Sutton, still popular today. Suttons always contain real silver-plate on their lures as silver gives maximum "warm color" reflection in low light as evidenced by a spectroscope. In 1929, Mr. Sutton passed on and the tools and dies were purchased by Mr. Stafford, the father of the current owner, Jim Stafford. In the early years of hand made Suttons, the company sold about 1200 spinners and 400 spoons each year. Now a days, according to Jim Stafford, they sell about 75,000 Sutton spoons each year.

The most popular Suttons today are the #s 44 and 61 in copper and silver that come in two versions. The most popular is a light hammered one that maintains its flutter even when trolling very slowly. The standard Sutton needs faster speed to maintain its action. The Sutton comes with a welded-in treble hook on the end. It comes in a variety of metals (silver, copper, and brass), sizes and thickness.

My favorite, and that of several other Master Anglers, is the Sutton, #61 with silver on one side and copper on the other. When I am trolling very slowly, when laker fishing, I like the thin Sutton as it will continue its action even at very slow speeds. Master Angler Mario DeCarolis and I like to put a small thin strip of red florescent tape on our Suttons to give them a bit of color, having learned this from our friend, Bean Counter from his empirical studies. It is said he caught a significantly higher number of fish on the Sutton with red stripe, which he fished on the right side of his boat (the experimental side) than he did on the "control" Suttons without the stripe which were fished on the left side of his boat over 6 years of trials. Mr. Sutton created a winner way back 150 years ago, which has stood the test of time. Last year the Vermont record lake trout, weighing 35 pounds was caught in Lake Willoughby on a Sutton.

This chapter gave the novice or expert angler a "heads-up" with the Chart of Secrets which is shared for the first time in this book with the average trolling speed, depths and best lures by month of the 15 Master Anglers in their six centuries of angling experience in Lake Winnipesaukee.

This information can save you years of experimenting to find what lures, speeds and depths work best in Lake Winnipesaukee, the well known Maine salmon lakes like Sabago, Moosehead, Grand Forks, or in any glacial lakes in North America. It will also save you considerable time and money, by our listing the best flies and lures to invest in for fishing Lake Winnipesaukee salmon and trout. Though there are interesting differences among the depths and lures of the 15 Master Anglers, this is the first time an average has been calculated from 15 expert anglers and shared for the public. These are secrets many have kept for generations. You will notice, however, that we're not giving away the places to fish. We want you to have some fun finding them and they are well distributed all over Lake Winnipesaukee. Watch for the angling boats!

CHAPTER 15

STATE OF NEW HAMPSHIRE RECORD FRESH WATER FISH

SPECIES	LENGTH	WEIGHT	PLACE	TOWN	DATE	ANGLER	STATE
Landlocked Salmon	36.00"	18 lbs. 8 oz.	Pleasant Lake	New London	8/30/1914	Mr. P.H. Killelea	MA
Landlocked Salmon	34.50"	18 lbs. 8 oz.	Pleasant Lake	New London	8/31/1942	Mrs. Letty M. Clark	NH
Brown Trout	32.50"	16 lbs. 6 oz.	Connecticut River	Pittsburg	7/4/1975	Ken Reed, Jr.	CT
Rainbow Trout	35.50"	15 lbs. 7.2 oz.	Pemigewasset River	Bristol	9/16/1996	Lance King	NH
Brook Trout	25.50"	9 lbs.	Pleasant Lake	New London	5/8/1911	A. Val Woodruff	NH
Lake Trout	39.50"	28 lbs. 8 oz.	Newfound Lake	Bristol	4/24/1958	Albert C. Staples	MA
Sunapee Trout	33.00"	11 lbs. 8 oz.	Sunapee Lake	Sunapee	10/2/1954	Ernest Theoharris	NH
Splake Trout	26.88"	9 lbs.	Crystal Lake	Eaton	2/20/1980	Thomas Barbour	NH
Largemouth Bass	25.80"	10 lbs. 8 oz.	Lake Potanipo	Brookline	5/1967	G. Bullpitt	NH
Smallmouth Bass	23.25"	7 lbs. 14.5 oz.	Goose Pond	Canaan	8/1970	Francis H. Lord	MA
Bluegill	11.25"	2 lbs. 0.64 oz.	Goodwins Pond	Acworth	6/18/1992	Justin S. Therieau	NH
Pumpkinseed	9.50"	12.48 oz.	Winnisquam Lake	Laconia	9/10/1984	Marcel R. LeBel	NH
Black Crappie	17.25"	2 lbs. 12.8 oz.	Bellamy Reservoir	Madbury	2/9/2000	Tom Noyes	NH
Rock Bass	13.50"	1 lb. 8 oz.	Island Pond	Stoddard	9/18/1982	Linc Chamberland	CT
White Perch	17.20"	3 lbs. 11.5 oz.	Winnipesaukee	Moultonboro	12/29/1986	John J. Ziolkowski	CT
Yellow Perch	15.50"	2 lbs. 6 oz.	Head's Pond	Hooksett	3/4/1969	R. Hebert	NH
Walleye	34.00"	12 lbs. 8.8 oz.	Connecticut River	Wells River, VT	5/4/1992	Anthony Bartolini	NH

Angling in the Smile of the Great Spirit

Species	Length	Weight	Location	Town	Date	Angler	State
Yellow Bullhead	16.00"	2 lbs. 8 oz.	Pecknolds Pond	Chester	8/1980	Gerald Menard	NH
Brown Bullhead	17.50"	2 lbs. 8.96 oz.	Wilson Pond	Swanzey	8/13/1998	Edward Grant	NH
White Catfish	23.00"	5 lbs. 11 oz.	Big Cub Pond	Danville	8/4/1996	Zachary Cross	NH
Chain Pickerel	26.00"	8 lbs.	Plummer Lake	Sanbornton	4/24/1966	Carroll R. Akeley	MA
Northern Pike	45.00"	24 lbs. 14.4 oz.	Moore Reservoir	Littleton	3/20/2002	Jacques Renaud	VT
Tiger Muskellunge	35.50"	11 lbs. 11.68 oz.	Connecticut River	W. Lebanon	6/27/1982	Brian Patch	NH
Round Whitefish	16.00"	1 lb. 1.44 oz.	Newfound Lake	Bristol	2/24/1994	Richard A. Dow	NH
Lake Whitefish	21.75"	5 lbs. 1 oz.	Winnipesaukee	Alton	8/23/1374	Paul E. Littlefield	NH
American Shad	No record - Minimum qualifying weight - 5 lbs.						
Carp	34.50"	30 lbs. 8 oz.	Mascoma River	West Lebanon	6/17/1985	Stephen Allan	NH
Carp (Bow Harvested)	34.00"	18 lbs. 15.84 oz.	Merrimack River	Manchester	6/29/1997	Todd Rivard	NH
Fallfish	20.75"	3 lbs. 8.96 oz.	Lake Winnipesaukee	Gilford	7/12/1991	John Conti	MA
Cusk	34.25"	11 lbs. 2.2 oz.	Sunapee Lake	Sunapee	3/4/1984	John MacKenna	NH
American Eel	44.50"	8 lbs.	Crystal Lake	Eaton	7/6/1975	Michael Hansharak	NH
Bowfin	28.00"	8 lbs. 13 oz.	Wilson Pond	Swanzey	8/24/1994	Kenneth L'Abbe	NH

Note the latest NH Fish records can be found at this web site: www.wildlife.state.nh.us/Fishing/fishing/htm)

The article below, excerpted from *Wildlife Journal,* May-June, 2002, the periodical from the New Hampshire Fish & Game Department, by Don Miller, fish biologist who is the keeper of the record fish in New Hampshire, is an interesting statement on how state records of fish are compiled:

Record Fish of New Hampshire and How They Jump from the Past into the Present

By Donald Miller, Large Lake Fisheries Biologist

Have you ever wondered how the NH Fish & Game Department (NHFGD) compiles the state record fish list? Many reports of possible record fish are obtained through our Conversation Officers in their patrol areas. Then there are the "fish tales" overheard at the breakfast diner or gossip at the local bait and tackle shops. This "grapevine" often reveals bits of information about a large fish caught by some angler, and through interviews and backtracking the story, the angler is found. Of course, many potential record fish are released or become the evening dinner.

As the official record-keeper for the NHFGD, I have heard my share of woeful stories. A few years ago, I met an angler who produced excellent photos of a largemouth bass and the scale that it was weighed upon that was approximately 12 pounds in size! That bass was released back into the southern oxbow pond where it was caught!

Ed Mosher was considered by many as the best lake trout angler in the Lakes Region, catching many large trout mostly by delicately jigging with a small piece of sucker on his jigs. He had won numerous Fish & Game sanctioned trophy fish awards.

Ed Mosher's 41.5 inch 24.97 lbs. lake trout, caught while ice fishing, Winnisquam Lake, in March 2000 He was also the subject of a feature article in the "Hawkeye when he landed this trout, the second largest laker ever landed in New Hampshire history. (Photo Courtesy of John A. Viar, NH F&G Dept)

Ed Mosher's 41.5 inch 24.97 lbs. lake trout, caught while ice fishing, in Winnisquam Lake, in March 2000 is the second largest laker taken in New Hampshire history. Ed passed away at the early age of 45 on November, 18, 2003.

One day [in the winter of 2002], I was pleasantly surprised when Dave Seybold of New London, stopped by my office at New Hampton with quite a story to relate. It seems that he discovered information that revealed a large landlocked salmon (18.5 pounds) was caught in Pleasant Lake, New London, NH, and was never entered or verified as a state record fish. I was aware that Pleasant Lake supported large fish, as our current state record landlocked salmon, angled in 1942 by Mrs. Letty M. Clark, hails from this lake. I expected Dave Seybold to tell me that this salmon was caught in the 1960's or 1970's, but I was flabbergasted when he said the salmon dated back to 1914!

This discovery has another interesting 'angle" to it, as former fisheries chief and executive director of the NHFGD, "Buck" Corson, had asked Dave Seybold to pursue this possible record salmon, in order to give the fish and angler its' place in the record books.

Letty M. Clark's 34.5 inch 18.5 lbs. state record (tie) landlocked salmon taken in Pleasant Lake, New London, 8/31/1942.

P.H. Killelea's (from Leominster, MA, 36 inch 18.5 lbs. state record (tie) Landlocked salmon taken at Pleasant Lake, New London, 8/30/14 (with his wife Mary) Caught on a Briston Rod, Vom Hofe reel with Kingfisher line on a shiner

Therefore, I am pleased to announce that New Hampshire has a new record landlocked salmon, caught by P.H. Killelea of Leominster, Massachusetts, on August 30, 1914!

Mr. Killelea will share the long held record with Mrs. Clark, Mr. Killelea was quite a sportsman and angler who made tracings of his large brook trout and salmon and hung them on the walls of his summer camp at Pleasant Lake. On another historical note, Mr. Killelea had a close lakefront neighbor, A. Val Woodruff, who caught and still holds the state record brook trout from Pleasant Lake in 1911!

I would like to thank both Dave Seybold and "Buck" Corson for their efforts in this interesting story. And, by the way, late August seems to be a great time to fish for salmon; Mrs. Clark caught her record on August 31.[37]

EPILOGUE

Fly fishing is to fishing as ballet is to walking. It is interesting that many men come to fly-fishing after they have been through other kinds of fishing, usually forms that involve powerful boats, heavy rods, and brutally strong fish. Perhaps this is because they are getting wiser and less hormonal. Or perhaps it is that as men get older, some of them develop holes in their souls. And they think this disciplined, beautiful and unessential activity might close these holes.[38]
- Howell Raines -

Why do I fish?

I asked the Master Anglers this question and each had his own manner of answering… or avoiding this elusive question. And they had some thoughtful answers. All made it clear that angling was not just about catching fish. Some loved being out with their fathers, grandfathers, or by themselves in solitude. Others see it as a way to spend special time with their own children and grandchildren. For some it began as a way to provide food for their families, which grew into something less easily explained. For others it was a way to escape and enjoy being with "the boys." Their real answers to this question, "Why do I fish?" are embedded within their colorful histories and legacies, shared with varied degrees of transparency within these pages.

I don't have an easy answer myself. But as the author of the question, I feel a responsibility to address it. An answer to this class of question is one that needs more than a rote response. And there is no one right answer. It requires a deeper search into the mind or spiritual forces which inhabit us as human creatures in the natural world. I'll explore this question here at the end of this book, but I'm less than confident that I'll come up with an answer acceptable to you or my angler friends.

An angler who can relax, surrendering to his craft and letting life's spirit flow through and around him will be sustained and rewarded by the experience. He will not fret about getting the fish to strike or forcing life to give him what he wants; it will just come. As the great Chinese sages taught, "Sitting quietly, doing nothing, everything is achieved." And the Zen saying aptly warns, "Don't push the river."

Perhaps there *is* a subtle but powerful difference between "fishing" and "angling."

Looking at angling, or life, in this way, I can see that I don't need to hammer life over the head (or myself) in order to get what I need. We can surrender and flow with the river of life instead of swimming against the current. Leave that for the salmon! I was taught always to try my best and never quit even when fishing. I still believe this. Yet trying hard is not the whole answer. There is much more in angling than that determination which will not be denied. After you acquire some of the tips and skills offered here by the Master Anglers and become a successful fisherman, more is needed to become an angler. Being at the right place at the right time is partly skill. But it is also partly luck with which God graces us when we bask in his smile.

I'm not willing to accept that the emerging technology now coming on the fishing scene should seek dominance over nature. The way to work with natural (or supernatural) phenomena is not to stand apart and try to penetrate their secrets through force, but rather to be a part of nature, reverently devoted to her. Being with nature has become something of a mystical experience for me. Some anglers already know about this. For others I can only assure you that there is a significant difference between this kind of angling and the more macho variety of fishing. I have done both.

Years ago I found that my Tlingit Indian brethren have also practiced blending with nature, animals and fish. I wrote about it in an earlier book, *Tenderness Is Strength*. I was told that I am a Tlingit Indian by reincarnation. This is different from being an honorary Indian, which is a recognition that occasionally an Indian tribe will bestow upon someone who has made a special contribution. The Tlingits told me that I *was* a Tlingit Indian named Doox in a former life. After this was corroborated by a wise chief of the Tlingit tribe, David Abraham (who died at the age of 103), I was told I have burial and angling rights on a river in Yakutat, Alaska.[39] I'm eager to go back again for some excellent salmon fishing.

Their belief is that the spirit of a deceased Tlingit will enter the body of a chosen person, bringing about the reincarnation of the Indian spirit. The Tlingit chief had several clues as to my identity, including my enthusiasm as an angler and hunter and my love of nature - traits held by

Doox, who, I had been in a past life. As this word spread among the Tlingit people, resistance toward me as a white man vanished and I was embraced as a brother. The Tlingits always thank the Great Spirit for every fish they catch or animal they shoot. They acknowledge the game for giving this ultimate sacrifice for their nourishment and well being. I had been doing that since I could remember.

I am not now a believer in reincarnation. However, opening myself to this spiritual phenomenon, after having been so closed to spiritual reality much of my life, was a transforming experience for me. A lesson in this is to blend with nature rather than trying to control or go against her.

We have traveled to the moon and to mars, yet we have not penetrated very far inside the human heart. Our own inner space is the next and the most challenging frontier for the adventurous among us. We are often ignorant of the inner mysteries of nature and spirituality. Yet our admission of ignorance is the beginning of our wisdom. To know that we do not know is to know a great deal. To know that there are mysteries about angling and that it is more than just the mechanical procedures of fishing is an important step in our search to connect with nature and our true inner strength.

When we are dealing with a mechanical process - how to use all the new technology being created - there is little choice but to become mechanical fishermen ourselves. That's our most appropriate and useful response. But, if we embrace angling as something of a spiritual mystery, then we will adopt a different angling attitude. How-to books of fishing tips, by themselves, will not bring about your transformation from fisherman to angler. Some measure of respect, and even of spiritual reverence, is required to become an angler as opposed to being a fisherman. If we treat the spirituality of angling lovingly, and with a certain tenderness, it will not be lost to us.

Once we have learned the basics, like those offered by the Master Anglers, we must also search for our sources of inner strength: for the photographer, his sense of vision, space, and color; for the race driver, his depth perception and reflexes; for the mountaineer, his balance, stamina, and timing. In every activity where strength is required, sensitivity also is required. Without it the strength will remain in its raw state as brute force. Sensitivity and spirituality are much more important in angling than brute force. This is one reason why in their twilight years many fishermen become anglers and gravitate toward catch and release and fly-fishing.

As I struggle with my new electronic downriggers, my downjigger, my jigging machine, and my sonar devices, I'm fishing more than angling. I recall from an English Literature lecture at West Point, a British guest author, John Masters, told us one afternoon: "A machine, no matter how complex looking, is the most simple of things. A man, no matter how simple looking, is the most complex of things." This message helped me choose the Infantry rather than a technical career such as an engineer or pilot. In the Infantry, human motivation and leadership are so much more important than technical know-how. Something like this may also be true in angling.

When I head out in my boat on Lake Winni on a beautiful summer morning with a view of Mt. Washington and the Ossipee Mountains to the north, I am freed from my macho ways and surrender to the beauty of the Great Spirit's smile, seeing the beauty of the sun rise.

There's a difference between "seeing" and "looking." Looking has an evaluative aspect to it. The overachiever is continually looking hard at things and people, trying to evaluate or judge them. Contrasted with "looking," "seeing" is a here-and-now process which might be described as connecting directly from eyes to heart rather than from eyes to brain. It means accepting the person you "see" with "soft eyes" rather than judging the person you "look" at.

Does it help me answer the question, why I fish, by suggesting that "looking" is to "fishing" as "seeing" is to "angling?"

I find that when I am fly-fishing the beds for bass in spring or fishing a trout stream, if I use "soft eyes" I can see camouflaged fish, which elude me if I strain to look at them. This helps me react when one rises to my fly. In a sense, I seem to flow with the fish and the water and become one with them. It's a blending with nature in a tender way rather than opposing or going after her in a hostile, invasive manner. The softer I become in nature as an angler, the more I can see, and the more she shows me. Now as a Christian believer, having opened myself to the spiritual possibilities of reincarnation in the past, I can better surrender to the Great Spirit's will. He has mysterious ways of using our mistakes, crises, and flaws for his purposes.

One August morning I got up alone at 5 AM to troll for lake trout on Lake Winni. For the previous 5 days I had been trolling 60 feet down in the cold depths, without a strike, where the lakers often suspend in

August. As dawn broke, the sun began putting on a spectacular display, painting the sky with feathers of golden oranges and reds. I was using an old antique Pearl Wobbler, one of my favorite lures for lakers. I was trolling with 10 colors of leadcore at the right slow speed and in a good place. All my techniques were perfect. Now it was up to the trout. For three hours I trolled through the old spots, each imprinted in my memory from past strikes, with no success. When I was about to head back to the dock suddenly I had a heavy strike. I knew it must be a large fish by the way it tore line off my reel.

With one hand I reached down and turned off the outboard motor, to stop my forward movement and to blend better with the morning quiet of the lake and the large trout hooked to my line somewhere down in the clear depths of the lake. Twenty minutes later, when I finally got him close to the boat, he sounded in one last deep run for freedom. Slowly I worked him back up. The hook held, and with one weary hand reaching the net under the now tired monster, I raised him out of the water and into the boat. I had not been practicing much catch and release, up until this moment. When I caught a trophy fish like this, I enjoyed taking it home for the admiring glances and compliments.

What a beautiful creature! The trout's spots were bright pink against the dark golden body, and his fat belly was pure white in the early morning sun. A precious moment to savor! I quickly removed the lure from his jaw, and carefully lifted him back over the side of the boat, working him back and forth to let water and oxygen pass through his gills. He stayed there looking up at me for a moment as if to say, "Thanks." With a powerful flip of his tail, he descended back to his home in the dark depths. I thanked the Great Spirit for this one more beautiful fish he had granted me and I could feel within me the strength of his smile. I had ceased trying to be a fisherman and had become an angler.

The Master Anglers of Lake Winnipesaukee

THE 15 MASTER ANGLERS OF LAKE WINNIPESAUKEE

Paul Philippe — in memoriam

Barbara Cotton

C/O son John Cotton
Phone: (603) 735-5724
Email: jcotton@tds.net

Bill Martel

Phone: (603) 524-1203
Address: 30 Ridgewood Ave, Gilford, NH 03249

Jim Warner

Phone: (603) 544-2325
Address: PO Box 417, Melvin Village, NH 03850
Email: flytyr@worldpath.net

Al Stewart

Phone: Massachusetts: 978-544-3907;
New Hampshire: cell: 520-1232;
Address: 60 Chestnut Hill Rd, Orange, Massachusetts, 01364
Call sign: "Percolator" on channel 16 or 70

Ted St. Onge

Phone: 625-8623
Address: 70 Warren Ave. Manchester, NH 03102
Email: C/O my daughter, Caroline Wiggin: amwiggin@yahoo.com

Mario DeCarolis

Phone: 279-6415
Address: 16 Dale Rd Meredith, NH 03253
Email address: amdecarolis@aol.com CB/VHF Call sign: "Angler"
channel 13 & 68

Harold C. Lyon, Jr. (Hal)

Phone: (603) 279-5882 (May-September on Bear Island);
(603) 524-1393 (October - May)
Address: 70 Carol Court, Laconia, NH 03246
Cell Phone: (603) 520-1214 Email address: Halclyon@yahoo.com
CB/VHS Call sign: "Aardvark" Channel: 16 or 12
Deep Waters Press Web site (for ordering book):
www.deepwaterspress.com

Charles B. French (Chuck)

Phone: (603) 524-6795
Address: 778 Gilford Avenue, Gilford, NH 03249
Email address: vispeak@metrocast.net

Carl F. Gebhardt

Phone: (603) 528-2369
Address: 22 Doris Drive, Gilford, New Hampshire
Email address: carlor@together.net

Richard L. Davis (Rick)

Phone: (603) 253-8689 (Derby) (603) 253-4473) (home)
Address: P.O. Box 267. Center Harbor, NH 03226-0267
Email address about Winni Derby: mail@winniderby.com
email: rickdavis@metrocast.net

Stephen G. Perry

Phone: (603) 271-2501
Address: NH Fish & Game Department,
2 Hazen Drive, Concord, NH 03301
Email address: sperry@wildlife.state.nh.us

Alan Nute

Phone: (603) 279-3152
Address):PO Box 486 Belmont N.H.
Email address ajbait@metrocast.net

Jason Parent

Phone: (603) 267-9476
Address: 20 Johnson Street Belmont, NH 03220
Manufacturer of "Jig BY J" — custom jigging machines
Email address: NHGuides@hotmail.com Guiding Web site:
http://www.nhguideservices.com/

Travis Williams

Phone: (603) 253-7530 or (603) 455-0268
Call sign: "CoolWater"
Email Address: coolwatercharters@yahoo.com Guiding Web site:
www.fishlakewinni.com

Notes

1. Harris, Bob, *Woods & Waters USA,* September 1999.
2. Nouven, Henri J. M. *Making all Things New – an Invitation to the Spiritual Life,* Harper Collins, San Francisco, 1981, p. 58.
3. Jack Noon: Excerpts from a personal letter to the author and *Fishing in New Hampshire — A History,* Volume Two in the *New Hampshire Fishing Series,* Moose Country Press, 2003.
4. Jack Noon: *The Bassing of New Hampshire,* Moose Country Press, Warner, NH, 1999. P. 66, 84-85.
5. Jack Noon: *Fishing in New Hampshire — A History,* Moose Country Press, Warner, NH, 2003.
6. Cleveland, Grover: *Fishing and Shooting Sketches,* (New York, 1906) p. 129-132, in Noon, pp.124-126.
7. Cleveland. pp. 133-135, in Noon, p. 126.
8. *Forest and Stream* (February 1, 1902), p. 93. Reprint of a Newspaper account in Noon, p. 112.
9. Noon, *The Bassing of New Hampshire,* p. 38.
10. Noon, *Fishing in New Hampshire — A History, ibid,* p. 102.
11. Scarola, John F. *Fresh Water Fishes of New Hampshire.* New Hampshire Fish and Game Department, Division of Inland and Marine Fisheries, 1973. p. 26.
12. Scarola. P. 28.
13. Noon, *Fishing in New Hampshire — A History, ibid,* p.147.
14. Noon, *Fishing in New Hampshire — A History, ibid,* p. 46.
15. Scarola. P. 36.
16. Scarola. p. 36.
17. Noon, *Fishing in New Hampshire — A History, ibid,* p. 47.
18. Noon, *Fishing in New Hampshire — A History, ibid,* p. 142.
19. Grasso, Pete. "Fish Tales — End of an Era." *The Weirs Times,* February 19, 2004. Pp.15-16.
20. Northern Cartographic, *The Atlas of New Hampshire Trout Ponds, 2nd Edition,* 1994, Burlington, VT. p. 18.
21. Northern Cartographic, p. 19.
22. Northern Cartographic, p. 20.
23. Northern Cartographic, p. 23.
24. Noon, *Fishing in New Hampshire — a History, ibid.* p. 45.
25. Noon, *Fishing in New Hampshire, a History, ibid.* p. 43.
26. Noon, *Fishing in New Hampshire — A History, ibid,* p. 142.
27. Noon, *Fishing in New Hampshire — A History, ibid,* pp. vi-vii.
28. Noon, *Fishing in New Hampshire — A History, ibid,* p. 211.
29. Noon: *Fishing in New Hampshire — A History, ibid.* p.126.

30. Noon, *Fishing in New Hampshire, a History. Ibid.* p. 126.
31. Nathan Hale, *Notes Made During an Excursion to the Highlands of New Hampshire and Lake Winnipiseogee,* Andover Mass. 1833. P. 7, as reported in Noon, *Fishing in New Hampshire,* p. 111.
32. J.W. Meader, *The Merrimack River; Its Source and its Tributaries,* Boston, 1869), p. 100, as reported in Noon, *Fishing in New Hampshire,* p. 111.
33. Scarola p. 81.
34. Scarola, pp. 76-77
35. Noon, *Fishing n New Hampshire — a History . ibid.* p.143.
36. Jetter, A. "One fish, two fish, red snapper, swordfish: a menace lurks in your 'healthy' meal." Reader's Digest, August, 2003, pp. 65-71.
37. Miller, Donald: "A Record New Hampshire Salmon: Jumping from the Past into the Present," *Wilflife Journal,* NH Fish & Game Department, May-June, 2002. p. 17.
38. Raines, Howell, "A Meditation on the Midlife Crisis and the Literature, Psychology, and Mystique of Fly Fishing", *Fly Fishing Through a Midlife Crisis.* 1993. William Morrow & Co. p. 112.
39. Lyon, Harold C. Jr. *Tenderness Is Strength,* Harper & Row, NY, NY, 1977. p. 42.

ORDER FORM

ANGLING IN THE SMILE OF THE GREAT SPIRIT
SIX CENTURIES OF WISDOM FROM THE MASTER ANGLERS OF LAKE WINNIPESAUKEE

by Dr. Harold C. Lyon, Jr.

"A very dynamic, inspiring, and a most entertaining adventure for the love of fishing in Lake Winnipesaukee." **Dr. Bruce Heald - historian and author**

"A "must have" book for anyone who wants to fish Lake Winnipesaukee or any glacial "big lakes". The historical accounts of Hal's childhood on Winnipesaukee evoked my own memories of fishing off the "big" rock at my grandfather's camp on Lake Winnisquam in the 1950's." **Don Miller, Big Lake Fisheries Biologist, New Hampshire Fish & Game Department**

"15 Master Anglers are interviewed, sharing their fishing experiences and expertise. The welcomed knowledge contained in this quintessential angling book will fascinate any reader." **Bob Harris — Outdoor Writer**

To Order: Price per softcover book: $24.95
Hardback limited gift edition: $29.95
Shipping and handling: $4 first book, add $1 for each additional book
Order via Internet: www.deepwaterspress.com

By mail: fill out the form below and send with your remittance or credit card information to:

Deep Waters Press
Suite 100. 77 Court Street, Laconia
New Hampshire, 03246
Phone: (603) 524-2585
FAX: (603) 825-0399
Via email: deepwaterspress@yahoo.com

Name: _____

Address: _____

City: _____

State and Zip: _____ **Email Address:** _____

Total enclosed: _____

Mastercard/Visa (circle): _____

Expiration date: _____

Signature: _____

Index

Aardvark, 56, 169, 176, 294
Abenaki, 1, 42
Abercrombie and Fitch, 146
Abraham, David, 288
Abrahamovich, Bill, 276
Abrahamovich, Stanley, 277
Achigan, 23
Adirondacks, 77
Adiwando, 2
An Unexpected Salmon Bonanza, 214
Arts, the New Hampshire Council of, 155
Award, Bunzel, 130

Bait & Tackle, AJ's, 49, 113, 243-244, 247, 276
Bait Store, Waldron's, 244
Bass, Largemouth Black, 0
Bass, Smallmouth Black, 0, 22-23, 141, 192, 200
Bass, Tournaments, 0, 11, 15, 126-127, 195
Bay, Melvin, 215
Bay, Paugus, 186-187, 222, 225, 233
Bay, Saunders, 214, 228
Beard, Henry, 13, 228
Bedee, Major E.E., 46
Beds, 24, 27, 34-35, 64, 85, 87, 107, 156, 194, 290
Benson, Charlie, 126
Bickerton, Jason, 126
Bishionette, Kent, 49, 69
Board, Message, 44, 56, 80, 129, 268
Boat Yard, Fay's, 56
Boats, Cigarette, 20-21, 226
Boats, High Performance, 20-21
Bonneau, Brad, 126
Bonner, Ryan, 125
Bridge, GovernorÕs Island, 232
Broder, Dave, 49, 250, 277
Brooks, Robert, 125
Brown, Shep, 9, 21, 29
Bryant, Dr., 27-28
Buoy Hopping, 40, 197
Burbot, 98
Bush, George W., 116

Canandaigua, 278
Carbone, Scott, 125
Carville, James, 116
catch and release, 3, 15, 30-31, 35, 45, 58, 95, 156, 176, 203, 220, 226, 234-235, 259-260, 270, 289, 291
Cattle Landing, 245
Center Harbor, 1, 123, 161, 222, 264, 295
Center, Sportsman's, 145
Chapman, Greg, 126
ChevChase, 151, 275-277
Chicken of the Sea, 55, 58
Chinese sages, 287
Church, First Methodist, 204-205
Clark, Letty M., 281, 284
Cleveland, Grover, 24-25, 27-28, 297
Clinton, Bill, 116
Cod, freshwater, 98
College, Dartmouth, 169, 189
College, Mt. Holyoke, 134
College, Plymouth State, 205, 244
Collier, Laural, 31
Collier, Miranda, 73
Conley, Grant, 125
Connecticut, 17, 27, 41, 63, 172, 281-282
Connecticut Lakes, 63
Copper Sulfate, 248-249
Corrigan, John, 127
Corson,
Cotton, Barbara, 0, 76, 129, 133-135, 137, 144, 213, 292
Cotton, Charles, 144
Cotton, Merton, 134
Counter, Bean, 50-51, 53, 55-57, 66, 71, 73, 131-132, 173, 199, 254, 279
Crappie, Black, 0, 97, 101-102, 281
Crawfish, 20, 24-25, 27, 31-34, 36-38, 40, 60, 89, 92, 98, 101, 107, 151, 156, 190, 194, 197, 244, 248
Crystal Lakes, 63
Cusk, 0, 22, 65, 97-99, 107, 111, 114-115, 123, 126, 141-142, 150, 152, 157, 160, 193, 201, 208, 224, 226, 246, 282

Dare Devil, 83
Davidson, Perry, 125
Davies, Dan, 126
Davis, Rick, 0, 21, 66, 117, 121, 189, 222-223, 225, 227, 249, 295
DeCarolis, Mario, 0, 5, 16, 47, 55, 59, 79, 95, 109, 114-115, 129, 131-132, 169, 171, 179, 279, 294
DeCarolis, Mark, 16

DeepWatersPress.com, 0, 57, 294, 299
Derby, Great Rotary Ice Fishing, 0, 94, 121-122, 124-125
Derby, Great Rotary Ice Fishing, 0, 94, 121-122, 124-125
Derby, Spring Salmon, 0, 21, 117, 121, 222, 227, 263, 276
Derby, Spring Salmon, 0, 21, 117, 121, 222, 227, 263, 276
Derby, Winni Salmon, 0, 21, 66, 117, 119, 121, 222-223, 227, 276
Dodger, 55, 246, 258
Donuts, Bear, 58-59
Doox, 288-289
DownJigger, 53-54, 290
Downrigger, 48-49, 51-55, 63, 66, 68-71, 73, 80, 148-149, 179, 185-186, 192, 206, 219, 223, 225, 231, 236, 245, 257-259, 261, 265-266, 271, 276-277
Downriggers, Big Jon, 192
Dr. Juice, 247
Dwight, Theodore, 10

Earwax, 191
Eelpout, 98
Egg Sucking Leech, 246

Fay's Boat yard
Feeney, James, 125
Fincky Fish Factory, 113
Fish and Game, 0, 11, 20, 22, 43, 87, 91, 104, 107, 117, 141, 165, 174, 186, 220, 225, 228-229, 236, 239, 270, 297
Fish Cheeks, 202-203
Fish Hatchery, New Hampton, 229
Fish, Fall, 46, 76, 106, 118, 143, 269
Fish, Forage, 43, 75, 92, 103-104, 106, 158-159, 198, 225, 235, 238-240
Fish, White, 0, 81, 85, 91-92, 94-95, 104-105, 141, 158, 175, 177, 202, 212, 224, 226, 233, 260, 269
Flash King, 206, 208, 210, 224, 246, 275
Flash King
Fly, Dobson, 36
Forest Management, 204, 217
French, C. Andrew, 0, 88
French, Chuck
Fulbright, 4, 263
Fuller, June, 245

Gallagher, Jimmy, 17
Gebhardt, Gottfred, 218

Gebhardt, John, 218
Gephardt, Carl, 0, 134, 189, 217, 219, 221
Gifted & Talented, 68
Gitzits, 246
Giuliano, Mike
Giuliano, Vincent, 0
Glen Morrill, 147, 154
Gordon, Chuckie, 162
Gore, Al, 116
Gosnell, Amanda, 80
Gosnell, Brittany
Gosnell, Crystal, 34, 80
Gosnell, Dan
Gosnell, John
Gosnell, Roy
Gosnell, Tiiersten
GPS, 48, 71, 132, 257
Grand PrizeWinners
Gray Ghost, 205, 208, 214, 216
Great Lakes, 1, 24, 44, 70, 81, 253
Great Spirit, 0-22, 24-40, 42-62, 64-73, 76-80, 82-90, 92-95, 98-108, 110-116, 118-119, 122-128, 130-188, 190-241, 244-272, 274-279, 282-305
Grey Ghost, 49, 232, 258, 275
Grey Ghost, 49, 232, 258, 275
Greyhound, 40
Gypsy, 56

Hack, Bruce, 55, 58
Hackl, George, 85
Hackle, Sparse Grey, 9
Hale, Nathan, 97, 298
Handrehan, Daniel, 126
Harbor, Center, 1, 123, 161, 222, 264, 295
Harbor, Winter, 146, 150, 152, 157
Harris, Bob, 1, 72, 101-102, 297, 299
Hartman, Jack, 20
Harwood, Martin, 206
hatchery, Powder Mill, 45
Hellgrammites, 26-27, 106, 156, 190, 197, 230, 244, 248
Herbert, Henry William, 86
Hightower, Jane, 203
Hines, Bill, 9, 14, 21, 36, 83-84
Hines, Uncle Gorden
Hippy Tad, Kent's, 49
Hook, Eagle Claw, 37, 197
Horned Pout

Ice-Fishing, 45, 115, 152, 238, 269
Indian, Algonquin, 23
Inland Fisheries, 45, 229, 297

Island, Bear, 0, 9, 13, 20, 22, 30, 56, 91-92, 94, 98, 107, 124, 169, 173, 182, 184, 188, 195, 245, 249, 294
Island, Little 2-Mile, 162
Island, Ozone, 173
Island, Rattle Snake, 152

Journal, New Hampshire Wildlife, 147, 180
Junior Division, 31, 118, 120-121, 225

Kane, Barbara, 204
Kane, Howard, 205
Kichline, Joseph, 218
Killelea, P.H., 43, 281, 285
Kvedar, Cyprian, 245

Lake Ontario, 258-259
Lake Waukewan, 24
Lake Winnipesaukee's First Downrigger, 68, 70
Lake, Champlain, 277
lake, glacial, 1-2, 8, 299
Lakes, Great, 1, 24, 44, 70, 81, 253
Lane, Lovejoy, 9, 19
lawyer, 33-34, 98
Leadcore, 47, 51-53, 149, 163-164, 166-167, 173-175, 192, 206, 224, 263, 271, 277, 291
Let's Go Fishing Program, 225
Ling, 98
Lyon, Col. Harold, 12
Lyon, Edith, 44
Lyon, Eric, 32
Lyon, Gregg, 14, 32, 64
Lyon, Robert, 0, 8, 40
Lyon, Taylor, 87
Lyon, Toni, 94
Lyons, Nick, 11
Lyon, Pete

Machine, Jigging, 72-73, 254, 258, 290
Martel, Bill, 0, 98, 129, 134, 138-142, 249, 292
Master Angler DVD, 57
Masters, John, 290
Maverick Mfg, 113
Mayer, Larry, 126
Mayflies, 78-79
Maynard Marvel, 41, 49, 163-164, 166, 210, 275
Maynard's Marvel, 49, 166, 210
McKie, Roy, 13, 228
McPhee, John, 85

Meader, 10, 65, 97, 298
Melvin Village, 44, 56, 136, 146, 293
Mercury, 99, 160, 168, 178, 188, 203, 226, 241, 252, 262
Meyerhoffer, Ed, 169-170, 177
Milfoil, 79, 212, 248-249
Miller, Don, 0, 43, 45-46, 62, 77, 92-94, 102, 104-105, 180, 187, 283, 299
Mineola, 2
Mongeau, Keith, 126
Moosalamoo, 55, 275-277
Moosalamoo, 55, 275-277
Moosehead, 1, 16, 205, 279
Mooselook, 42, 49-50, 131, 141, 151, 182-183, 205, 208, 224-225, 275, 277
Mosher, Ed, 283-284
Moulton, Bob, 145, 147
Moultonboro, 56, 102, 130, 281
Mountains, Hohe Tatra, 4
Mountains, Ossipee, 20, 290
Mountains, Ossipee, 20, 290
Mt. Washington, 1, 20, 60, 290
Muddlers, 86
Mussels, Fresh Water, 108

National Forest, White Mountain, 217-218
Nature, 0, 4, 15-16, 79, 93, 108, 165, 177, 198, 205, 288-290
Nault, Oscar, 181
Neck, Meredith, 9, 19, 21, 29, 59, 84, 94, 190
Needlefish, 49, 58, 182, 193, 232, 267, 274-275
Nelson
Newfound Lake, 42, 66, 82, 185, 281-282
Nightcrawlers, 102

Noon, Jack, 0, 10, 24, 27-28, 42, 46, 63, 82-85, 114, 297
Nouwen, Henri, 2
Nute, Alan, 0, 49, 113, 243-245, 247, 249, 275-276, 296

Orvis, 7, 133, 135, 137
Overachiever, 290
Paine, Dr., 59-60
Parent
Parent, Harrison Hunter, 254
Parent, Jason, 0, 53, 72-73, 243, 253-254, 261, 277, 296
Parker, Benjamin Franklin, 82
Pearl Wobbler, 67, 193, 205-206, 291
Pepsi Cola, 123

Perch, White, 0, 22, 47, 82, 88, 91-95, 104-106, 111-112, 114-115, 123, 126, 175, 178, 196, 198, 202, 224-226, 244, 246, 248, 269, 281
Perch, Yellow, 0, 9-10, 20, 22, 65, 85, 88, 91-94, 104-105, 123, 150, 152, 157-158, 160, 177, 186, 198, 202, 211, 226, 228-229, 235, 248, 260, 270, 281
Perry, Henry and Ena, 229
Perry, Stephen, 0, 295
PH, 0, 76-79
Pheobe, 246
Philippe, Paul, 0, 50-51, 129-132, 173, 175, 292
Pickerel, 0, 10, 22, 43, 65, 81, 83-86, 88, 92, 111-112, 114, 123, 126, 152, 160, 202, 228, 249, 282
Pickerel, Chain, 83, 85-86, 282
Piragis, John, 122, 125
Poacher, 158
Point, Black, 145, 147, 154
Point, Clark, 152, 156
Pond, Goose, 24, 281
Pond, Melanesian, 156
Pond, Plummer, 83
Pond, Rust, 24
Poor Man's Shrimp, 95, 115
Posson, Mark, 125
Pumpkin-head, 247

Quimby, Bill, 21

Recipe, 39, 178, 252
Recipes
Red & White, 83, 85, 100-101, 131, 169, 202
Red Ghost, 49, 232
Red Maribou, 23, 275
Richards, Michael, 125
River, Deschutes, 191
River, Merrymeeting, 136
River, Pemigewasset, 41, 281
Roach, 81, 106, 137
Rocky's Rangers, 16
Rotary Ice Fishing Derby, 0, 77, 94, 111, 121-122, 124-125

Salmo salar, 41
Salmon Meadows, 83
Salmon, Atlantic, 0, 22, 41-42, 118, 222
Salmon, Landlocked Atlantic, 0, 22, 41-42, 222

Salmon, smoke, 0
Salmonitis, 129
Salmonitus, 55
Sanderfoot, Jerry, 113
Sargent, Jr., Weymouth, 125
Scarola, John F., 0, 297
sewed on bait, 182
Seybold, Dave, 284-285
Shad, 10, 22, 81-82, 143, 158, 177, 202, 226, 232-233, 260, 282
Shoe-horn, 275-277
Shop, Lakes Region Sports, 145
Silver Buddy, 246
Slovakia, 4
Smelt Assessment, 239
Smelt, Bicentennial, 155
Smelt, DB, 49, 194, 246, 250, 257-258, 261, 274-277
Smelt, Fire, 49, 275
Smelt, Lake Winni, 44, 104, 144, 155, 160, 257, 275
Smelt, Lil Warner, 144
Smelt, Magog, 155
Smelt, Rainbow, 103, 105, 208, 237, 239
Smelt, Winni Fire, 49
Smelt. DB, 49, 194, 246, 250, 257-258, 261, 274-277
Smithsonian Hirschhorn, 61
Spawn, 10, 41-42, 44, 64, 81, 93, 103, 106-107, 118, 158, 187, 226, 267
Speed, Trolling, 22, 48, 50, 52, 141, 148-151, 155, 164, 182, 193, 207, 223, 231, 245, 257, 267, 279
Spinners, Dave Davis, 55, 67, 179, 190, 276
Sporting Goods, Paugus Bay, 222, 225
Spring Winni Salmon Derby, 0, 21, 117, 121, 222, 227
Squam lakes, 42, 63, 81, 158
St. Onge, Ted, 0, 48, 79, 129, 179-180, 183-184, 187-188, 293
Stafford, Jim, 278
State of New Hampshire Record Fresh Water Fish, 0, 279, 281
Steelhead, 6, 191, 217-218, 259
Stewart, Al, 0, 129, 161-166, 168, 293
Sucker, White, 106
Suckers, 64, 106, 143, 185, 225, 260
sunfish, 9, 35, 107, 229
Sunfish, Pumpkin Seed, 107
Supernatural, 288
Sutton, 49-50, 55, 80, 131-132, 175-176, 224, 246,

250, 258, 267, 271, 275, 277-279
Swedish Pimple, 175, 208, 210-211, 246, 269

Tag, 59, 80, 115, 178, 250
Tenderness Is Strength, 0, 288, 298
The Atlas of New Hampshire Trout Ponds, 77, 297
The Catch & Release Nazis, 58
The Chart of Secrets, 0, 273, 279
The Compleat Angler, 86
The Concord Monitor, 127
The Guide Learns A Valuable Lesson, 215
Thermocline, 47, 181, 185, 247, 268
Thermometer, 113, 179, 182-185
Tlingit, 200, 202, 288-289
Tobin, Emory, 126
Top Lake Winni Salmon Lures, 0, 273
Top-Gun, 277
Top-Gun, 277
Tortoise, 40
Tournaments, Bass, 0, 11, 15, 126-127, 195
Tournaments, Derby, Ice Fishing
Trading Post, Kittery, 53
Trading Post, Opechee, 133-134, 136, 213
Trading Post, Opechee, 133-134, 136, 213
Trefethen, Gregory, 126
Trotto, Frank, 172
Trout Unlimited, 205
Trout, Rainbow, 0, 10, 22, 47, 75, 77-78, 92, 125-126, 131, 148, 152, 156, 165, 197, 204, 207, 221, 230, 233, 238, 244, 270, 281
Turner, Fred, 191

Ulm, Steve, 264
Uncle Gordon, 9, 11-13, 19, 22, 27, 29-30, 32, 37, 57, 67, 73, 190-191
Under the Cover of Darkness, 43, 70, 213
University, Michigan State, 229

Viar, John, 0, 61-62, 93, 104-105, 284

Wallace, Jim, 122-123
Walton, Izaak, 86
Wanaton, 2
Warner, Jim, 0, 44, 49, 76, 129, 134-135, 138, 144-146, 150-151, 153, 155, 159-160, 249, 275, 293
Warren, Dr., 26
Weeks, 36, 64, 113, 199, 219
Weirs, 10, 42, 72, 136, 297

West Point, 14, 16, 18-19, 56-57, 189, 290
West Point, 14, 16, 18-19, 56-57, 189, 290
Whall, Bill, 0, 55-56, 130
Whall, Bill
Whittier, John Greenleaf, 23
Williams, Bob, 264
Williams, Ted, 146
Williams, Travis, 0, 52, 55, 243, 253, 263-265, 267-268, 276, 296
Winni-Smelt, 49
www.deepwatewrspress.com, 22
www.NHGuideservices.com, 73, 296
Zen, 19, 288
Zen, 19, 288
Zern, Ed, 9, 29, 39